IMAGES OF THE NATION

Different Meanings of Dutchness
1870-1940

edited by

Annemieke Galema
Barbara Henkes
Henk te Velde

CIP-GEGEVENS KONINKLIJKE BIBLIOTHEEK, DEN HAAG

Images

Images of the nation : different meanings of
Dutchness, 1870-1940 / ed.: Annemieke Galema, Barbara
Henkes, Henk te Velde. — Amsterdam - Atlanta, GA 1993 : Rodopi.
Ill. - (Amsterdam studies on cultural identity, ISSN
0925-2746 ; 2)
ISBN: 90-5183-430-6 (Bound)
Trefw.: Nederland ; culturele identiteit.

©Editions Rodopi B.V., Amsterdam - Atlanta, GA 1993
Printed in The Netherlands

Contents

Preface

It could be argued that the discipline of history was born out of nationalism. The social relevance of history was linked to the fact that many people in the nineteenth century hoped that study of a nation's past would stimulate the national consciousness. The cordial relations between history and the nation were long-lived. It was only after World War II, and in many cases not until the 1960s, that historians became critical of the myths of nationalism, an aspect of the critique of ideology which was applied at the time to all kinds of traditional, conservative ideas. The dominant idea of the nation suggested unity and harmony instead of difference and conflict. Nationalism was revealed to be an ideology which wrongly suggested that the members of a 'nation' formed an indissoluble, coherent whole. Nowadays there are not many historians left who still regard the nation as a natural 'being' or organism with properties of its own. Nonetheless, nationalism remains a significant social phenomenon. As we have seen in recent years, not only in Eastern Europe and in the former Soviet Union but also in the reactions to the unification of Europe here and there in Western Europe, nationalism is still a force to be reckoned with. However, if feelings of national identity and belonging together cannot be conceived as natural links, what are they? What is their significance and function? It is in response to such questions that we present this collection of studies, a quest for the significance and function of national consciousness.

All of the authors in this volume relate national consciousness to the circumstances in which it arose and the meaning which it had for a specific group or individual. A common point of departure is the notice that carefully defined representations of the nation served to legitimise or support the political or social claims of specific groups. These representations were the stake in public debate; for example, various groups could try to reserve the same 'image of the nation' for themselves. These can be called the *articulated* representations or images of the nation. In addition, however, under certain conditions representations of the nation could play a significant role in the lives of individuals or groups who hardly participated in the public debate, if at all, such as emigrants. Images of the nation had a different meaning in this context. They no longer served to back up socio-political demands, but they served, for example, as something to hold on to or as a model of interpretation in a new setting. They were seldom formulated systematically; they can be called the *unarticulated or less articulated* images of the nation.

Each article in the collection and the collection as a whole focus on both of these categories. Images of the nation are thus no longer presented as the result of indoctrination by a social elite. They acquire significance in a specific socio-cultural setting and cannot be evaluated divorced from this context.

The articles in this collection concentrate on a single country - the Netherlands. Depending on the theme of the article, the non-Dutch world makes its appearance because the group in question moved between Germany and the Netherlands, or between the Netherlands and the United States, or in the form of an international comparison. The period chosen is 1850-1940, the period of democratisation and the rise of the mass society.

The articles are arranged as follows. After a general introduction to the development of an articulated national consciousness in the Netherlands, two articles concentrate respectively on a professional group closely connected with the national state and on a politico-religious group. They are followed by a contribution on the discussion of a national stereotype and one on images of the nation in a border province. Then come two articles on the less articulated images of the nation held by different groups of emigrants. The collection is concluded by a contribution in which the articles on both articulated and less articulated images of the nation are discussed and assessed by comparison with British developments.

This collection arose out of a seminar on 'images of the nation' held in Lunteren, the Netherlands, in March 1990. This seminar was held under the auspices of the Nineteenth and Twentieth Century History Post-Doctoral Training Programme (PONTEG), Amsterdam. This publication has become possible by the financial support of PONTEG. We would like to express our thanks to Peter Mason for his elegant and indispensable correction of the English. We were fortunate to have had the excellent professional help of Tjalling de Vries, who made the text camera-ready. Finally, Richard Johnson furnished extensive constructive comments on earlier versions of the articles. His dedication was particularly stimulating.

VARIETIES OF DUTCHNESS

Nicolaas C.F. van Sas

Nationalism is back, there is no doubt about it, both as a political force to reckon with and as a subject for historical research. Twenty years ago the concept of nationalism was hardly a fashionable field of study. In the aftermath of the Second World War, nationalism had come to be identified with excesses of national-socialism such as aggressive xenophobia and vulgar notions of *Blut und Boden*. At the same time, the historical profession moved away from practising history in overtly national or nationalistic terms. In the long run, however, the latter development may well have been favourable to the study of nationalism, making it possible to look at it more dispassionately. During the 1980s a number of innovative studies on the subject were produced in various disciplines. In the preface to the second edition (1991) of one of these seminal works, *Imagined Communities. Reflections on the Origin and Spread of Nationalism* (first published in 1983), its author, Benedict Anderson, writes about the startling transformation of the study of nationalism in recent years, in which the traditional literature on the subject has been made largely obsolete. In this respect he refers to the 'extraordinary proliferation of historical, literary, anthropological, sociological, feminist, and other studies linking the objects of these fields of enquiry to nationalism and nation'.

I should perhaps stress that I am using the term 'nationalism' in a broad and neutral way to include not just nationalism as an *idée force* but the whole complex of ideas and conceptions of the nation, ranging from the highly articulated to the almost subconscious level: the 'images of the nation' referred to in the title of this collection.

Until some 15 years ago, traditional studies of the nation, national identity and national character showed an almost instinctive inclination to simplify these phenomena and to employ a relatively homogeneous, monolithic concept of the fatherland, which was also regarded as more or less constant over time. Present-day studies, on the contrary, tend to take the view that there is a bewildering variety of *images* of the nation at one and the same time. Far from being seen as a monolithic entity, the nation is now considered as a highly complex phenomenon, experienced differently according to period, social group, geographical region etc. Various groups and individuals identified with the nation in a wide variety of ways. In sharp contrast with the time-honoured essentialist approach, modern studies are often markedly anti-essentialist - they are not about ways of *being* but about ways of *seeing* - to such an extent that one is sometimes led to believe that the nation (any nation) is merely a motley of images and fictions. There is a danger here of postmodernist derailment with relativism holding absolute sway. Historians in particular should stress that the image is not everything. Indeed, the 'images of the nation' in this volume are all firmly rooted in reality of one sort or another.

Does this renaissance of studies of nationalism imply that such a study is also warranted in the case of the Netherlands? When the concept is defined broadly, there is obviously much to gain and much to learn, especially when one takes into account comparable studies from other countries. As for nationalism narrowly defined, there have been only too many in the past - and still are in the present - who have concluded that this type of nationalism was something the Dutch happily did not indulge in, or rather could not be accused of. I am afraid I do not share this view. Perhaps Dutch nationalism has been somewhat different from nationalist manifestations in other (especially larger) countries, but that is obviously part and parcel of the phenomenon as such. Far more than the great border-crossing ideologies of liberalism, socialism and communism, nationalism by its very nature has been stamped by the traditions and developments particular to individual nations, while displaying at the same time many common characteristics.

The present volume, the result of a conference held in Lunteren in the spring of 1990, is particularly welcome for those wishing to gain an understanding of Dutch nationalism in the broad sense. Not only does it reflect the renewed interest in nationalism as a phenomenon, but the separate articles also illustrate several possible approaches. There are examples of a well-articulated elitist view of the nation alongside almost commonsensical notions. In a sense, all the studies presented here - though some are perhaps more 'traditional' than others - belong to the new approach, if only in their recognition of the very plurality and multifariousness of the image of the nation.

Focusing on the social function of conscription, Wim Klinkert deals with the army as a school for the nation in an emerging mass society. Roel Kuiper examines the highly paradoxical position of Abraham Kuyper, on the one hand a fierce nationalist, indeed a champion of the so-called neo-nationalism of the period, on the other hand a neo-calvinist and as such one of the main instigators of the socio-religious compartmentalisation <Verzuiling> of the Netherlands. Henk te Velde tries to expose the ambiguities of the time-honoured but all too facile equation of 'bourgeois' and 'national' in the Netherlands. Rico op den Camp looks at Limburg, the last territorial addition to the Dutch state, to examine its integration into the Dutch nation. Finally, there are two studies, both by women, Annemieke Galema and Barbara Henkes, which display a strikingly original approach. Both add a new complexity to the images of the nation by introducing the concept of emigration-immigration and trying to unravel the interactions between images of the old nation and of the new one, while stressing at the same time the importance of factors like the age and social background of the emigrants involved. They complement the view from above with one from below - ingeniously extracted from the sources - but in doing so they make it clear how wrong it would be to see both sets of views as reflecting a simple social dichotomy. Most of the studies presented here are taken from a relatively short time span, stretching from the last quarter of the nineteenth century to World War II. This includes the crucial decades of transition leading up to the phase of 'integral' nationalism (in an evolving mass society), the subsequent outburst of fierce nationalism around 1900, and the 1930s when, in the face of the fascist challenge, an inward-looking sense of nationality was being rediscovered. To provide some background and context for these manifestations of nationalism it may be useful to give a brief sketch of the development of Dutch national consciousness during the era of modern nationalism, from the late eighteenth century onwards. It should be noted that, in view of the present state of research, this sketch is heavily biased in favour of relatively articulated and elitist notions of the nation.

It is something of a truism that by nature Dutch culture has always been very open to outside influences. No doubt this poses a problem when trying to define a specific Dutch identity, or rather identities. However, though the Dutch were indeed very open to outside influences, they were also highly successful in keeping both their culture and their political culture to themselves. They did so by 'nationalizing' the external pressures and temptations to which they were exposed. This is true for the eighteenth-century Enlightenment, which they adapted almost beyond recognition; for the ideology of the French Revolution, carefully tailored by

Batavian revolutionaries to suit their own national purposes; and for the modern imperialism of the late nineteenth century, which did not pass the Dutch by as has often been assumed. The basis from which they operated (particularly the upper strata of society) was a firm and self-evident national consciousness. Indeed, part of the problem sometimes experienced in defining Dutch national feeling is precisely this self-evidence, since what is self-evident does not have to be reasserted all the time, and may even seem absent in retrospect. This self-evident sense of nationality of the Dutch was nonetheless clearly noticed by observant foreigners. Ernest Renan, for instance, whose 'Qu'est-ce qu'une nation?' (1882) is one of the classic texts of nationalism (enjoying a new lease of life in recent studies), singled out the Netherlands as one of his archetypical nations.

Dutch national consciousness between the 1780s and the present day has been constantly changing its guise and manifes-tations in a continuous interplay between development inside the country and the outside world. There was not simply a linear, evolutionary development from the rather vague (though unmis-takable) national consciousness of the seventeenth century toward the so-called 'integral' nationalism of the late nineteenth century. The stream of national consciousness never stopped flowing, but it kept on changing its appearance. Phases of fierce aggressive nationalism (in the 1780s, the early 1830s and around 1900) alternated both with periods in which the sense of nationality was more inward-looking (e.g. between 1800 and 1813, and during the 1930s) and also with times of apparent national self-doubt. Besides, to say that nationalism of one sort or another is typical for a certain period does not mean that it applies to all Dutch alike during that period. Not only have there been many fluctuations in the intensity and orientation of national feeling over the years, but there are also appreciable differences in national consciousness to be found among various classes, social and religious groupings and in different parts of the country.

A sense of Dutch *national* consciousness (as distinct from,

but not in conflict with, local or provincial patriotism) was already
present during the seventeenth century and was based on memories
of the heroic struggle for national independence against the
Spaniards. Indeed, the Dutch Revolt and the subsequent Golden
Century remained an important part of Dutch national consciousness ever after, often as a source of inspiration for later generations, though sometimes also as a golden weight on their shoulders.

Modern nationalism in the Dutch Republic as elsewhere
entered its formative phase in the second half of the eighteenth
century. The all-important factor here is the Dutch Enlightenment.
The development of a modern national feeling and of the Dutch
Enlightenment went hand in hand. A truly national 'communication
society' was created by means of new media like the spectatorial
weeklies and an impressive range of clubs and societies. A new
enlightened public came to the fore, which reached well into the
middle ranks of society, though it was still confined to no more
than perhaps the upper 5 per cent of the population.

During the 1760s and 1770s an ideal image developed in the
bosom of this new 'communication society' of an enlightened
Dutch society, an 'imagined community' in the happy phrase of
Benedict Anderson. This vision was based on a fusion of universal
enlightened values and uniquely Dutch features, especially the
burgher virtues (such as industriousness, thrift and an innate sense
of freedom and tolerance) which had made the Dutch great in their
glorious seventeenth century. Cosmopolitan trends and national
traditions were skilfully welded together. This ideal image of
Dutch nationhood was shored up by a potent political myth. The
Dutch were told over and over again that their nation had entered a
free fall of constant and apparently mortal decline. This concept of
the decline of the Dutch Republic is probably the main constitutive
myth of modern Dutch national consciousness. These professions
of decline were, however, not so much a matter of despondent
doom-mongering as a clever way of advertising the Dutch national
Enlightenment. They were both an expression of enlightened
thought and of national feeling. Thus, paradoxically, talking about

national decline in fact signified positive thinking and active participation in the cult of an enlightened fatherland.

This cult of the fatherland in the 1760s and 1770s was essentially non-political. The new 'national' emotions were shared by educated Dutchmen of all political leanings. Unwittingly, however, they laid the foundation for the very political nationalism of the 1780s during the Fourth Anglo-Dutch War and the so-called Patriot Period. The fatherland, only recently depicted as an idyllic imagined community, now became a highly charged political concept. It possessed all the characteristics necessary to qualify as modern-style nationalism: activist, ideologically motivated, oriented toward the future, imbued with a strong sense of the national past. Typically it also carried a secularized religious fervour, which was neatly captured by the poet Jacobus Bellamy when he called the fatherland 'my heaven on earth'.

During the second phase of the 'Dutch revolution of the eighteenth century', after the French invasion of 1795, this rampant partisan nationalism had burnt itself out. From about 1800 onward a new national feeling - 'vaderlandsch gevoel' as it was called - started to develop, shared by Dutchmen of all political shades. This 'vaderlandsch gevoel' cannot be called nationalism in the narrow sense. It completely lacked the necessary activist zeal and ideological content. Indeed, it developed in an 'End of Ideology' atmosphere and bore a strong cultural imprint. It was marked by a heightened sense of history. The glorious seventeenth century, which the Patriots of the 1780s had still been confident they could regain, was now considered lost and gone forever, past history to be moulded and mythologized according to the needs of the nineteenth century: the age of nationalism.

Thus, two distinct manifestations of Dutch nationality had been put forward in the course of a mere thirty years: the overt nationalism of the 1780s and the 'community of feeling' of the early 1800s. Both in a sense served as models for the future, or were the two poles between which later expressions of Dutch nationality tended to vacillate.

An important moment in the history of Dutch nationalism was the year 1830, when the union of Dutch and Belgians established in 1814-1815 fell apart. This rupture was not so much the *consequence* of nationalist antagonism between the Dutch and the Belgians. It was almost the other way around: the Belgian Revolution itself was the catalyzing factor in promoting both Belgian and Dutch nationalism. In the North there was an outburst of narrowly political nationalism, urged on by elementary xenophobia against the Belgians and fuelled by some spectacular acts of military bravado.

It has been suggested, on the basis of contemporary sources, that the Dutch experienced a sort of crisis of national identity during the 1830s (after the nationalist agitation of 1830-32 had died down) and 1840s. I prefer to treat these expressions of national self-doubt with some caution. In a sense they may be interpreted in much the same way as the eighteenth-century wailings about the decline of the Dutch Republic. Both then and now there was a debate going on about the present state and the future of Dutch society. An almost ritual element of this debate was the depiction of the actual situation in the darkest possible colours. However, these expressions of gloom also served as a programme of national renewal, both in a cultural and in a political sense. This programme was being developed, for instance, in the well-known monthly *De Gids*, founded in 1837. Here the glorious past of the seventeenth century was presented once more as the main source of inspiration, embroidering on themes already put forward in the years between 1800 and 1813. Potgieter, one of the editors of *De Gids*, summarized his manifesto in three catchwords: 'Voorgeslacht, Vaderland, Vrijheid' <Ancestry, Fatherland, Liberty>.

Thorbecke's constitutional revolution of 1848 put an end to these feelings of national unease. On the other hand, the very success of this political catharsis inaugurated an era of national-liberal complacency. This in its turn was challenged in the last decades of the century by newly-emancipated segments of society like the Roman Catholics and the Protestant 'kleine luyden' <small people> led by Abraham Kuyper. The so-called School Battle and subsequent *Verzuiling*, which began in the 1880s, created an atmosphere of political and religious conflict which at first sight looks highly detrimental to national unity. In reality, however, the politico-religious tensions of the 1880s may well have contributed to a heightened sense of national awareness and even have served as a catalyst for the integral nationalism of the nineties.

Many theories and interpretations of the *Verzuiling* have been put forward, but the relationship between the process of *Verzuiling* and the evolution of Dutch nationalism remains a strangely neglected topic. Great play has been made of the growing organisational 'apartheid' of Dutch society, without acknowledging that at the same time feelings of Dutchness were penetrating ever deeper into that society. Perhaps it was a shared sense of nationality that kept Dutch society together, despite its all too evident fragmentation. The various past relationships which are so important in the self-images of the different groupings may help to prove this point. Historians from every grouping, especially those still in an emancipatory mood, were actively rewriting the Dutch past in terms of their own in-group. However, this battle about the Dutch past was always fought on the understanding that in a deeper sense this past was shared by all Dutchmen alike.

The years around 1900 were a period of fierce and unalloyed nationalism, supported by an upsurge in the economy which in the 1890s finally took the leap toward modern industry. This fits in neatly with Ernest Gellner's well-known and provocative theory advanced in *Nations and Nationalism* (1983), which sees (integral) nationalism basically as a function of the process of modernization. In an industrializing society, according to Gellner, there is a compelling need for a highly mobile population or workforce. This mobility can only be ensured through the creation of a 'universal high culture', based on a modern educational system and equally modern mass media.

In terms of Gellner's theory of modernization, the wave of nation-alism in the Netherlands around 1900 should not come as a sur-prise. However, another constitutive factor of late nineteenth century nationalism must not be overlooked: the interplay between internal and external developments. With some explanation, and perhaps some special pleading, these expressions of nationalism can even be made to fit into the analytical framework of modern imperialism. It has been argued that, during the era of modern imperialism, the Dutch developed their own specific variety of this phenomenon, distinct perhaps from that of other, larger countries, but still similar enough to qualify as a form of modern imperial-ism. The main difference was that the Dutch did not take part in the race for new colonies. Their variety of modern imperialism consisted of effectively establishing their authority in those ter-ritories that were already theirs: it was essentially a defensive form of imperialism. All the same, enforcing authority overseas often went hand in hand with fits of jingoistic nationalism at home, a combination typical of the age of imperialism. A case in point is the Lombok expedition of 1894-95, which excited great popular enthusiasm in the mother country.

During the same period the Boer Wars, especially the Second Boer War of 1899, were a source of great nationalist excitement in the Netherlands, based on feelings of ethnic and linguistic solidarity with the oppressed Boers. These ethnic and linguistic sentiments are also typical of the kind of nationalism (sometimes dubbed neo-nationalism) of the late nineteenth century. Furthermore, the monarchy now became a truly national symbol with the accession of the young and adorable Queen Wilhelmina, expertly stage-managed during the nineties by her mother Queen Emma. Finally, the Golden seventeenth century was still a source of nationalistic inspiration, with the Dutch school of painting, particularly Rembrandt, taking pride of place.

This wave of nationalism around 1900, which has gone unrecognized for a long time, ended with World War I, but it was already on the wane before that. It may have been partly the defensive reaction of a bourgeoisie which felt threatened by developments in society that eluded its control. On the other hand, much of this nationalism was constructive in the sense that it pointed to the future and that it played a positive part in the process of nation-building.

That this shared sense of nationality was the cement in an increasingly compartmentalised society is clearly seen in the 1930s, the last phase in the development of Dutch nationalism under discussion here. In those years of grave economic crisis and serious doubts about the effectiveness of parliamentary democracy (in the Netherlands as elsewhere), the idea of a national 'community of feeling' was taken up again. There was a long tradition of studies of Dutch national character in the Netherlands, going back to the late eighteenth century. In this tradition, virtues like an innate sense of liberty, tolerance and moderation were extolled to establish the uniqueness of the Dutch nation and to keep at bay the dangerous world outside. This time-honoured national self-image was now put forward as a way out of the crisis of parliamentary democracy and as a means of warding off the dangers of fascism. On all sides of the political spectrum, from the social-democratic left to the conservative right, there were professions of national unity, using a shared language and expressing a common ambition to try and bridge the dividing lines - as it was said at the time - within the Dutch nation.

Over the century and a half which I have been discussing, from the 1780s to the 1930s, the national factor has consistently played an important or even essential part in the shaping of Dutch culture and society, and particularly of political culture. It is by no means easy to establish this role. The proverbial openness of Dutch society ensured that there was a constant need to define and redefine what Dutchness really meant over the centuries. Indeed, during that century and a half - the age of nationalism - the most conspicuous manifestations of nationality - either in the shape of overt nationalism or in the guise of a more inward-looking national feeling - were always in response to external influences of one sort or another. This was as true of the phases of aggressive nationalism in the 1780s, 1830 and around 1900, as it was of the rather different climate of the early 1800s and the 1930s.

The articles presented in this volume exemplify some of the many varieties of Dutchness. In that sense they are symptomatic of present-day studies of nationalism and the nation. The key-word here is diversity as opposed to a homogeneous, monolithic, unchangeable sense of nationality. This is perhaps the big paradox of nationalism which is now being discovered in many nations. Far from stressing the unity of the nation, modern research tends to focus on its highly complex appearance. In the final analysis, everybody has his or her own 'image of the nation', anchored in the unique reality of his or her own particular life and experiences.

THE SALUTARY YOKE OF DISCIPLINE...[1]
MILITARY OPINION ON THE SOCIAL BENEFIT OF CONSCRIPTION 1870-1914

Wim Klinkert

Between 1870 and 1914 a number of heated discussions took place in Dutch military circles on how to spread the burden of national defence more evenly over the population. The majority of the officers disapproved of the existing army organization. If the Dutch state wanted to have any chance of survival, a larger part of its population should contribute to national defence. This could be achieved by the introduction of personal conscription, which happened in 1898, or general conscription, which was never realized.

The final decision in such unpopular military matters naturally rested with the Dutch parliament. This article, however, is not concerned with the political struggle. This has already been covered

---

[1]   F.A.V.W.H. van Tuerenhout, *Over de invoering van het pruisische systeem van legervorming in Nederland*, ('s-Gravenhage 1871) 19.

in a number of publications on military legislation.[2] Within the framework of this volume, it is more interesting to focus on the non-military arguments put forward by military officers because they shed some light on the image of the Dutch nation from the perspective of this particular group: the officer corps. Two aspects attract special notice: first, it was taken for granted that the Dutch had become a non-military nation, but it was assumed that the unsoldierly material could be transformed into efficient fighting men. Second, it was continually pointed out that 'the salutary yoke of discipline' would yield results beyond the military sphere. A well-trained and disciplined (male) population would benefit the state in many ways.

The officers who expressed their opinion were on the whole dissatisfied with the existing structure of the Dutch army and nation as a whole. They were no disengaged onlookers. Their writings were intended to change the existing relationship between army and nation and to strengthen the army. Thus their image of the nation had a function: it propagated a strengthening of the position of the army within the nation. However, they could not reach agreement on an image. Their different models of military organisation were also models of socio-political organisation. Fear of an internal socialist threat and of a build-up of international tensions (economic, political and military) made officers look for ways of enabling the nation to survive. Some thought the solution was to be found in a democratisation of army and nation in which both would integrate and strengthen each other. Other officers believed in a stronger, larger army, which could only be realized when the nation was prepared to adjust the education of its male youth[3] to this purpose.

---

[2]   A.L.W. Seyffardt, *Ons krijgswezen in de Staten-Generaal* ('s-Gravenhage 1899-1902); W.E. van Dam van Isselt, *De ontwikkeling van ons krijgswezen sedert november 1813* (Haarlem 1902); R.H.E. Gooren, *Krijgsdienst en krijgsmacht in de Nederlandse politiek 1866-1914* (Utrecht 1987).
[3]   It goes almost without saying that all references to the burden of defence apply to the *male* population only. In military circles there was hardly any discussion of female participation. Exceptions are H.P. Staal,

After outlining the main reasons for military discontent, this article points out the solutions put forward by some officers within the framework of their image of the Dutch nation.

The Dutch army 1870-1914

The Netherlands had a cadre-militia army, i.e. a small body of regular officers trained a large number of conscripts. Once a year a draft of 11,000 was called up for a 12-month period of service, 600 of them for the Navy.[4] About two-thirds of the army consisted of infantry. The second largest branch was the garrison artillery, about 15%, which reflects the major role that fortresses used to play in the defence of the Netherlands. The cavalry, the mobile, élite arm, was very small in comparison with foreign armies.

The year of national service will have been a dull time for most conscripts. They were subjected to a hardly inspiring routine of drill, shooting practice and other military exercises and fatigue duties in dilapidated barracks, mostly in small garrisons. Each September the training was rounded off with large divisional field manoeuvres which were held on the heaths in the eastern part of the country. After that, they just idled away a long winter.

The draft was filled by drawing lots. However, substitution was allowed, i.e. a conscript could pay somebody else to serve in his place. It was also possible to pay someone who had acquired exemption and swap lottery numbers. The latter form of substitution was called exchange of numbers. In practice, 20% of each draft consisted of substitutes, many of whom served as such for several

---

'De persoonlijke dienstplicht der vrouw', *De Gids* (1908 II) 241-267; *Vereeniging ter beoefening van de krijgswetenschap* (1907/8) 395; and *Militaire Spectator* (1904) 552.

[4]   Conscripts who joined the field artillery, cavalry and some sections of the pioneers had to serve longer. On the other hand, there were many possibilities for a reduction of the period under arms.

years in succession. These substitutes, who were a kind of professional soldier, left a lot to be desired as regards their intellectual,
physical and, in contemporary opinion, moral standards. Many who
had drawn a place by lot but who could afford to pay 600 guilders
made use of this way of evading national service. The well-to-do and
the well-educated part of the male population could thus easily keep
clear of the army, but at the expense of its quality.

The number of those who could keep aloof was bound to
diminish when substitution was banned in 1898. Moreover, the annual
draft was raised to 17,500 in 1901, and to 23,000 in 1912. Furthermore, from 1901 onwards suitable conscripts could be assigned to be
trained as Non-Commissioned Officers, and from 1912 even as
commissioned officers.

This was not all. Another reason why the military burden
became heavier to bear for the Dutch people was the abolition of the
municipal civic guard in 1901. This guard was not controlled by the
Ministry of War, but by the Ministry of Home Affairs. Not every
conscript became a member of this civic guard. There was another
drawing of lots. In small municipalities these corps were dormant and
never had any training at all. It was only in the larger towns that
some training took place, but this was insufficient to attain any
worthwhile level of military skill. Between 1901 and 1907 the civic
guard was gradually replaced by a system in which every conscript
was liable to be called up for army service for eight whole years[5] -
instead of five - after which he automatically became a member of
the national guard (landweer) for the next seven years.[6] In times of
crisis or war both parts of the armed forces could be called up
simultaneously, but the conscript army and the national guard had
different tasks. As the national guard soldiers were older than the
army ones, they were not incorporated in the mobile field army, but
were employed to guard objects and points of strategic interest and

---

[5]   Reduced to six in 1912.
[6]   Reduced to five in 1913.

to man fortresses and fortifications. The national guard depended on conscripts from the educated classes for its cadre.

Thus from 1901 onwards the population had a heavier military burden to bear. The yearly draft became larger. Substitution was no longer allowed, the civic guards were replaced by the national guard, training as an NCO became compulsory, and a conscript could be called up during a period of fifteen years. Those who gained exemption were spared all this. This meant that, in the event of war, many older men had to leave their families to join the national guard, while the young men who had drawn a lucky number could stay at home. Many officers considered this an unfair consequence of the cadre-militia system, and not only for military reasons.

The army was not held in great esteem in the Netherlands. Since 1830 it had had no opportunity to prove itself. Besides, the Dutch had never taken a great interest in army matters. It was not a question of an anti-military attitude, but rather of a non-military one, strengthened by the possibilities open to the well-to-do to keep away from the army. Moreover, the Dutch parliament kept the cost and the individual burden of national defence low. The number of army volunteers had always been meagre. The pay was low, which did not help to make a military career attractive. Not much research has been done on the standing and social background of the nineteenth and twentieth century officers corps, but it seems that the higher classes did not aspire to a military career, with the exception of some families with a martial tradition. The officer's profession was not held in high esteem. On the other hand, for a young man from the middle class, the army offered a chance to rise socially.

By the end of the nineteenth century people slowly began to be more interested in matters of defence. This change can be explained by the abolition of substitution as well as by an awareness of increasing international tension. By the turn of the century it was realized that the Netherlands found itself caught between two rivalling blocs, engaged in an arms race on land and at sea. Moreover, the impact of the Boer War was such that the nation began to have doubts about its own ability to defend itself. However, this high level of concern was short lived. The relation with long-term processes such as democratization and a rising sense of nationalism calls for further research, but it is a fact that from 1900 onwards defence matters began to play a greater part in Dutch party politics, and that politicians began to show more interest in their compatriots under arms.[7]

Military discontent

The victories of the Prussian army between 1864 and 1871 and the sobering experience of the Dutch mobilization of July-September 1870 caused a growing insistence on the need for drastic improvements in the army and the military pressure on the politicians to take action. A large number of officers resented the low esteem the army enjoyed, the low expectations of its performance, the lack of trained cadre and the small military value of the civic guard. Although their solutions to the problems varied considerably, they agreed on a number of essential points: the army should be bigger; financial privileges should be abolished, and the entire population should contribute to the defence of the nation. The officers noted an alarming gap between the people and the Army. The army was like a foreign body, a 'costly, wilting, exotic hothouse plant'[8], cut off from the society which it claimed to defend, while the nation did not seem to be inclined to make any effort to integrate the army.

All these problems could be corrected if a larger and more representative part of the population participated in the defence of the country. Then, however, the questions arose as to what was the most

---

[7]   R.P.F. Bijkerk, 'Naar een gewapend volk? Het defensiebeleid van de Vrijzinnig-Democratische Bond bij het aantreden van het kabinet-De Meester (1905-1908)', *Mededelingen Sectie Militaire Geschiedenis Landmachtstaf* 9 (1986): 7-30.

[8]   ***, 'Militaire opvoeding en de moderne oorlog', *De Gids* (1904 III): 297.

suitable type of army organization and how a disinterested people could be convinced that change was necessary. Roughly speaking, one can distinguish two systems of army organization that were put forward as possible solutions.

The first was the existing cadre-militia army, without substitution and without the worthless civic guard. This can be called the 'military' option. Its main features are one annual draft selected by lot, and a long period of training inside army barracks. Allowing for the country's limited resources, this system closely resembled that of the surrounding great powers. This option was eventually adopted by the Dutch parliament. In military circles, it has always been preferred to the alternative system: general conscription.

Perhaps an even greater variety of proposals was launched for general conscription than for the cadre-militia army. The much (mis)used term 'people's army' will be avoided here, because it would only lead to greater confusion. It would be better to call this option the 'democratic' one, because general conscription was considered to be a solution to two distinct, undemocratic disadvantages of the cadre-militia army. First, the latter failed to create close ties between the army and society, since a separate military caste of professional soldiers remained in existence. Second, with its system of drawing lots it put a disproportionate burden on a limited part of the male population. The advocates of general conscription wanted to increase the number of men called up for the army and to provide some other sort of military training for the rest. The period of training had to be short to prevent the development of a military caste and to keep down costs. Furthermore, it had to take place as little as possible in such isolated and unhealthy strongholds of militarism as the army barracks. The cadre should consist of conscripts rather than professional soldiers. In addition, the supporters of general conscription put great emphasis on all kinds of physical training in civilian life. They contended that, unlike the model based on the armies of the great powers, this option was in accordance with the Dutch national tradition of a mobile army in the field plus local or regional defence forces.[9]

The non-military arguments put forward from 1870 onwards for abolition of the substitution were very similar to those used afterwards to support general conscription. All the same, there was a great gap around 1900 between the majority who wanted to keep the existing cadre-militia army and a clamorous minority who wanted to proceed along the democratic road. Why the majority of the military were unwilling to take this step, although it would make for a larger army, will be dealt with later.

Fairness and national unity

The usual argument for the participation of a larger part of the population in national defence was that it was only fair to spread the burden more evenly. Substitution was objected to, not only on military grounds, but also as being socially unjust.[10] The Prussian victories were largely attributed to the very fact that well-to-do citizens, the economic and intellectual leaders of the nation participated in the army. An infantry officer, Van Tuerenhout, an admirer of the Prussian military system, wrote in 1871: '...these days

---

[9]   A.L.W. Seyffardt, 'Wat nu? Beperkte of algemene dienstplicht?', *De Gids* (1888 I): 115.

[10]   The most active proponents of this view between 1870 and 1880 were: W.J. Knoop, M.D. van Limburg Stirum, F.A.V.W.H. van Tuerenhout, F.E.L.A. Abel, F. de Bas, C.D.H. Schneider, L.J.M. Glasius and W. Hoogenboom. Between 1880 and 1890 the military members of parliament W. Rooseboom and A. Kool came to the fore, supported by the *Militaire Spectator* and *De Gids*. Support from academic circles came from the professors C.B. Spruyt, J. de Louter, J. van Vloten, J.Th. Buys, G. Kalff and S.R. Steinmetz.

no army is able to achieve its aims, unless those educated, thinking elements form part of it which are kept out by substitution.'[11]

But there were more reasons to involve the well-to-do citizens in national defence. Did not they have every interest in the continuation of the existing social structure? Since they benefited most from that existing order, it was only fair to expect them to bear a proportionate share of the burden of the defence of that order. Moreover, article 177 of the constitution of 1848 defined participation in the defence of the nation as a *duty* of every citizen. For the higher classes that duty should mean proving leadership in the army. Since they also held the leading positions in society, why could one not expect the same from them in the army?

On the other hand, some compensation for the heavy burden of leading the army seemed reasonable, especially considering since military service might interfere with their university studies. It was therefore justifiable to grant some privileges such as choice of place and time of service, the right to live outside barracks, and better food and clothes. These privileges, which were copied from the Prussian army, were to be paid for by the conscripts themselves. Because they would mean the participation of the well-to-do in the army, they would lead to a fraternization between the social classes and would refine the manners of the lower classes. Shoulder to shoulder, all classes would fight together for the defence of the fatherland. 'Without compulsory personal conscription the army will never be what it should be: a part of the body of the nation.'[12] After all, was not it dangerous to entrust all weapons to the proletariat, who had nothing to lose, while the propertied class remained on the sideline?[13] Personal conscription could unite the nation and, '... is not

---

[11]   F.A.V.W.H. van Tuerenhout, *Over de invoering van het pruisische systeem van legervorming in Nederland* ('s-Gravenhage 1871), 21.

[12]   *Militaire Spectator* (1876), 261. A similar remark in the *Militaire Spectator* (1880): 76.

[13]   W. Hoogenboom, *Ontwerp van wet tot regeling van de nationale militie, de schutterij en den landstorm* (Utrecht 1879).

that, especially in these days of envy and hatred, socialist agitation and signs of revolution, a social advantage of major importance?'[14]

The same arguments were still used after 1898, but now in support of compulsory cadre training.[15] Soon it become clear that the introduction of personal conscription in itself was not sufficient. The educated class did not show any inclination to serve as cadre. Many used the loopholes in the law to evade the longer period of training for NCOs, and until 1912 there was no legal way to compel conscripts to become commissioned officers. So new rules and legal coercion were needed to overcome the deep-seated indifference to military matters.

A more virile and disciplined nation

As was pointed out above, for the officer corps it went without saying that the Dutch were a non-military nation. However, it was not necessary to acquiesce in this situation. Potentially, the Dutch were a strong people, both physically and morally; it was only that certain circumstances had obscured this quality. One of the most authoritative international military technical journals, *Von Löbells Jahresbericht*, wrote in 1887 in its 'Bericht über das Heerwesen der Niederlande': 'The Dutch love their personal freedom, that is the reason why they hate all things which are compulsory. They have a dislike for the life in military barracks and large parts of the population disapprove of personal conscription. But, the moment they are in uniform, they have no problem with military discipline, the courage of their army proves

---

[14]   H.L. van Oordt, *De persoonlijke dienstplicht. Een nationaal belang bij uitnemendheid n.a.v. de motiën der R.C. kiesverenigingen ten gunste der plaatsvervanging* (Leiden 1889), 46.

[15]   Among others: W.E. van Dam van Isselt, *De Nederlandsche kadervorming in het licht van Denemarken's oorlogservaring* ('s-Gravenhage 1908), 58-59 and W. Hasselbach, 'Militiekader en kaderplicht', *Vragen des tijds* (1908 II): 64-65.

'The goose step, or ... is Holland able to defend herself?'
'High those legs! Think of independence!'
(W.F. Winter in *De Ware Jacob* February 1906)

that. The Dutch even like military exercises.'[16] There was no need to despair. Moreover, had not their revolt against the Spanish and several wars against France been an inspiring example of the military capabilities of the Dutch?

According to many officers, the Dutch had become weak and spoiled because of certain circumstances: a long period of peace, growing material prosperity[17], the lack of interest shown by the ruling classes[18], and the spread of anti-national ideologies - socialism, pacifism[19] or 'cosmopolitanism'[20]. On top of all that, the current educational system, with its emphasis on intellectual book-learning, was supposed to produce 'weak, scholarly, nervous little fellows'.[21] That did not make things any better.

Only a military and at the same time national impulse could counteract this deplorable state of affairs. Therefore more attention had to be paid to physical education and the generation of patriotic feelings among Dutch young people. But how were the army and school to divide this task? What role should private rifle clubs and bodies of volunteers play? Opinions were divided, but all parties agreed that discipline, devotion to duty, patriotism and an excellent physical condition should become important characteristics of the population. The army felt itself pre-eminently suited to contribute to

---

[16]   *Von Löbells Jahresberichte* (1887) 207.

[17]   '...the Dutch people (...) is a people that, because of prolonged prosperity, has become indolent and dull in every sense.' L.J.M. Glasius, *Beschouwingen over het vraagstuk onzer landsdefensie in den zomer van het jaar 1873* ('s-Hertogenbosch 1873) 26. The same argument is put forward by P.K.P.J. van Sloten, *Het beginsel van den krijgsdienst* ('s-Hertogenbosch 1876) 3.

[18]   W. Hasselbach, 'Militiekader en kaderplicht', *Vragen des tijds* (1908 II): 55.

[19]   Which includes what the military regard as a naive faith in arbitration and world peace. E.g. W.G.F. Snijders, 'Het leger', *De Tijdspiegel* (1911 III): 113.

[20]   Staal named 'assimilation' as a dangerous anti-national tendency. H.P. Staal, 'Het ontwerp-militiewet', *De Gids* (1911 III): 463.

[21]   *De Tijdspiegel* (1901 III): 477.

this goal, not only for its own sake, but for that of society as a whole:
' ... a national army like ours is not only a guarantee for the continuation of our institutions and freedoms, but also the big national
school, where order and duty are practised and transferred to civilian
life.'[22] In other words: '...the army (...) is the best school to learn
obedience and devotion to duty, the pillar of order and regularity.'[23]

The majority of the officers held the opinion that all these
qualities should preferably be taught during military training in army
barracks. They thought at least one year of military training was
required. They strongly disapproved of the reduction of the training
to 8½ months, which was introduced in 1901. Such a short period
would never suffice. Their opposition continued until the outbreak of
the First World War. Some of them even went so far as no longer to
guarantee the fighting quality of the Dutch soldier.

Their emphasis on training in the army barracks did not imply
that these officers rejected physical training prior to conscription. On
the contrary, they thought it necessary to compensate for the short
period under arms. However, the advocates of the cadre-militia army
judged training outside the army barracks differently from the
advocates of general conscription, who attached more value to it on
the whole.

The supporters of the cadre-militia army thought that military
discipline, i.e. the essence of military education comprising obedience, devotion to duty, a spirit of sacrifice, etc., could only be taught
properly within a purely military environment. 'In the large army we
want, in that advanced training school, discipline must be strict and
duty onerous. Iron officers and severe laws will mould the nation.
That will make it a strong one,'[24] stated a rather extreme article in

---

[22]   ***, 'Het vraagstuk der defensie in 1889', *De Gids* (1889 II) 260-
261. The same argument is given by G.J.C.A. Pop, 'Nogmaals een woord
voor den persoonlijken dienstplicht', *Militaire Spectator* (1890): 207.

[23]   P.K.P.J. van Sloten, *Het beginsel van den krijgsdienst* ('s-Hertogenbosch 1876), 44. The same argument is given by W.G.F. Snijders, 'Het
leger', *De Tijdspiegel* (1911 III): 122.

[24]   BE, 'Een gelukkig volk', *Militaire Spectator* (1899): 30.

the *Militaire Spectator* in 1899. Especially from the nineties onwards, when the Dutch parliament seemed inclined to reduce the period of service, the military emphasized the absolute need for training in army barracks: 'Local exercises don't breed soldiers. The soldier must feel the strong but just hand of the relentless military discipline upon him for a prolonged period of time. Outside the army barracks civilians can be taught how to play soldiers, but real soldiers are only made in the army.'[25] The soldier was only expected to acquire military virtues, knowledge and qualities. The idea of the infantry officer Buys to teach the conscripts history, geography and an elementary knowledge of political science, as in France, was not adopted.[26] A few years before the mobilization, on the other hand, a programme was begun to teach recruits the basic principles of hygiene, especially foot hygiene, but this was due to the bad performance of many units during marches.

As was pointed out above, the officers who advocated general conscription valued other aspects. Prominent representatives of this group were father and son Van Dam van Isselt, an infantry and an artillery officer respectively, and the artilleryman Polvliet.[27]

In 1895 J.T.T.C. van Dam van Isselt wrote *Volksopvoeding en volksweerbaarheid* (Education and the nation's ability to defend itself) in which he reproached the ruling class for having taken no initiative whatsoever to strengthen the nation since coming to power in 1848. Consequently, the country now found itself in a deplorable state, with the army unpopular and the population weakened. Unless drastic educational reforms were introduced and people were urged to volunteer for military training, it was doubtful whether the Netherlands could remain an independent nation. The young should leave

---

[25]   W.C. Schönstedt, *De Nederlandsche infanterie* ('s-Gravenhage 1898), 30.

[26]   T.W.J. Buys, 'Eene overdenking', *Militaire Spectator* (1903): 566-575.

[27]   G. Polvliet, 'Legervorming', *De Gids* (1908 IV): 55-92 and 223-252.

the stuffy schoolrooms and play outdoors. Factual knowledge should be replaced by self-reliance, love of freedom and readiness to make sacrifices. That would restore the right 'moral strength' the Dutch nation needed to ensure its survival. Van Dam thought that the English public schools set an example that should be followed.[28]

Van Dam, whose first brochure on this subject dated from 1880[29], was not the only person to hold such opinions. Since 1888 the gymnastics teacher of the Rotterdam Erasmus grammar school, S. van Aken, had been pleading for more physical education in schools so that the time under arms could be reduced.[30] In 1900 Van Aken wrote: 'The education in the family and the instruction in the schools and more in particular in the gymnasium and on the playground teach military qualities on a much sounder basis than the army can.'[31] This physical education had to go hand in hand with the cultivation of patriotic feelings. Polvliet, for instance, suggested that national days of commemoration should be celebrated with sports and games for the people.[32] The same opinions were held by W.E. van Dam van Isselt, who followed in his father's footsteps from about the turn of the century.[33] He added to his father's and Van Aken's ideas a detailed plan of an army organization, which he propagated in many

---

[28]   Elaborated in J.T.T.C. van Dam van Isselt, *De samenwerking van leger en volk* (Utrecht 1897).

[29]   *Een voorstel tot versterking der levende strijdkrachten in school en leger* (Amsterdam 1880).

[30]   The connection between physical education and a reduction of the period under arms dated from the sixties. It was pleaded by members of parliament in 1861, but also by De Roo van Alderwerelt and by J.C.C. den Beer Poortugael in *Neerlands legervorming bij vermeerdering van militie* ('s-Gravenhage 1867). Some regulations made the reduction in fact possible, but a coherent policy covering all military and educational angles of this subject did not materialize.

[31]   S. van Aken, 'Volksweerbaarheid', *De Gids* (1900): 308.

[32]   G. Polvliet, 'Legervorming', *De Gids* (1908 IV): 233.

[33]   W.E. van Dam van Isselt, *Volksweerbaarheid* (Amsterdam 1901[2)]) en *Een Nederlandsch volksleger* (Schiedam 1904).

articles and brochures and through the *Vereeniging Volksweerbaarheid* (society for national defence).

Van Dam emphasised that a successful defence of the country could only be effected if it was based on a close union of people and army, on the nation's own traditions, and on the fullest use of the great defensive value of the Dutch polder terrain: 'The army should be an organic part of the state, which, in its own but effective and powerful way, contributes to our moral, physical and material prosperity.'[34] The foundation for such an army should be laid in every family and at each school. It should comprise physical and moral education and a thorough knowledge of Dutch history.[35] The organization of the army was to be a purely national one. It should not be a copy of the system adopted by the major powers, nor of the Swiss militia army, as propagated by the liberal politician S. van Houten. According to Van Dam, a militia army suited the Swiss, who were naturally martial and strong, but not our non-military 'peasants'[36]. The former inspector of the infantry, W.G.F. Snijders - though otherwise reaching conclusions opposite to Van Dam's - agreed with him on this point. Snijders wrote: 'The endless space of our plains, lakes and seas implant in our national character the seeds of a desire for freedom, and also the seeds of its excesses of

---

[34]   W.E. van Dam van Isselt, *Volksweerbaarheid* (Amsterdam 1901[2]), 23.

[35]   "By way of our own history, by pointing out the heroism and heroic deeds of our forefathers (...) the weakening of our self-confidence can be replaced by a buoyant and deeply felt patriotism." W.E. van Dam van Isselt, *Volksweerbaarheid*, (Amsterdam 1901[2]), 27.

[36]   *Militaire Spectator* (1900) 408. F.E.L.A. Abel used the same arguments against copying the Swiss model in *Iets over burgerwapeningen en militielegers* (Utrecht 1873). He too pleaded for "an organization which fitted Dutch circumstances and satisfied Dutch needs", but concluded that a cadremilitia army more or less along Prussian lines met these requirements.

lawlessness and the lack of restraint.'[37] How different had been the effect of their environment on the Swiss.

A small number of officers thought the problem of the non-military character could only be overcome completely by a military and patriotic education totally outside the army barracks.[38] The majority of the advocates of general conscription, though, had more faith in a combination of military training in barracks and physical training together with the instillation of patriotic notions in civilian life. They gave more attention to problems concerning the education of recruits[39], before and during their military service, not only because in general there was a greater interest in teaching methods and educational psychology, but also as a result of personal conscription[40], of the fear that the nation as a whole became weaker, and of changed opinions on the role of the individual soldier on the battlefield. Future wars would demand more individual initiative and self-reliance on the part of the lower cadre and soldiers. A number of officers strongly resisted the existing education which overvalued parades, drill and blind obedience to a superior. These were outworn notions, suited to an army that lacked all ties with society, but they did not correspond to the character of the Dutch soldier.[41]

According to Van Dam, the national army should consist of a well-trained mobile field army and a large reserve army, which could

---

[37]   W.G.F. Snijders, 'Het leger', *De Tijdspiegel* (1911 III): 148. Van Aken was of the same opinion: 'The indolence and inertness, the obstinacy and love of contradiction, all of which are called Dutch characteristics, cannot be tolerated in the army.' *Militaire Spectator* (1903): 588.

[38]   G. Polvliet, 'Legervorming', De Gids (1908 IV) 59 and 225. C. Gerretson, 'Leger en school', *De Tijdspiegel* (1912 III): 1-23.

[39]   D.J. Ruitenbach, *Militaire opvoeding* ('s-Gravenhage 1906).

[40]   'We now have (...) a new army, consisting of new elements and requiring a totally different treatment. The cursing, drinking substitutes have disappeared and intellect has entered with all its virtues but also with all its faults.' E.J. Korthals Altes, *Een nieuw leger!* (Amsterdam 1910), 18.

[41]   L.W.J.K. Thomson, 'Leger-psyche en leger-samenstel', *Vragen des tijds* (1907): 59-85.

fight a stubborn guerrilla-like war in the polders and lines of fortifications.[42] In this way the entire male population would participate in the national defence.[43]

Van Dam's views were a combination of ideas that had been circulating for some time among certain officers. He repeated the emphasis put on the field army in the sixties and seventies by military politicians like W.J. Knoop and the leading progressive liberal member of parliament J.K.H. de Roo van Alderwerelt. He also felt a strong link with the Roman Catholic Minister of War A.E. Reuther - especially in the latter's opposition to the government commission on conscription chaired by J.W. Bergansius[44] - and with the progressive liberal Minister of War A.L.W. Seyffardt. Their insistence on military training for the entire population largely outside Army barracks, on stubborn resistance in the Dutch polders and a short period of military service, is also found in Van Dam's writings, but neither of the ministers was successful in persuading the Dutch parliament to change the structure of the military organization in such a drastic way.

The majority of the officer corps also rejected such proposals, although in the seventies the idea of a military training for the entire population had formed part of the proposals for reform put forward by a large number of officers who - still impressed by the Prussian victories - had advocated the abolition of substitution.[45]

---

[42]   W.E. van Dam van Isselt, 'Nationale oorlogsvoorbereiding', *Orgaan van de vereeniging ter beoefening van de krijgswetenschap* (1911-1912): 5-107.

[43]   Van Dam made one exception: '... it is advisable to exempt the lowest class of the population, the dregs of the cities, from military duties. This class has nothing to lose and has little interest in the continued existence of freedom and our institutions of state...' (Van Dam van Isselt, *volksleger*, 9.)

[44]   *Verslag der staatscommissie tot voorbereiding der wettelijke regeling van den militairen dienstplicht* ('s-Gravenhage 1889).

[45]   For instance: J.C.C. den Beer Poortugael, *Neerlands legervorming bij vermeerdering van militie* ('s-Gravenhage 1867); F.A.V.W.H. van

The major objections raised by the supporters of the cadre-militia army against Van Dam's views were that the period of training within the army barracks was too short and training outside the army could never make up for it. A strong army with well-trained conscripts demanded - also in the soldiers' own interest - intensive military training. At best, gymnastics at school might provide a welcome addition. It did not make the military training in any way less important. 'The realization of a 'people's army' will be no more than citizens with weapons. It will lack individual proficiency, discipline, cohesion, self-confidence, a skilful cadre and qualified leaders, in short everything that distinguishes a regular army from an armed mass.'[46]

There was yet another objection. The officer corps was influenced by the prevailing military European view, which favoured offensive actions with big army units[47]. In the Dutch context this meant that the defence strategy was increasingly based on a large, well-trained, highly mobile field army operating on the sandy, high grounds in the south and the east of the country. This was diametrically opposed to a stubborn but passive defence in the polder by armed citizens.

Tuerenhout, *Over de invoering van het pruisische systeem van legervorming in Nederland* ('s-Gravenhage 1871); L.J.M. Glasius, *Beschouwingen over het vraagstuk onzer landsdefensie in den zomer van het jaar 1873* ('s-Hertogenbosch 1873); P.K.P.J. van Sloten, *Het beginsel van den krijgsdienst* ('s-Hertogenbosch 1876).

[46]   J.M. Benteyn, *Volksleger?* ('s-Gravenhage 1907), 44.

[47]   See T. Trevors, *The killing ground. The British Army, the Western Font and the emergence of modern warfare 1900- 1918* (London 1987); P. Paret (ed), *Makers of modern strategy from Machiavelli to the nuclear age* (Oxford 1986).

War as a fact of nature

On a more abstract level, arguments of a Social Darwinist nature were widely used to emphasize the value of a broad participation of the population in the defence of the state. Without such a national effort the laws of nature would inevitably lead to further weakening and the ultimate dissolution of the nation. Struggle in many forms was held to be an unavoidable part of human existence. This fact should not by definition be judged negatively. Struggle led to destruction, but it also had a very constructive influence on the nation as a whole. Struggle strengthened society in all its aspects and the ultimate struggle, war, was the affirmation of the right of the nation to exist.[48] The state derived this right solely from its ability to stand up for itself.

One of the first Social Darwinist statements came from the infantry officer Van Sloten. In 1876 he wrote: 'Struggle is a natural law. As long as there are two men, there will be struggle and war. No civilization without struggle, no struggle without civilization; this is what we learn from history. It is the way it has always been and it is the way it will remain, until the last man has died. Who thinks otherwise is no human being!'[49] Remarks of this nature became very frequent later in the century.[50] This attitude was frequently combined

---

[48]   '...the theatre of war is (...) an international sporting arena, in which nations contest each other with unequal teams; and war is for the proud, self-conscious a great struggle in which both sides put *all* their moral, spiritual and physical strength...' W.E. van Dam van Isselt, *Eene militaire vraag van den dag* (Schiedam 1911), 45.

[49]   P.K.P.J. van Sloten, *Het beginsel van den krijgsdienst* ('s-Hertogenbosch 1876), 25.

[50]   Among others: J. van Dam van Isselt, *Een voorstel tot versterking der levende strijdkrachten in school en leger* (Amsterdam 1880), 20; J.T.T.C. van Dam van Isselt, *Volksopvoeding en volksweerbaarheid* ('s-Gravenhage 1895), 25; H. Oolgaardt, "Strijd in tijd van vrede", *Militaire Spectator* (1898): 688; S.R. Steinmetz, 'Oorlog of eeuwige vrede?', *De Tijdspiegel* (1899 III): 121-144; BE, 'Een gelukkig volk?', *Militaire Spectator* (1899): 29-30.

with a very cynical view of international relations. Arbitration, disarmament and international law did not have many supporters among the military. They did not trust treaties on paper, because states always acted out of self-interest and because war was both ineradicable and necessary.

To give just one example: the prominent artillery officer H.L. van Oordt, an authority on the laws of war, disagreed wholeheartedly with the opinion held among lawyers that in the near future arbitration and a kind of world police force would end all conflicts. Van Oordt contended that it was a good thing the lawyers were wrong, not only because competition and struggle were a part of nature, but also because they had a beneficial influence on peoples and nations. A large military effort would enhance self-confidence and through this the economic development of the state.[51]

So the Social Darwinist argument had a military and a social element. Society as a whole was to be urged to strengthen itself and to make the army an integral part of itself, because the permanent 'struggle for life', whether in the economic, intellectual or military field, had to be fought with success. In the end participation in this struggle made the nation stronger.

Conclusion

Many of the arguments pointing out the social advantages of military training remained in use for a long time and the same arguments were put forward in different discussions. Moreover, the officers were in agreement about the problems of society. The criticism that an important part of the male population was unwilling to participate in the defence runs through this period like a continuous thread. Only laws could solve this problem. Coercion was apparently the only means to change the unwillingness and lack of interest.

---

[51]   *Militaire Spectator* (1913): 298-299.

Secondly, the unfitness of the Dutch for military tasks was a problem. It was supposed to be due to the long period of peace, material affluence and 'wrong' ideologies, but the national character did not help either: 'Our young are, in general, dissolute and insolent, they lack every respect for authority and are known for their destructiveness; the number of breaches of the law by young malefactors rises terribly.'[52] Despite these negative characteristics, however, major changes in society, viz. the introduction of an ideal form of manliness and anti-individualism, could give the Dutch back their former strength.

From approximately 1900 on interest in defence slowly grew. The old arguments in favour of a larger participation of the population in defence remained, but new arguments were put forward and other aspects began to attract attention. More emphasis was laid on the need for an integration of army and nation as a means of surviving as an independent state. Shortly after 1870 the military focused on technical adjustments in the organization of the army following the example of Prussia. Later the discussion dealt with questions of drastic social change and a radically different position of the Army within society. It became obvious that a majority of the officer corps was not prepared to go that far. They would probably have endorsed the Social Darwinist arguments, but not the far-reaching proposals of the advocates of general conscription. That would have meant a completely different defence strategy and the end of military training of recruits as they thought necessary. They were only prepared to go along with ideas of physical and moral strengthening as long as these ideas furthered the cause of a larger and stronger army along the lines of the great powers. They were neither prepared to accept a democratisation of the army itself nor of society as a whole.

The image of the nation advanced by the officers shows not only the close relationship between their opinions on technical

---

[52]   J. Eysten, 'De positie van het leger in de maatschappij', *De Tijdspiegel* (1906 II) 54.

military matters and the social changes they wanted, but also that the function of their 'ideal' society was to produce an 'ideal' army. The disagreements between the officers on how these 'ideals' should be realized considerably weakened their influence.

ORTHODOX PROTESTANTISM, NATIONALISM AND FOREIGN AFFAIRS

Roel Kuiper

Introduction

This article is an examination of how Dutch orthodox Protestants conceived their nation in the second half of the nineteenth century, concentrating on the Dutch Calvinists. Although divided in several groups, they all looked back with pride on their position of dominance in the seventeenth and eighteenth centuries, the era of 'Dutch Israel', as it was called. At their height, they felt themselves to be a chosen people, and the idea of a religious mission still smouldered in their minds. However, orthodox Protestants did not play a decisive role on the political stage in the first half of the nineteenth century. Moderate liberals and conservatives with a modern and pragmatic outlook shaped the Kingdom of the Netherlands after the liberation from the French in 1813. Orthodox Protestants found themselves marginalised in the new constitutional monarchy and resented their lack of influence.

They also lacked capable leaders in the first decennia of the nineteenth century. Orthodox Protestantism had its basis in the middle and lower classes. Most orthodox Protestants lived their quiet lives in rural areas. In the 1830s and 1840s, however, some stirrings of a political awakening could be observed within a small group of aristocrats and wealthy citizens in The Hague who had undergone conversion and had turned to orthodox pietism. This was part of a general European movement of religious awakening among the upper classes, which could be observed among the Prussian and Swiss nobility and clergy too. As in Prussia, an intense religious zeal led the Dutch revivalists to political action.[1] To turn orthodox Protestantism into an important political force meant to overcome a great deal of ambiguity with regard to modern society and constitutional rule. New concepts of the nation and the role of orthodox Protestants in modern society had to be developed.

In looking at the concepts of the nation which were developed to overcome this ambiguity, one might ask how it was possible to maintain that the Dutch were a Protestant nation? What were the political implications of the conceptualisation of the nation? How were they to give concrete form to their concept of the nation in parliament and legislation? In dealing with these questions, I also hope to show that their concept of the nation also had implications for the perception of the Netherlands in an international context and for Dutch foreign policy.

In dealing with orthodox Protestantism, nationalism and foreign affairs, I shall first consider the concept of the nation as held by those Protestants who became politically active in the middle of the nineteenth century. Then I shall focus on the ideas of the nation entertained by Abraham Kuyper and his adherents in the last decennia of the nineteenth century, before indicating the

---

[1]   Robert M. Bigler, *The politics of German protestantism. The rise of the protestant church elite in Prussia, 1815-1848* (Berkeley/Los Angeles/ London, 1972), pp.125-155. Cf. M.E. Kluit, *Het protestantse Reveil in Nederland en daarbuiten, 1815-1865* (Amsterdam, 1970), [1] passim.

relevance of these ideas for the perception of the Netherlands in the European scene and for Dutch foreign policy.

Constitutional change and political action

In the 1840s there was much public debate concerning the amendment of the constitution. Progressive liberals asked for more political rights, but the King refused to meet their demands. The European revolutions of 1848 made him change his mind. In March 1848, afraid of losing his position, he gave the liberal leader J.R. Thorbecke (1798-1872) instructions to deliver a new constitution. This was not greeted with enthusiasm in all parts of Dutch society. Conservative voices could be heard saying that the King had capitulated under the threat of revolution and pressure from abroad. Orthodox Protestants had their own reasons for being anxious. They did not believe that a new constitution would improve the situation.

Among orthodox Protestants there had always been a strong aversion to the constitution. It was seen as a product of the French Revolution, and condemned especially because it gave equal rights to several existing religious groups in the Netherlands, and thus separated the state and the old Reformed Church. The existing constitution denied the realities of Dutch history, they argued. Their legitimate position and tradition were not recognised in the constitutional framework of the state. This position closely resembled the historicist and romantic views of Prussian conservatives like Ludwig and Leopold von Gerlach, with whom they sympathized. There was a common orientation on the Historical School of Von Savigny and the work of the Swiss political thinker Von

Haller, who stated in his *Restauration der Staatswissenschaft* that the identity of each nation was a product of history.[2]

In 1843 J.W. Gefken, an attorney in The Hague, wrote to his friend G. Groen van Prinsterer (1801-1876) that the Netherlands was a Protestant nation and, he argued, this was a 'historical truth stronger than the constitution'.[3] This 'historical truth' was a rather vague idea, but he expressed a deeply felt conviction: the Protestant nation was a reality which could not be established or repudiated by a mere act of the state.

Gefken and Groen van Prinsterer both belonged to the Dutch revivalist movement in The Hague, a movement which had adherents among the leading circles of Dutch society. There were important revivalist communities in The Hague and Amsterdam. In these communities there was a strong sense of the former position of orthodox Protestants, which played an important role in the political debates of those years. The orthodox intellectuals wanted to play a role on the political stage, but on the other hand, they did not want to accommodate themselves to the constitutional framework, which they considered to repudiate the original Protestant character of the Dutch state. A solution was formulated by Groen van Prinsterer. This historian and political leader of the revivalists accepted the constitution as a political charter, but wanted it to be determined by historical Dutch Christian principles.[4] To defend Dutch society against modernism, secularisation and liberalism, there had to be a strong awareness of what the Netherlands stood for in the past. Isaac Da Costa (1798-1860), a converted Jew with great influence in the Amsterdam revivalist community, delibera-

---

[2]   On the influence of Von Haller in revivalist circles see: R.M. Berdahl, *The politics of the Prussian nobility. The development of a conservative ideology, 1770-1848* (Princeton, 1988), pp. 246 ff. Cf. J.L.P. Brants, *Groens geestelijke groei; onderzoek naar Groen van Prinsterer's theorieën tot 1834* (Amsterdam, 1951), pp. 61 ff.

[3]   J.W.Gefken, Autobiography, 23-24, Reveilarchief, Amsterdam.

[4]   Cf. R. Kuiper, 'Het Reveil en de grondwet van 1848', *Radix*, 14(1988): 112-126.

Kuyper as seen by his supporters
(A.C. de Gooyer and R. van Reest, *Kuyper de geweldige ... van dichtbij*
(Baarn, s.a.)

De politieke parvenu.

...and by his opponents
(the socialist *Notenkraker* 25 October 1908)

tely took up the concept of the Dutch as God's chosen people in the modern era. In 1844 he wrote to Groen van Prinsterer that he wanted a constitution based on the 'principles of Belief and History'.[5]

These men opened the way to overcoming the problems and frustrations with politics. Groen van Prinsterer said that he was 'antirevolutionary' in rejecting the principles of the French Revolution, but would accept the historical outcome of the revolution. He wanted to fight ideas, not facts. Da Costa followed him on this path. The difference with conservatism was, according to Groen van Prinsterer and Da Costa, that the anti-revolutionaries attacked the principles, not the outcome of the revolution. So the anti-revolutionary politician was a 'historical Christian' politician who would try to realise Dutch identity as a Protestant nation in parliament and legislation. The liberal constitution was formally accepted by the anti-revolutionaries in 1848, but they wanted it to be changed into the constitution of a Protestant nation. They therefore engaged in political action and entered the first parliament that was elected under the new constitution.

At that time, their ideas about the Protestant nation were a complete abstraction. It was a banner to wave, and they did so militantly. The anti-revolutionaries proclaimed the historical rights of the orthodox Protestants, but their concept of a Protestant nation presupposed a unity which did not exist. The nation had become a pluriform society. Catholics, for example, were no longer a politically deprived minority in the Netherlands. There were also other practical problems as well. The anti-revolutionaries claimed to have a clear insight into the essential needs of the Dutch nation, but the difficulty was that their ideas still had to be translated into actual political concepts. In particular, the vague relation between state and church became problematic. Could the Dutch Reformed

---

[5]   G. Groen van Prinsterer, *Brieven van mr. I. Da Costa I* (Amsterdam, 1872), p. 161.

Church maintain a dominant position in a constitutional state? However, the main concern of anti-revolutionary or historical Christian political action was clear: the Netherlands should stick to its Protestant history in order to recover its moral strength and national prestige. This was a reactionary ambition, but it had to be achieved by modern means: parliamentary action, direct suffrage and constitutional development.

Some brethren in Amsterdam saw this in a positive light and argued that Dutch political freedom and constitutional development were the fruits of historical Protestantism. H.J.Koenen, a member of the city council in Amsterdam and friend of Da Costa, wrote to Groen van Prinsterer that in English and Dutch history monarchical principles had been mitigated by 'the democratic element in the reformation of Geneva'.[6] Consequently, autocracy and repression were seen as features of non-Protestant countries, as could be observed in France, Spain, Italy, Austria and Russia. In this 'liberal' wing of the revival, constitutional development was seen as an index of a political and cultural process of civilisation. When the Risorgimento fought for freedom in Italy, Koenen, Da Costa and other revivalists saw this as divine judgement on political autocracy and Catholic repression.[7]

These were spiritual and also self-affirming opinions. They showed a tendency to present the Dutch nation as an example and model for other nations, but one orthodox Protestant group remained sceptical about this model. This was the Secessionist movement ('Afscheiding'), which left the Dutch Reformed Church in 1834. They were persecuted for a time, because there was no absolute freedom of religion until 1848, since the existing constitu-

---

[6] G. Groen van Prinsterer, *Schriftelijke Nalatenschap, Briefwisseling, II* (The Hague, 1964), pp. 640.

[7] G. Groen van Prinsterer, brieven van Da Costa, III, 214. This point of view was also stressed in the newspaper of the revivalist community in Amsterdam, *De Heraut*, 1859, no. 23 and 30. Koenen expressed his view in a letter of 21 October 1861, Briefwisseling, III (The Hague, 1949), pp. 504-505.

tion only recognised the established denominations. The persecuted minority wanted to be free from government intervention in religious affairs. One of their leaders H.P.Scholte, declared the state to be a product of the devil.[8] It is not surprising that they had been striving for a complete separation of church and state throughout the nineteenth century. The influence of the state was something to be feared. Many of the Secessionists left the country in the 1840s and emigrated to the United States. In their eyes, the Protestant nation was not an ideal that could be pursued in the Netherlands.[9]

The history of the Secession showed the political weakness of the Protestant nationhood. Did it make sense to link historical identity and actual positions? What were the perspectives of orthodox Protestantism and the Protestant nation? It was a historical truth, as Gefken maintained, but was it also a contemporary political and social reality? These questions acquired a certain relevance after the introduction of direct (though restricted) suffrage in 1848. Would the Protestant nation be reflected in parliament? The anti-revolutionary faction proved to be very small. Groen van Prinsterer and his friends in parliament often referred to the 'people behind the voters'. In order to enlarge their influence, the anti-revolutionaries became supporters of more extended suffrage. In 1850 Da Costa wrote to Groen van Prinsterer that enlargement of the influence of the ordinary people on the government would be healthy for the country. 'Among the Dutch people there is a religious element and faithfulness to the monarchy'[10]. But it was still a judgement on a theoretical level. The true touch-

---

[8]   A.A. de Bruin, *Het ontstaan van de schoolstrijd* (Barneveld, 1985), pp. 179-180.

[9]   He did this in the Separatist journal *De Reformatie*. See also: H.W.J. Mulder, *Mr. G.Groen van Prinsterer* (Franeker, 1973), pp. 78.

[10]   G. Groen van Prinsterer, Brieven van Da Costa,II,12. In *Het Oogenblik* (Amsterdam, 1848), Da Costa had already put forward the view that the nation and the Orange dynasty had always supported each other in Dutch history, so extension of the suffrage would not weaken the position of the monarchy.

stone was the ballot-box, but since suffrage was limited to the wealthiest tax-payers, the elections gave no clear picture of the real extent of the Protestant nation.

Orthodox Protestants and national education

In parliament, the anti-revolutionaries tried to implement their political ideology, agitating against the dominant liberals and pleading for a national school. The school issue became very important in the decennia after 1848. The constitution of 1848 made it necessary to draft a new law for a primary school system. Initially, Groen van Prinsterer and his friends pleaded strongly for a state school system, with separate schools for Protestants, Catholics and Jews, because it was obvious to them that a Protestant nation should have Protestant institutions. However, their attempts failed, and in 1857 parliament accepted a school law which stipulated that the state schools should have no specific religious character. The state was not going to be responsible for religious education.

Disappointed by this law, Groen van Prinsterer changed his tactics. He now undertook a political struggle for 'special' (denominational) schools, protected from the influence of the 'neutral' state. If the state was not going to organize religious education in a Protestant way, it should at least facilitate religious education in Protestant schools, he argued. This struggle brought him closer to secessionist leaders, who for reasons of their own tried to build up schools for their followers without state interference. Their efforts implied a different concept of the nation, in which the Protestants did not claim first rights but formed part of the population. In 1860, Groen became chairman of the Association of Christian National School Education, which tried to organise special schools. Many of his friends and followers considered this a very radical position and refused to follow their political leader on this path.

There was much debate on the subject in the following decennia. Should the national school be repudiated or defended in the name of historical rights? And what would this imply for the position of orthodox Protestantism within the nation as a whole? What was desirable: a policy of separation or integration? In particular, many clergymen of the old Dutch Reformed Church, the former 'state church', did not want to abandon the national school. They denied that state education had become all that bad, and pointed to the influence which they had in local situations.

Many Protestant critics accused Groen of breaking up the unity of the Dutch nation. The reformed clergymen, who portrayed the church and the school as national symbols, were reluctant to follow this separatist path. They therefore demonstrated a paternalistic confidence in the opportunities available for educating the people within the existing structure. They clung to the idea of the unity of the nation. As Bronsveld, one of their leaders, put it: 'The church is the historical institution, desired and wrought by God, in which here on earth God's realm had taken shape, and although it ceased to be the state church it remained to this very moment the church of the people'[11]. In this conservative conception, the church of the people had to reform society; it should influence the national schools and the nation.

The political tactic of Groen van Prinsterer and the concept of Protestant nationhood held by many reformed clergymen clashed in May 1869 at a meeting of the Association of Christian National School Education in Utrecht. The young clergyman Abraham Kuyper (1837-1920), a friend of Groen van Prinsterer, intervened in the discussion to say that state education was satanic. After that, a group of clergymen, who traditionally supported the national school, left the meeting room. They were not prepared to support anti-revolutionary political action in order to get special schools,

---

[11]   *Stemmen voor waarheid en vrede* (Utrecht, 1868), pp. 958. Bronsveld wrote a monthly column in this journal. See also L.C. Suttorp, *A.W.Bronsveld* (Assen, 1966).

which would separate the orthodox Protestants from the nation as a whole. This protest against Groen van Prinsterer and Kuyper was also a demonstration of conservatism. This clash revealed an important discrepancy, not only in tactics but also in views. For many politicians associated with Groen and Kuyper, the concept of the Protestant nation had lost much of its political relevance. They tried to achieve rights for the Protestant part of the population. For many traditional clergymen, however, school, state and church were not to be separated.

A fresh point of view

This is the background to the views of Abraham Kuyper, who tried to give orthodox Protestants a more pronounced role in Dutch society. In the 1870s, the aged Groen van Prinsterer announced Kuyper as the new 'leader' of the anti-revolutionary movement. This young theologian demonstrated much ambition and energy in mobilising orthodox Protestants in society and politics. Adopting the consequences of Groen van Prinsterer's position, he deliberately transformed the idea of the historical Dutch Protestant identity in a far more fruitful way than Groen van Prinsterer was able to.

His personality, influence and ideas are of great importance for the understanding of orthodox Protestantism in the last decennia of the nineteenth century. He wanted to unite the orthodox elite and nobility with the middle and lower classes on the basis of a newly formulated Calvinist creed. In 1879 he was the founder of the Antirevolutionary Party (ARP) and author of its political programme. A year later he was also the founding father of the Free University in Amsterdam and of the Reformed Church, which broke away from the old Dutch Reformed Church in 1886. In effect, he was the creator of an orthodox group, holding firmly to its beliefs in Dutch society, with its own church, university, special schools, political party and newspapers. In this way he contributed to the compartmentalisation of Dutch society.[12]

Kuyper wanted this Calvinist section of Dutch society to be influential on the nation as a whole. The mobilisation of the Calvinists was meant to have a national effect. Kuyper therefore considered the Dutch as a spiritual unity. In 1869, at the meeting in Utrecht, he said that 'a nation is a divinely created moral being, which received its talent and gift, its calling and commandment from Him, but as a people, a nation, as a whole'.[13] A nation was a unity, a coherent organic being. Although I use the word 'nation', there are some difficulties in the translation. Kuyper preferred the Dutch (and German) expression 'volk' to the term 'natie'. A 'natie' was formed by blood and birth, something used in an ethnological sense, while a 'volk' was formed by common language, beliefs and history. This made a 'volk' a connected spiritual unity. Indeed, there were some mystical elements in Kuyper's opinions, derived from Romanticism.

The next step was to emphasize the influence of Calvinism on this unity. In 1869, Kuyper stressed that the 'conscience', the spirit of the Dutch nation, was formed by Calvinism. In 1874 Kuyper gave a proof of his political theory by emphasizing that constitutional development in the Netherlands, England and the United States was enabled by Calvinism.[14] The programme of the ARP professed that Calvinism was the 'basic feature' of the character of the Dutch nation.[15] Kuyper admitted that Calvinism had a less dominant position in his own time, but he held that the Dutch 'volksgeest' still resembled Calvinist customs and morals. This all sounded arrogant, but Kuyper needed this to give his

---

[12]   See A. Lijphart, *The politics of accommodation: pluralism and democracy in the Netherlands* (Berkeley, 1968).

[13]   A. Kuyper, *Het beroep op het volksgeweten* (Amsterdam, 1869), pp.6.

[14]   A. Kuyper, *Het calvinisme, oorsprong en waarborg onzer constitutioneele vrijheden* (Amsterdam, 1874).

[15]   A. Kuyper, *Ons program*, pp. 22.

adherents the self-confidence to operate as representatives of the true spirit of the nation. In the meantime, this was a challenge to liberalism, which was dominant on the political level and conceived as the political enemy of the awakened anti-revolutionary movement. Kuyper, however, did not want to influence and reconvert the nation through the state, but he tried to organize and strengthen a militant orthodox Protestant group in society. In his opinion, this group was the true core of the nation and would influence the nation in an organic way.[16] He put the old and difficult discussions about the relationship between state and church aside, arguing that not the institutions of state and church as such, but the conscience and character of the nation were of decisive importance.

Calvinist character and Dutch culture

According to Kuyper, Calvinism had marked the character of the whole nation in Dutch history. It is interesting to see how he defined this character of the Dutch people, because he did not do so in a psychological description but in terms that could imply a social and political programme.[17] In 1869 he mentions five features of this national character[18]:
   1. Religiousness
   2. Appreciation of Dutch history
   3. Thriving family life
   4. Civic self-government
   5. Respect for freedom of conscience.

---

[16]   See the article in this collection by Henk te Velde.

[17]   In his *Stemmen voor Waarheid en Vrede* of 1881, 252, Bronsveld gives an example of a 'psychological' description. He denied that the Dutch people was 'phlegmatic', as was often said at the time. Kuyper seldom considered the character of the Dutch nation in this way.

[18]   *Het beroep op het volksgeweten*, 15. Also: L. Praamsma, *Abraham Kuyper als kerkhistoricus* (Kampen, 1945), pp. 104-109.

These national features were spiritual factors, as can be observed, not historical descriptions. Kuyper derived these spiritual factors from his conception of Dutch society in the seventeenth century. That was the period of Calvinist heroes and Calvinist culture. Kuyper often praised this Dutch Golden Age, when Calvinism was the dominant religion and determined Dutch culture. In its spiritual content it should be a model for the Calvinists in the nineteenth century. The mirror of history showed that nineteenth-century Calvinists had to win back a position and fulfil their 'national task'. Kuyper wanted his adherents to be proud of their religion and to remember their cultural influence in the past. The historical picture must lead them to political and social action. The anti-revolutionary newspaper *De Oranjevaan* wrote in 1883: 'Thank God, we have a history to mirror ourselves'[19].

Besides the self-affirmation of spiritual notions, this mirror also revealed the civic and political notions of self-government and freedom of conscience. These notions were not specific for Kuyper and his adherents. The liberals also stressed these values from their own point of view. They were the values of emancipating citizens, demanding political rights in modern society. Kuyper, however, explained to his adherents that these values were historically linked with Calvinism. This explanation supported anti-revolutionary opinions about constitutional development and their concern to restrain the influence of the state. Calvinism was a guarantee, Kuyper repeatedly said, of constitutional freedom. The constitutional framework was fully accepted and incorporated in Kuyper's conception of the nation.

Kuyper and his neo-Calvinist band appealed to the Calvinist character, will, and conscience which were considered to be a constant feature of the Dutch 'volksgeest' (spirit) and could be demonstrated in Dutch history.[20] In fact they broke with tradi-

---

[19]   *De Oranjevaan* (Utrecht, 1 September 1883).
[20]   Cf. G.J. Schutte, *Het calvinistisch Nederland* (Utrecht, 1988), pp.7-8.

tional forms. In the context of the compartmentalisation, new forms and traditions were created up to raise the orthodox people to the height of modern society. A well-organized political party, special schools and a new reformed church with its own set of morals had been created. These new institutions, forms and morals formed the stumbling block for clergymen such as Bronsveld, Hoedemaker and others who adhered to the national schools and the old national church. According to them, the Netherlands should be a Protestant nation preserving its traditional institutions and forms. In the opinion of the theocratic Hoedemaker, who was for some time professor of theology at Kuyper's Free University, state and church should bring people back to orthodox principles. The church should be the rudder of the ship of state[21]. In this political concept, which underlined the normative nature of history, there was not much room for freedom for other religious groups. The only legitimate position was reserved for Protestants, who could claim first rights. The fact that the ARP in 1888 formed a coalition with the Catholics to obtain government power was objectionable in their eyes, but it was clear that Kuyper's romantic and spiritual concept of the Protestant nation was far more fruitful in a pluriform and constitutional state than Hoedemaker's dogmatic concept.

Morality and neutrality in foreign affairs

These orthodox Protestant notions had some impact on the field of foreign policy and perceptions of the Dutch role on the international scene. There is, of course, a link between the image of the nation and the perception of the role of this nation on the international stage. With regard to the international developments, we can demonstrate the transformation of Kuyper's idea of the Protestant nation.

---

[21]   G. Abma and J. de Bruijn, *Hoedemaker herdacht* (Baarn, 1989), pp. 179, *passim.*

However, foreign policy was not a major preoccupation of either the ARP or of the other Dutch political parties. The Netherlands was neutral and nobody questioned this. There was no separate chapter on foreign policy in the party programme written by Kuyper in 1879; it was included in the chapter on diplomacy and military defence. However, there were strong statements on international law, Western culture and the international community. Kuyper considered the European nations as 'baptized nations', knit together by a Christian type of international law.[22] Europe was conceived as a connected organism. The nations had to act as brothers and care for each other. In the European organism, each nation had its place and function. Violations of international law should not be tolerated. These were the basic rules for the Christian community of European nations.

This was an appealing conception of how states ought to behave, derived from German romanticism and supplied with contemporary notions about international arbitration, but at the practical level of policy-making Kuyper and the members of his party did not believe in peaceful and harmonious relations between European states. Kuyper himself was a vigorous supporter of a strong army and doubted the fruitfulness of the movement for international peace, disarmament and arbitration for a long time.

Still, other opinions were of greater relevance. Kuyper had a weak spot for the *vox populi*, in which he heard the cry of conscience. As we have seen, Kuyper had deep respect for the historical spirit of the people. We can follow his opinions in his newspaper *De Standaard*. In 1882 he supported the revolt of Arabi Pasha in Egypt.[23] He compared the Egyptian fellahs with the Dutch in their struggle against Spain. He believed in the cry of the national spirit of the Egyptians who resisted British imperialism and capitalism. The Protestant press contained a polemic with Bronsveld and his colleague Buytendijk, who regarded England as

---

[22]   A. Kuyper, *Ons program*, pp. 303-307.
[23]   *De Standaard* in the summer of 1882, *passim*.

a Protestant nation, in this case the representative of Christianity in its struggle with Islam.[24] Kuyper, however, did not focus on state systems but on the spirit of a nation.

A similar position was apparent in 1898. In that year Kuyper sympathized with the struggle of the people of Cuba, strongly supported by the Americans against the Spanish colonialists. Although there was doubt in Protestant newspapers about the legitimacy of the American intervention, Kuyper, who visited the United States in the summer of 1898, declared that the 'conscience' of the American people had reacted against the injustice of Spanish rule in Cuba.[25] In 1900, after the outbreak of the second Boer War, Kuyper definitively broke with his old sympathy for England. Previously, just as in the Netherlands and the United States, he had viewed the conscience of the people as a mirror of Calvinist opinions about law and justice. Now he felt that England had become a country of imperialist money-makers and profit-hunters.[26]

According to Kuyper, the cry of the conscience of a people could only be heard when a people was a comprehensive unity. People must be one in customs, opinions, morality and language. In this way the national character could be maintained and rendered influential. These notions were used in Protestant newspapers in their response to the emigration movement in the last decennia of the nineteenth century. Emigrants were told that they could be good patriots abroad by trying to maintain their national character and by propagating their Calvinist principles. They must therefore stick together. Emigrants were advised to go to South Africa or

---

[24]   Bronsveld expressed this view in his column in the *Stemmen* 1882, pp. 327. S.H. Buytendijk expressed his view in his *Wageningsch Weekblad*, 1882, *passim*.

[25]   A. Kuyper, *Varia Americana* (Amsterdam, 1899), pp. 71, 18-5-191.

[26]   A. Kuyper, *De crisis in Zuid-Afrika* (Amsterdam, 1900).

North America, where they would meet and strengthen Dutch culture.[27]

These ideas, which betrayed a kind of cultural imperialism, originated in the years after the outbreak of the first Boer War in 1880, which caused an outbreak of nationalism in the Netherlands. It also led to a re-evaluation of the margins of Dutch foreign policy. Kuyper and other members of the ARP in particular argued that the Dutch government could not keep silent while the Dutch people - the conscience of the nation - was clamouring for action.[28] A prominent ARP member of parliament, Keuchenius, noted in his personal papers that the Boers 'had shown us the strength with which our fathers have fought for the Gospel and for freedom'.[29] A question was raised in parliament on 7 March 1881. Keuchenius argued that the Netherlands had to do something on behalf of the Dutch Boers. He understood that the government was concerned about British action against the Dutch colonies in the East, but stated that the government should not be guided by fear but by national feeling.[30] Keuchenius' intervention was called 'manly' and 'brave' in the Protestant press.[31]

This attitude of the ARP reflects the ambivalence of many orthodox Protestants toward Dutch neutrality. Deep down they did not like neutrality because they saw the Netherlands primarily as a Protestant nation. The Netherlands should stand for certain prin-

---

[27]   This can be seen in *De Standaard*, as well as in newspapers which were published in rural areas, such as the *Nieuwe Provinciale Groninger Courant*.

[28]   In January and February Kuyper repeatedly argued in *De Standaard* that the Dutch government should do something, while many governments in Europe supported the Boer cause. On 9 February he asked: 'what has been done so far, except signing addresses?'

[29]   Royal library, The Hague, collection-Keuchenius, nr.118.

[30]   Handelingen van de Tweede Kamer der Staten-Generaal, 1880--1881, 950-951. A record of this intervention in *De Standaard* of March 11 1881 and *De Protestantse Noord-Brabander* of 12 March 1881.

[31]   *Ibidem.*

ciples in the world. This should also be reflected in Dutch diplomacy. In *De Standaard* Kuyper repeatedly stressed that ambassadors must not distance themselves from their nation and national culture.[32] The nation had to speak through them, so they had to be in contact with the nation. This also implied a more pronounced foreign policy. In spite of its neutral status, the Netherlands should not be silent when international law was violated or people were massacred. In the 1890s, parliamentary members of the ARP pleaded for international protest against the Turks, who were persecuting and murdering the Armenians.

When Kuyper became Prime Minister in 1901, opposition newspapers voiced the fear that he would compromise the policy of neutrality. He was known as a supporter of a more active foreign policy, which he did indeed try to shape. In 1901 he offered Dutch mediation to the British government on behalf of the South African Boers, which indirectly led to the end of the war. He also intensified contacts with Brussels and Berlin. In the press he was called 'Minister of foreign travel'. He was subjected to questions in parliament by the opposition in 1904, because they did not trust all these contacts and travels. Nevertheless, it is not really clear what he wanted.[33] I think that he simply tried to advance a more active foreign policy, considering himself as the leader and the embodiment of Dutch national spirit.

---

[32]   *De Standaard*, November 1896, *passim*.
[33]   Cf. J. Fokkema, 'De buitenlandse politiek van Kuyper of Kuyper en de buitenlandse politiek?', *Antirevolutionaire Staatkunde*, 42 (1972): 289-300; E.H.Kossmann, *De Lage Landen, 1780-1940* (Amsterdam/Brussels, 1979), pp. 322-323; C.J.A. van Koppen, *De Geuzen van de Negentiende Eeuw. Abraham Kuyper en Zuid-Afrika* (Wormer, 1992), pp. 11-25; R. Kuiper, *Zelfbeeld en Wereldbeeld. Antirevolutionairen en het Buitenland* (Kampen, 1992), pp. 225-228.

Conclusion

We may conclude that two political concepts of the nation played a dominant role in orthodox Protestantism in the second half of the nineteenth century. Firstly, there was the old point of view that the Netherlands should be attached to its Protestant history, adhere to its old institutions of church and school, and try to win back the people to the old Protestant church by state influence. Political experiences after 1848 led to serious doubts about the possibilities of this route. From the 1870s on, Abraham Kuyper developed another concept, based on the political ideas of Groen van Prinsterer.

There was a remarkable difference in views between the political generation of Groen van Prinsterer and Kuyper's adherents. Not the state or history, but the Calvinist people itself was to influence the nation. Orthodox Protestants should not insist on their historical rights, but demonstrate their spiritual strength within the nation. It was their duty to do so because the conscience and culture of the Dutch people were held to be Calvinist in essence. Kuyper denied that the state as such had a religious character, but he believed in political influence when the conscience of the nation should speak through the institutions, organs and officials of the state. Kuyper defined the culture, customs and conscience of nations and people in the world in a romantic (Herderian) way.

His conception of the nation, however, could not be grasped by historical descriptions and sharp lines. Its purpose was to motivate and inspire his own people, not to convince others. Calvinist nationalism was meant for cultural practice. It was not translated in political theory, but it gave a spiritual meaning to anti-revolutionary action. It was the translation of Protestant nationalism for modern society. The anti-revolutionaries saw themselves as performers of a national mission, not conservative sticklers for old traditions and institutions. They were not attached to historical forms, because they felt themselves to be the true representatives of the historical Dutch nation in all circumstances.

This idea of Calvinism as a basic feature was dynamic and proved to be enduring. Because the anti-revolutionaries believed themselves to be in touch with the spirit of the nation, they could abandon old-fashioned opinions and adapt to new circumstances time and again. As late as the 1930s, the ARP leader and Prime Minister Colijn stressed repeatedly and strongly that the ARP just supported the national interest. 'Therefore', he said in 1937 when his party had achieved a position of dominance in Dutch politics, 'the way to the renewed viability of Dutch Calvinism for the benefit of the fatherland does not lead through the sultry atmosphere of a political lumber-room, but forges its way in the service of the fatherland in its greatest, highest and deepest national interests'.[34]

---

[34]   H. Colijn, *Voor het Gemeenebest* (Utrecht, 1938),   p. 36.

Zij en .... wij.

'Them and ... us'.
The degenerate bourgeois student and the fit, respectable AJC boy.
(The socialist *Notenkraker* 29 May 1926)

HOW HIGH DID THE DUTCH FLY? REMARKS ON STEREOTYPES OF BURGER MENTALITY

Henk te Velde

To say that the Dutch are 'burgerlijk'[1] or that the Netherlands has a 'burgerlijke' tradition[2] is to trot out a cliché, but what does it mean? This article will deal with a feature of Dutch national character that is difficult to translate: the word 'burgerlijk'. Whoever tries to find an English equivalent will probably choose *bourgeois*. Like bourgeois, though slightly less, *burgerlijk* has a ring of materialism and can be used as a term of abuse or as a (more or less neutral) term to characterize the nineteenth or twentieth-century middle classes. Indeed, *burgerlijk* refers to the values, spirit and attitude of the

---

[1]   E.g. A. Chorus, *De Nederlander uiterlijk en innerlijk. Een karakteristiek* (Leiden, 1967), passim or, recently, G. Hofstede, *Gevolgen van het Nederlanderschap. Gezondheid, recht en economie* (s.l., s.d.), p. 9 and P. Thoenes, P.B. Cliteur and S.W. Couwenberg in *Op de grens van twee eeuwen. Positie en perspectief van Nederland in het zicht van het jaar 2000*, ed. S.W. Couwenberg (Kampen, 1989), pp. 11-13, 35-37, 192-196.
[2]   E.H. Kossmann, 'Eender en anders. De evenwijdigheid van de Belgische en Nederlandse geschiedenis na 1830' in Id., *Politieke Theorie en Geschiedenis* (Amsterdam, 1987), p. 379.

middle classes. *Burgerlijk* also refers to the burgher estate of the Ancien Régime. 'Burger' though, the noun that accompanies *burgerlijk*, sounds more neutral than 'bourgeois'. 'Burger' signifies not only bourgeois, but also burgher or inhabitant of an early modern town, and especially *citizen* of a country.[3] So 'burgerplicht' should be translated as civic duty. Whoever uses the words 'burger', 'burgerij' and 'burgerlijk' should be very careful. Are the Dutch *burgerlijk*, and have they always been *burgerlijk*? It depends on the definition of terms and their range. Who are *the* Dutch and what is *burgerlijk*? One has to bear in mind that the writer who uses these words often has a political or cultural purpose in doing so. Many interesting discussions start with the question: what do you mean?

It is not enough to determine the meaning of the word in general. Its meaning in each historical period requires examination. The following discussion traces the evolution of the term from the nineteenth century on. The point of departure will be the work of Johan Huizinga, the leading historian of the period between the wars. As will be made clear, he played a pivotal role in the discussion. The story will then go back from Huizinga to the previous century before returning to the thirties. The article focuses on the political and social significance of the way the word *burgerlijk* was used by the political and intellectual elite; the sources for this story will be the comments of intellectuals on Dutch culture and politics. Thus the term *burgerlijk* will be placed in its historical context.

Huizinga used the word *burgerlijk* to characterize the Dutch with great emphasis and very explicitly: 'Whether we fly high or low, we Dutchmen are all *burgerlijk* - lawyer and poet, baron and labourer alike. Our national culture is *burgerlijk* in every sense that you can legitimately attach to that word.'[4] According to Huizinga, in his

---

3   The same goes for the German 'Bürger'.

4   J. Huizinga, 'The spirit of the Netherlands' in Id., *Dutch Civilisation in the Seventeenth Century* (London, 1968), p. 112. The translator uses the word 'bourgeois' and also makes a small mistake. In literal translation

'Spirit of the Netherlands' (1934), the dominant *burger* spirit narrowed the distance between the classes and was the basis of the national community: it inspired not only the bourgeois but also the 'baron' and the 'labourer'. The Dutch were neat and proper, and the flaws in the national character were petty-bourgeois stinginess and rudeness. Dutch history testified to civic freedom and civic virtues, to lack of military spirit and a paramount spirit of commerce. The Dutch respected the rights and views of others and Dutch nationalism was not irredentist; most of all, the Dutch were 'unheroic' and not liable to political extremism.

Huizinga did not annotate his essay; he probably wrote it off the cuff. He was summarising common knowledge, not presenting a new view of Dutch culture. Nevertheless, his essay did not resemble the average sociological study of the Dutch national character.[5] Huizinga did not dwell on the influence of the climate and the Frisian or Saxon 'race' on the national character; he did not aim for positivist exactitude but deliberately wrote a moralistic article - the intention of his essay will be discussed below. This intention made him use the *word burgerlijk* to sum up Dutch national character.[6]

---

the phrase would read: 'Whether we like it or not..' However, I liked the translation and kept it for the title. Thanks to Wessel E. Krul for comments and discussion.

[5]   B. van Heerikhuizen, 'What is typically Dutch? Sociologists in the 1930s and 1940s on the Dutch national character', *The Netherlands Journal of Sociology* 18 (1982): 103-125; cf. G. van Veen, 'Nederlands geestes-merk in verband met opgaven van deze tijd', *Volksontwikkeling* 16 (1934-1935): 266-280.

[6]   Cf. *after* his essay A.J.C Rüter, 'De Nederlandse natie en het Nederlandse volkskarakter' (1941-1945) in Id., *Historische studies over mens en samenleving* (Assen, 1967), pp. 318-320 and A.C. Josephus Jitta, *Het Nederlandsch volkskarakter* (Maastricht, s.d.), p. 21.

Before the 1930s

Although they did not always use the word *burgerlijk*, Dutch writers of the intellectual elite had attributed similar characteristics to their national culture throughout the nineteenth century. In the Biedermeier period of the early nineteenth century they praised the 'typically' Dutch homeliness and moderation. The classical liberals of the middle of that century rejected stuffy petty-bourgeois values, propagated a revival of the 'typically' Dutch civic spirit of the Golden Age, and thought that the middle classes were the 'core' of the nation.[7] The liberal bourgeoisie of the nineteenth century believed it embodied the *essence* of the national tradition. Although it was a minority, it would have to lead the Dutch in the right, national, and therefore bourgeois liberal direction.[8] The orthodox Calvinists of the end of the nineteenth century also emphasized civic spirit and civic freedom. They, however, believed that the orthodox lower middle class constituted the core of the nation.[9] By then the leading role of the liberal upper middle class in politics and cultural life was no longer self-evident.

The Roman Catholics, the Calvinist lower middle class and, somewhat later on, the Socialist lower class demanded a fair share of political power and a place on the cultural scene. This entailed a socio-political struggle that ended provisionally in an amendment of the constitution of 1917 to allow universal male suffrage[10] and full subsidy for denominational schools. The reactions of the classical liberals to the beginning of this process may be illustrated by the

---

[7]   Cf. R. Aerts, 'De nationale cultuur: een intellectuele discussie in de negentiende eeuw', *Comenius* 38 (1990): 236-255.

[8]   See *De Nederlandsche Spectator* 1 (1860) no. 1 for a fine example of liberal pretence (national = liberal).

[9]   A. Kuyper, *"Ons Program"* (Amsterdam, 1880), pp. 19, 307-308, 413. See the contribution to this volume by Roel Kuiper.

[10]   It entailed universal female suffrage in 1919. This essay focuses on political parties and their context; women did not form a separate party and the women's movement will be left aside here, though a gender analysis of *burger* and *burgerlijk* could be useful.

work of the historian Robert Fruin. He feared the uneducated masses and the dogmatism of the religious parties as threats to the national unity, tradition and identity. In 1870 Fruin had written an essay on Dutch national character. Although only the first signs of the emancipation movements could be seen, liberalism had already lost its initial zest and Fruin's essay was pervaded by quiet scepticism. In his view, the Dutch were reliable but conventional workers. Dutch intellectuals dutifully assimilated the fine achievements of foreign cultures, but they were rarely brilliant: though it had its own identity, Dutch culture lacked greatness. In a spirit of liberal arrogance, Fruin let slip an additional remark about the 'people': 'Everywhere, in all countries, the lower classes (lagere klassen des volks) are un-civilized.' And everywhere they would be uncivilized in a similar way. It would therefore be almost pointless to look for a national identity in the slums of the big cities. Clearly, Fruin thought that only the bourgeoisie kept up the national tradition. As long as the liberal bourgeoisie determined the course of the nation, this conviction posed no problems.[11]

In the face of the growing political influence of the masses, however, a calm and sceptical attitude no longer seemed enough to maintain the national heritage. From time to time a call for vigorous political and national leadership might be heard. In 1890, one of the editors of the important liberal review *De Gids* called for a leader to mark a new era of national greatness. In line with the national *burgerlijke* history, he preferred this leader to be a 'Raadpensionaris', a Dutch Secretary of State of the Old Regime, not an emperor or even a king.[12] No such leader appeared, and the liberal elite looked

---

[11]   R. Fruin [with S. Vissering], 'Het karakter van het Nederlandsche volk' in Id., *Verspreide Geschriften* 1 (The Hague, 1900), pp. 1-21. On Fruin and the problems of the conservative liberals see P.B.M. Blaas, 'The touchiness of a small nation with a great past: the approach of Fruin and Blok to the writing of the history of the Netherlands' in *Britain and the Netherlands* 8, ed. A.C. Duke and C.A. Tamse (Zutphen, 1985), pp. 133-161.

[12]   W.G.C. Byvanck, 'Rembrandt-legende', *De Gids* (1890): II 298.

for another way to safeguard the national future. After about 1880, the upper middle class hesitantly and gradually began to accept the modern age of mass politics where the 'people' played a new part. Sometimes, as in the case of Huizinga, this acceptance remained qualified, and sometimes it was the outcome of a painful process of adjustment.

In a country without an independent, powerful nobility, the upper middle class constituted the elite. In the nineteenth century this elite regarded itself as the personification of the national tradition - which was presumed to be tolerant and liberal - and wanted to educate the people. This education was to inculcate the national values into the people: according to the upper middle class, these were the values of the serious, responsible, decent and broad-minded *burger*. This did not include zealous Calvinism, not to mention ultramontane Catholicism or revolutionary Socialism. The emancipatory movements of the lower middle and lower classes that embodied these ideologies were considered by the liberal elite as a threat to the national tradition and a source of the disintegration of the fatherland. As elsewhere in Europe, the *fin de siècle* was the period of the crisis of liberalism.

In the nineteenth century liberals had wanted to educate the people, but they had usually refrained from questioning the rigid structure of social groups. Now they realized that in a modern society national unity implied a breakdown of the walls between the classes. After 1900, not only the dangerous international situation but also the hundredth anniversary of the kingdom (1913) and the impending universal suffrage gave rise to reflections on the national character. Many of these reflections deplored the lack of cultural community[13] and social unity and the distance between the classes.[14] In 1913 the

---

[13]   J. Havelaar, 'Holland. Wezen en waarde van ons nationaal karakter', *De Gids* (1916): II 275-277.

[14]   E.g. Th.M. Roest van Limburg, *Ons volkskarakter. Een studie in volkspsychologie* (Amsterdam, 1917), pp. 53, 55; Cf. H.Th. Colenbrander, '1848' (1905) in Id., *Historie en Leven* 2 (Amsterdam, s.d.), p. 193.

complaint could be heard that the gap between the respectable, distinguished middle classes and the 'coarse and undomesticated' lower class was much deeper than in Italy, France or Germany. No joint national culture linked the civilized bourgeoisie to the people.[15] According to the liberal historian Colenbrander, the emancipation of the proletariat meant a 'crisis of civilization'. The worker had lost all sense of community except class-consciousness. When the worker would get the vote, however, he would learn how to use it: parliamentary politics was a 'school' and children behaved better at school than out on the street.[16] Colenbrander was a prominent commentator. His views, and the opinion of those who mourned the rift in the Dutch people, did not go unnoticed. All the same, only twenty years later Huizinga, who was editor of *De Gids* like Colenbrander, wrote in his *Spirit of the Netherlands* that the Dutch people were *more* homogeneous than the people of other countries. In an article that paid tribute to Huizinga, the liberal educationalist Kohnstamm wrote that the Dutch should pay more attention to national tradition and national unity. However, after three-quarters of a century in which the Dutch people seemed to be falling apart, there were signs of improvement.[17]

What had changed? Had the lower classes been educated and domesticated in the meantime? In 1938 a historian compared the Dutch people of the thirties to the rough Dutch emigrants to South Africa at the end of the nineteenth century, and concluded that an 'important and constructive work' of education had been done,[18] but

---

[15]   C. Scharten, 'De roeping onzer dichtkunst', *De Gids* (1913): II 184-186.
[16]   H.Th. Colenbrander, 'De staatkundige ontwikkeling der Nederlanders voor honderd jaar en thans' (1913) in Id., *Historie en Leven* 2 (Amsterdam, s.d.), pp. 98-107.
[17]   Ph. Kohnstamm, 'De geestelijke gevaren van het nationaal-socialisme', *De Opbouw* 17 (1934-1935): 345, 347.
[18]   P.J. van Winter, *Onder Krugers Hollanders. Geschiedenis van de Nederlandsche Zuid-Afrikaansche Spoorweg-Maatschappij* 2 (Amsterdam, 1938), p. 81.

he did not pretend that this work had been done in only twenty years. Before examining this problem, it will be useful to compare Dutch views with foreign comments on the same subject.

Burger, Bürger, bourgeois

Huizinga called the Dutch *burgerlijk* and he obviously thought that the Dutch were more *burgerlijk* than others. One wonders what his opinion would have been of the following statements. In 1918 Thomas Mann wrote in his *Betrachtungen eines Unpolitischen*: 'das Deutsche und das Bürgerliche, das ist eins'. Six years later, René Johannet, a French *homme de lettres*, wrote a best-selling essay in which he stated that France was 'la plus bourgeoise des nations' and that of all the countries in the world France had the greatest right to call herself an 'Etat bourgeois'. Finally, among the Swiss it was not unusual to say 'Wir sind alle Bürger'. What does this mean?[19]

Evidently not all writers meant the same when they used the word 'bourgeois' or 'Bürger'. Mann wrote his rather rambling book in the exciting years of the First World War. He defended German *Kultur* against English and French *Zivilisation* and *bürgerliche Bildung* against *bourgeois* materialism. Bound by historical tradition, the *Bürger* lived in an ideal balance. The German *Bürgertum* could rely on a great tradition created by scholars and writers like Kant, Goethe and Schiller. This tradition included Schopenhauer, Wagner and Nietzsche, and Mann wondered whether the German nature wavered between the *Bürger* and the artist and contained the best of both worlds. He criticized the rationalistic 'antiheroism' of *Zivilisation*... and seemed to advocate almost the opposite to Huizinga's

---

[19]   T. Mann, 'Betrachtungen eines Unpolitischen' in Id., *Gesammelte Werke* 12 (Frankfurt am Main, 1960), p. 107. R. Johannet, *Eloge du Bourgeois Français* (Paris, 1924), pp. 16, 62; cf. A. Daumard, *Les bourgeois et la bourgeoisie en France depuis 1815* (Paris, 1987), pp. 41-42. A. Tanner, 'Bürgertum und Bürgerlichkeit in der Schweiz. Die 'Mittelklassen' an der Macht' in *Bürgertum im 19. Jahrhundert. Deutschland im europäischen Vergleich* 1, ed. J. Kocka (Munich, 1988), p. 194.

views; for Huizinga had stressed the 'unheroic' element in the *burger*.[20]

Johannet proudly stated that his country could rely on the French *bourgeois*, much more than their respective countries could depend on the German 'baron' or the 'businessman' from Manchester or Chicago. The moderation and love of the *juste milieu* guarded him from the plutocracy of his German, English and American counterparts. It was almost the case that without the bourgeoisie no French tradition existed and no French government was possible. However, the bourgeoisie should defend its position and free France from the Socialist and proletarian threat, and should fight and win the battle between the elite and the masses, between civilisation and barbarism. Johannet praised Maurras and Sorel, hoped for a new Napoleon or a French Mussolini... and seemed to advocate almost the opposite to Huizinga's views: Huizinga had not called for class struggle, but had stressed the *burgerlijke* unity of the people.[21]

Obviously, there were many different perceptions of the bourgeoisie. All writers, however, expected something from the bourgeoisie, or perhaps one should say from a bourgeois life-style. Did the interbellum period mark a revaluation of the bourgeois style of living? Many a historian has described the *Belle Epoque* as the end of the bourgeois period,[22] but the period after the Great War witnessed a revival of bourgeois self-confidence.[23] This self-confidence probably decreased after the roaring twenties. In the face of the Great Depression and the totalitarian threat, pessimism spread. However, the interest in the bourgeoisie remained. Many publications

---

[20]   Mann, 'Betrachtungen eines Unpolitischen', pp. 72 ff., 104, 111, 501 and passim. Th. Mann, 'Gedanken im Kriege' in Id., *Friedrich und die grosse Koalition* (Berlin, 1915), p. 8; cf. p. 16 where he uses the past participle 'verbürgerlicht' in a pejorative sense.

[21]   Johannet, *Bourgeois Français*.

[22]   E.J. Hobsbawm, *The Age of Empire 1875-1914* (London, 1987), pp. 165-191 and passim; J. Romein, *The watershed of two eras. Europe in 1900* (Middletown, 1978), e.g. p. 37.

[23]   At least in France: Daumard, *Bourgeois et bourgeoisie*, pp. 41-42.

on the bourgeoisie appeared in the interbellum period. Those that did not *attack* the bourgeoisie were conservative in one way or another: they looked back to the golden age of the bourgeoisie, or they wanted to preserve and protect the endangered bourgeois values. Virtually all these writers concentrated on the bourgeois life-style, not on the economic or social position of the bourgeoisie. They all praised the bourgeoisie as a cultural or moral model, not as a social class.[24]

The different perceptions of the bourgeoisie had several things in common. Huizinga, Mann and Johannet all rejected both the American and the Soviet way of life and praised the discipline of the responsible, serious, economical and decent bourgeois. Mann wanted to protect the key values of the bourgeoisie from the materialism of the French, Johannet from the materialism of the Germans and communists, Huizinga from the materialism and pseudo-heroism of the Communists and the Nazis. This is the heart of the problem. Those that did not want to join the Communists and still wanted to fight the Nazis fell back on the bourgeois values. They tried to separate those values from their social background and pass them off as national values for the entire population. Having accepted 'Western' democracy in the meantime, Thomas Mann again advocated *Bürgerlichkeit*, but to protect Germany from the Nazis he underlined the simplicity, thrift and discipline of great German authors like Goethe.[25] For the first time since the Biedermeier

---

[24]   E. Goblot, *La barrière et le niveau. Etude sociologique sur la bourgeoisie française moderne* (Paris, 1967 [1925]), p. 2, thought that a class only existed in the 'moeurs' and 'opinions' and O. Gmelin, *Naturgeschichte des Bürgers* (Jena, 1929), p. 5, confronted the *bürgerliche* attitude with the 'ecstatic' or 'vagabond' attitude, not bourgeoisie with proletariat or nobility.

[25]   T. Mann, 'Goethe als Repräsentant des bürgerlichen Zeitalters' (1932) in Id., *Gesammelte Werke* 9 (Frankfurt am Main, 1974), pp. 297-332; cf. 'Bürgerlichkeit', *Ibidem* 11, pp. 411-413. In 1918 he had seen such qualities in Schopenhauer and had emphasized the typically German artist-with-*bürgerliche*-qualities: 'Betrachtungen eines Unpolitischen', pp. 104, 107. However, in 1932 the accent was different. Cf. on the problematic

period, leading intellectuals recommended conservative and quiet bourgeois values almost without reserve. Huizinga in particular did so. Fruin had written in resignation that Dutch culture only had the style of respectability, whereas Huizinga was delighted with the Dutch lack of an urge to greatness.

Huizinga in the Dutch thirties

Even some critics of the bourgeoisie mended their ways. In 1931 the well-known Dutch essayist Menno ter Braak had published a book that applauded the 'poet' and pilloried the stiff, narrow-minded, insipid 'burger'. In his eyes, not only the *burger* as bourgeois, but also the *burger* as citizen was an impersonal and conventional 'atom' in the crowd. He rejected Huizinga's essay but was very active in the Dutch anti-Fascist movement. Finally, even he changed his opinion of the qualities of the *burger:* he appealed to all 'honest and decent men' to fight the Nazis. In his fight against Nazism, Ter Braak defended parliamentary democracy without illusions and without great enthusiasm. In those years, only liberal political parties did not question the parliamentary system. Even Ter Braak shared to some extent the common misunderstanding that equated parliamentary democracy with materialistic politics in which quantity counted instead of quality. A liberal-minded intellectual like Huizinga did so even more than Ter Braak, for instance in *The Spirit of the Netherlands*. Huizinga did not like party politics or proportional representation, so in his defence of the quiet and tolerant Dutch tradition against Fascist 'heroism', he advocated not democracy but *burgerlijkheid*.[26]

German *Bürgerlichkeit* e.g. L. Gall, ''...Ich wünschte ein Bürger zu sein'. Zum Selbstverständnis des deutschen Bürgertums im 19. Jahrhundert', *Historische Zeitschrift* 245 (1987): 601-623.
[26]   M. ter Braak, *Het carnaval der burgers. Een gelijkenis in gelijkenissen* (Amsterdam, 1967 [1931]), pp. 19-21 and passim. See on the intellectual relationship between Huizinga and his great-nephew Ter Braak: W.E. Krul, 'Menno ter Braak contra Huizinga. Over de grenzen van de

Now it is clear why Huizinga underlined *burgerlijke* values, but how could he pretend to depict what united all the Dutch? As is well known, the Dutch were divided into religious and political groups that did not seem to have much in common. Socialists, Catholics and Protestants lived in separate worlds. They had their own sports clubs, broadcasting corporations and youth movements. These propagated Socialist, Catholic and Protestant world views respectively. Apparently it was only tolerance and 'accommodation' which prevented the Netherlands from civil war and falling apart in rival groups. The leaders of the various political and religious denominations appear to have succeeded in keeping their supporters quiet and in reaching compromises.[27]

Was this the whole truth? Huizinga did not think so: 'We Dutchmen are all *burgerlijk*'. Of course, Huizinga's liberal intellectual milieu possessed this quality, but was this also true of the Dutch people at large? How could he say so at a time when the end of the bourgeoisie was announced?[28] How could he say so in the midst of the mass unemployment and the proletarian poverty of the thirties?

---

ironie' in Id., *Historicus tegen de tijd. Opstellen over leven en werk van J. Huizinga* (Groningen 1990) pp. 264-287. E.H. Kossmann, *The low countries 1780-1940* (Oxford, 1978) p. 574; A.A. de Jonge, *Crisis en critiek der democratie. Anti-democratische stromingen en de daarin levende denkbeelden over de staat in Nederland tussen de wereldoorlogen* (Utrecht, 1982), esp. p. 11. It was not until after the Second World War that all the main political parties accepted parliamentary democracy without reservations. Huizinga's colleague Pieter Geyl did advocate democracy; according to him, nowhere was democracy more in line with national character and tradition than in the Netherlands: P. Geyl, 'Historische wortels van de Nederlandse democratie' (1940) in J. van Gelderen etc., *Nederland. Erfdeel en taak* (Amsterdam, 1946), p. 64.

27   The classic study of the subject is A. Lijphart, *The politics of accommodation: pluralism and democracy in the Netherlands* (Berkeley, 1968); cf. Kossmann, *Low countries*, pp. 568-574. But see S. Stuurman, *Verzuiling, kapitalisme en patriarchaat. Aspecten van de ontwikkeling van de moderne staat in Nederland* (Nijmegen, 1983).

28   E.g. Goblot, *Barrière et niveau*, pp. 105-108.

Obviously, he did not mean to say that all Dutch belonged to the middle classes, but that all Dutch shared the same middle-class mentality. He thought Dutch culture had expressed in the past and in the present civic (and middle-class) *ideals*. Significantly, Huizinga did not confront bourgeois values with proletarian ones, but with the attitude of the Bohemian *artist*.[29] He presented the *burger* not as a social but as a cultural type. He advocated not the capitalist materialist bourgeois, but the values of the traditional, steady burgher. In the age of mass democracy when the attitude and values of the 'people' mattered more than before, Huizinga wrote about national values without linking them to social position as Fruin had done in 1870. Of course, it was no coincidence that he chose the word *burgerlijk*. Deliberately, however, he took the word *burger* with its suggestion of seventeenth-century tradition, and not bourgeois that was linked to the nineteenth-century class society.

One has to bear in mind that Huizinga wrote his essay in the 1930s.[30] In Simon Schama's view, Huizinga's bourgeois ideals did not fit what Schama sees as the heroic and insatiable Dutch of the Golden Age.[31] Nor were the ideas of the 1930s identical with the liberal ideals of the nineteenth-century bourgeoisie. The liberal ideal was progressive; Huizinga's ideal was conservative. Huizinga was not looking for a small vanguard that embodied the *essence* of the national tradition and could guide the nation; he was looking for the

---

[29]   Huizinga said as much in a letter of 18.12.1927: Id., *Briefwisseling* 2, ed. L. Hansen, G.A.C. van der Lem and W.E. Krul (Utrecht, Antwerp, 1990), pp. 181-182.

[30]   Peter Gay did not realize this and did not distinguish the bourgeoisie as a class from *burgerlijkheid* as an ideal when he criticized Huizinga on this point: P. Gay, *The Bourgeois experience. Victoria to Freud. vol. 1. Education of the senses* (New York, Oxford, 1984), pp. 17-35, esp. 29. Perhaps the translation of Huizinga's text caused a misunderstanding: bourgeois (noun + adjective) is not the same as *burgerlijk* (adjective: *like* a *burger*).

[31]   S. Schama, *The embarrassment of riches. An interpretation of Dutch Culture in the Golden Age* (London, 1987), pp. 4-7, 568-569.

common denominator. In the 1930s, Socialists, Liberals, Catholics and orthodox Protestants all advocated some *burgerlijke* values. As they were supposed to be dangerous enemies of the (liberal) bourgeoisie, the attitude of the Socialists merits special attention.

Socialist and burger

In the nineteenth century the liberal elite had feared that the politics of the religious parties would bring about the disintegration of the fatherland. In the period between the wars the denominational politics proved to be respectable and conservative. Since the end of the nineteenth century some liberal and denominational politicians and intellectuals had feared the revolutionary potential of the Socialist masses. As late as 1918, Socialist revolutionary rhetoric scared the conservative bourgeois. Gradually, however, the Socialist Party proved to be a party like the others. Moreover, Socialist leaders turned out to be respectable and decent politicians. After the introduction of universal suffrage, they certainly had something to lose; the organization built up to conduct the class struggle began to live its own life. Writing about Dutch national character, a prominent liberal educationalist even postulated that the Dutch people was bound to have a sense of unity: everyone had equal rights so that no one could feel oppressed.[32] He ignored the real social inequality and the fact that until 1939 there were no Socialist ministers, but as far as Socialist leaders were concerned, there was something in it.

The structure of Dutch society had changed. In the nineteenth century society had been split horizontally. The upper middle class pulled the strings and lived in relative isolation from the lower middle and lower classes. Though that structure remained in existence in the twentieth century, at least to some extent, it was complemented by a vertical division of society. The separate worlds that lived side by

---

[32]   R. Casimir, 'Ons volkskarakter en tegenwoordige stromingen', *De Opbouw* 17 (1934-1935): 350.

side constituted a number of blocks. Now there were several rivalling elites, whereas previously there had been a united (bourgeois) elite. Dutch society was thus hopelessly divided, but then again there was more unity than before. The Catholic and orthodox Protestant elites bridged the gap between the world of the bourgeoisie and the religious lower middle and lower classes. The Socialist elite bridged the gap between the middle classes and the proletariat. This is not to say that the proletariat became bourgeois, but that the Socialists *translated* proletarian demands in a formula that could be discussed in the middle-class world of politics and intellectual culture.

Some commentators even thought that all European Socialists were *burgerlijk* because they strove, even more than others, for bourgeois ideals like order, justice and safety.[33] The Socialist movement or, for that matter, the religious parties certainly contained elements of a *burgerlijke* world view. A sense of responsibility, refusal of hedonism, a certain abnegation and the wish to realize long-term ideals could be classified as *burgerlijk*.[34] But all blocks were founded on these basic assumptions. In spite of their different political ideals and organizations, the blocks were united in a common effort, more structured than ever before, to educate and civilize the people and initiate it into the world of the serious *burger*. Of course they did not succeed completely, but every confirmed adherent of a block had to adopt some *burger* values.

In the nineteenth century liberals had accused Socialists of hedonism and materialism. Actually, the Socialist movement had been serious and ascetic from the beginning and as soon as it gave up its revolutionary pretensions, it fitted perfectly well into *burgerlijke* Dutch society. The cultural ideals of the youth movement of the Socialist elite, the AJC (Arbeiders Jeugd Centrale, Workers' Youth Movement), testified to this. The AJC wanted to fight the capitalist bourgeois mentality. Its aim, however, was in fact an improved

---

[33]   The German Otto Gmelin in his perceptive essay *Naturgeschichte des Bürgers*, p. 21.
[34]   *Ibidem*, pp. 14-15 and passim.

burgerlijke culture. The AJC attached great value to self-control, maintained strict - though somewhat unconventional - morals, rejected swearing, drinking, smoking, sensual dancing and was more interested in educating the people than in fighting its oppression. The AJC turned against the individualism of capitalism and aimed for a new cultural community.[35]

The AJC was a sign of the loss of social and political radicalism of the Socialist movement. The Socialists began to underline their solidarity with the national community and they changed their attitude to the royal family.[36] This alteration led to remarkable similarities between Socialist views of the national character and Huizinga's opinion. The Socialist sociologist Kruyt thought that democratic, humanistic, ethical Socialism fitted the Dutch national character, whereas a dictatorship of the proletariat did not. According to him, the ecstatic and revolutionary Socialism of the nineteenth century had never stood a chance of winning over the Dutch people. The practical Socialism of the current Social Democratic party was in line with the sober, level-headed Dutch mind. This Socialism could give the individualistic Dutch the sense of community they needed.[37] Kruyt did not use the word *burgerlijk*. The Marxist historians Jan and Annie Romein did. In their book on the great figures of Dutch history, they stressed the *burgerlijke* character of many of them. Writing in 1938, they hoped that Europe would learn something from Dutch 'moderation'.[38] Jan Romein even wrote that the freedom, tolerance and human dignity of *burgerlijke* tradition

---

[35]   G.J. Harmsen, *Blauwe en rode jeugd. Een bijdrage tot de geschiedenis van de Nederlandse jeugdbeweging tussen 1853 en 1940* (Assen, 1961), pp. 186-200; L. Hartveld, F. de Jong, D. Kuperus, *De Arbeiders Jeugd Centrale AJC* (Amsterdam, 1982), passim.

[36]   P.J. Knegtmans, *Socialisme en democratie. De SDAP tussen klasse en natie (1929-1939)* (Amsterdam, 1989), pp. 201-203, 253.

[37]   J.P. Kruyt, *Het Nederlandsche Volkskarakter en het Socialisme* (Arnhem, 1934), pp. 68-69, 76-81.

[38]   J. and A. Romein, *Erflaters van onze beschaving. Nederlandse gestalten uit zes eeuwen* (Amsterdam, 1979 [1938]), pp. 7, 14, 177, 182.

Dutch and Belgian Limburg since 1839

J. Craandijk, 1834-1912.
(*Eigen Haard* 1912, vol. II, p. 377)

had instilled 'liberalism' into all great Dutch politicians. Socialist, Calvinist or Catholic, in a certain way they had all been nineteenth-century liberals.[39]

Comparison

With certain restrictions, Dutch political culture of the thirties can be termed *burgerlijk*.[40] The Socialist, orthodox Protestant and Catholic blocks rejected the individualistic nineteenth-century *laisser faire* liberalism, but in doing so they virtually continued and even intensified the old, liberal and *burgerlijk* process of civilization. The ideals that were expressed in political or social activities bore a *burgerlijk* mark. But was Dutch culture more *burgerlijk* than other cultures? Romein had written about the 'liberalism' of Dutch history but, along the same lines, it has been argued that 'the strange death of liberal England' after the First World War meant that many liberal ideals had been absorbed by all parties.[41] Johannet and Mann thought that their respective national traditions were bourgeois.

At least after 1933, Germany was no longer *burgerlijk* in the meaning Huizinga gave the word, but were Britain or France? Obviously, one has to take into account the respective national traditions. One could cite the Dutch burgher of the Golden Age or the relatively harmonious Dutch history as proof of the *burgerlijke* spirit of the Dutch, but then perhaps one would miss the point. It is

---

[39]   J. Romein, 'Oorsprong, voortgang en toekomst van de Nederlandse geest' (1940) in Id., *In opdracht van de tijd. Tien voordrachten over historische thema's* (Amsterdam, 1946), pp. 163-167.

[40]   Cf. J.C.H. Blom, 'Nederland in de jaren dertig: een 'burgerlijk-verzuilde' maatschappij in een crisis-periode' in Id., *Crisis, bezetting en herstel. Tien studies over Nederland 1930-1950* (The Hague, 1989), esp. pp. 14 ff.

[41]   D. Smith, 'Englishness and the liberal inheritance after 1886' in *Englishness. Politics and Culture 1880-1920*, ed. R. Colls and P. Dodd (London etc., 1986).

illuminating to compare Huizinga with Mann. Mann interpreted the
Bürgerlichkeit of such great artists as Goethe and Kant as the *essence*
and the *height* of German culture. Huizinga considered the *burgerlijk*
element in Dutch culture to be essential, but not only or even mainly
its height. Mann stressed the *great* tradition of Germany and, though
he was proud of the great Dutch history, Huizinga stressed the
modest, perhaps partly even the *small*, tradition of Dutch *burgerlijkheid*.

One could argue that Mann tried to characterize the spirit of
German *high culture*, and Huizinga the spirit of the entire Dutch
society. This is not surprising. Kossmann has argued that the Germans
- like the English or French - possess a great and continuous cultural
tradition, whereas the Netherlands does not have such a tradition, but
comments on, interprets and absorbs the outstanding foreign cultural
products.[42] Kossmann probably exaggerates the difference between
the Dutch and the German or English traditions. However, one does
not have to deny the continuity of the Dutch cultural tradition to
acknowledge that the Dutch elite often considered itself as a cultural
crossroads. It was thus almost natural in the divided society of the
thirties for the intellectual to single out middle-of-the-road *burgerlijkheid* as the character and the common denominator of Dutch
society, whereas the German or French intellectual would be inclined
to point to the greatness of their respective national high cultures. It
would be interesting to compare the Dutch to the Swiss case. The
Swiss elite regarded Swiss society as *bürgerlich*, and in the Netherlands it has been customary to compare the two countries superficial-
ly.[43] A comprehensive comparison has never been made.

As stated above, from a *cultural* point of view 'burgerlijk' was

---

[42]   E.H. Kossmann, 'How to write Dutch cultural history?', *Dutch
Crossing* 38 (1989): 3-15.
[43]   E.g. Roest van Limburg, *Ons volkskarakter*, pp. 6-7; Chorus *De
Nederlander uiterlijk en innerlijk*, pp. 58, 158; Couwenberg, 'Culturele
identiteit' in Id. ed., *Op de grens van twee eeuwen*, pp. 192-193.

mainly a term of abuse (though less so than the French and English 'bourgeois' and only rarely before the last quarter of the nineteenth century[44]). The outstanding author Multatuli attacked *burgerlijk*, narrow-minded and 'distasteful stiffness'. The Socialist artist Herman Gorter denounced the 'petty-bourgeois meanness' (klein-burgerlijke laagheid) of Dutch nineteenth-century culture, and even included Multatuli in his condemnation. In 1923 Colenbrander wanted to give the Dutch people, who had grown lonely and *burgerlijk* (verburge-rlijkt), the great political historiography that it needed to deal with and grasp its discontinuous history. Colenbrander wanted to give consistency and continuity to Dutch society and national tradition by putting up a great cultural performance. He apparently wanted to *overcome* the sleepy *burgerlijkheid*.[45]

From a *political* point of view things looked different. In 1875 the romantic liberal Quack could not resist citing a 'brilliant page' of Renan predicting a new community life after the current 'narrow-minded, bourgeois, mediocre society' had been swept away, but Quack rapidly continued his historical argument and left Renan to 'dream about the future'.[46] Sometimes Dutch bourgeois felt tempted to live dangerously, but they never gave in to the temptation. In the face of the totalitarian threat in the 1930s, the dull cultural mediocrity seemed a political golden mean.[47] The dull *burgerlijke* Dutch could turn out to be reliable, responsible citizens. After the nineteenth-

---

[44]   In 1896 the well-known portraitist Jan Veth even defended the word 'bourgeois' as long as it implied having a goal and consistency: J. Veth, *Portretstudies en silhouetten* (Amsterdam, s.d.), p. 60; cited with sympathy by Huizinga, *Verzamelde Werken* 6 (Haarlem, 1950), pp. 376-377.

[45]   Multatuli, *Verzamelde Werken* 8 (Amsterdam, ca. 1890), p. 3. H. Gorter, *Verzamelde Werken* 3 (Amsterdam, 1949), p. 311. H.T. Colenbrander, *Vooruitzichten voor Nederland en den Nederlandschen Stam in 1898 en in 1923* (Leiden, 1923), pp. 14-15.

[46]   H.P.G. Quack, *De socialisten. Personen en stelsels* 1 (Amsterdam, 1875), p. 88.

[47]   On 'mean' and mediocrity in Dutch history see: E.H. Kossmann, 'Anderhalve eeuw Nederlandse cultuur', *De Gids* 150 (1987): 104-111.

century consensus of the elite had been broken, Dutch (conservative and liberal) intellectuals had looked for a common national mission and a national common denominator. They found it in respectable *burgerlijkheid*. This *burgerlijkheid* was conservative and intolerant towards outsiders who did not share the often narrow rules of decency.

What was the meaning and function of this *burgerlijkheid*? To answer this question one should look for the opposite of the term. In the thirties *burger* was not opposed to proletarian, but to Fascist (and Communist) and to the irregular and undisciplined social outcast. The way in which authors from liberal, denominational or Social Democratic backgrounds used the term suggests that they wanted to defend a Dutch tradition of unheroic but solid quality against the onslaught of totalitarian politics. They used *burgerlijkheid* to characterize the national tradition. This did not mean that the bourgeoisie had 'beaten' the proletariat, however, but that authors from different political backgrounds looked for consensus and stability; *burgerlijkheid* suggested historical continuity and harmony. The large groups that did not participate in politics (or were only the object of politics) were not part of the *burgerlijke* society, and the consensus only existed through the elastic, cultural rather than primarily social meaning of the term. Liberals, orthodox Protestants, Catholics and Socialists condemned not only 'irresponsible' (Fascist or Communist revolutionary) politics but also 'irresponsible' (social) behaviour. They wanted to inculcate the values of respectable politics into their adherents. To the extent that they succeeded, Dutch society was a *burgerlijke* society.[48]

---

[48]   Not (necessarily) bourgeois. After all 'burger' also means citizen and cf. the interesting discussion of the question whether the 'civilization' of the lower classes implied 'embourgeoisement' in A. de Regt, *Arbeidersgezinnen en beschavingsarbeid. Ontwikkelingen in Nederland 1870-1940* (Meppel, Amsterdam, 1986), pp. 242-248.

G.J. Schutte, *Het Calvinistisch Nederland* (Utrecht, 1988) discusses the Calvinist Dutch stereotype. Many of the allegedly Calvinist qualities are sometimes classified as *burgerlijk*. After the war intellectuals held on to the *burger* image, stressing its passive democratic component. Once again the praise of 'civic culture' was not an exclusively Dutch affair (see the book with that title from 1963 and G.A. Almond and S. Verba, *The civic culture revisited* (Boston, Toronto, 1980). From the sixties on, conservative essayists have mourned the broken moral code of the *burger* (Chorus, *Nederlander innerlijk en uiterlijk*, pp. 176-182 and esp. Id., 'De Nederlandse volksaard' in *De Nederlandse Natie* ed. S.W. Couwenberg (Utrecht, Antwerp, 1981), pp. 33-43) though recently the Dutch have been called *burgerlijk* again (Couwenberg cited in note 1).

TOWARDS ONE NATION
THE PROVINCE OF LIMBURG AND THE DUTCH NATION DURING THE EIGHTEEN-SEVENTIES

Rico op den Camp

On the occasion of the termination of his office as chancellor of the University of Groningen in 1870, the liberal lawyer B.H.D. Tellegen delivered an oration entitled 'Germany and the Netherlands'. Against the background of the Franco-German war which was raging just outside the national borders, Tellegen intimated to his audience that he did not give much credence to rumours of German intentions to annex the Netherlands or parts of it. But he did point out a different, more surreptitious danger to which the Netherlands ware exposed: the loss of national identity. According to Tellegen, Germany was ruled by the principles of monarchy and aristocracy, while constitutional parliamentarianism was characteristic of the Dutch political spirit and system. Tellegen expressed the differences between his own country and Germany thus: 'We do not fight, but vote; we do not shoot, but argue; we do not kill, but decide'.[1] His oration was a call to muster the moral power to stay on 'the road of political freedom' which had led to 'free government' in the Netherlands since 1848.[2] If the country were to maintain its characteristics of freedom and tolerance, the slogan 'no authority but self-government, not German but Dutch!' would remain valid forever.[3]

In this speech Tellegen evoked the picture of a small state called to render account of its specific national identity under the threat of being forced to surrender its political and cultural independence. The question of what constituted that Dutch national identity has already been partially answered. The present article is not intended to discuss whether this (liberal) picture of Dutch national identity as tolerant, peace-loving and freedom-loving is true. Instead, it pursues the question of *how* feelings of national identity were experienced, and how self-evident an image of 'the Dutch nation' was to the inhabitants of the country. Particular attention will be paid to a part of the Netherlands that occupied a peripheral position within the Dutch state in the nineteenth century (and in some respects still does today): the province of Limburg. I shall examine the image of the Dutch nation as it existed in Limburg during the Franco-German war of 1870-71, as well as the image of Limburg in the Netherlands during these and succeeding years.

Limburg and the Netherlands before 1870

Tellegen's opinion was representative of the civic nationalism that ruled in Dutch liberal circles. Before the Franco-German war the

---

[1]   B.H.D. Tellegen, *Duitschland en Nederland. Rede uitgesproken bij gelegenheid der overdragt van het rectoraat der Hoogeschool te Groningen* (Groningen, 1870), p.35.

[2]   Tellegen: *Duitschland en Nederland,* p.30.

[3]   Tellegen: *Duitschland en Nederland,* p.39.

Netherlands adopted an uncertain and ambiguous attitude toward Germany, but fear for Germany became predominant during the autumn of 1870.[4] This fear was caused by the threat of a territorial annexation of the Netherlands or parts of it by Germany, but many dreaded more 'the moral impact of the Prussian preponderance than the Prussian arms', to quote Thorbecke, leader of the Government and a member of the same political camp as Tellegen.[5]

In an attempt to explain why people in the Netherlands in the nineteenth century viewed the struggling, dynamic nationalist movements in countries like Germany and Italy with suspicion, the Dutch historian Boogman adduced the fact that the Dutch themselves 'were part of an historical nation-state', which he qualified as 'satiated': the country was complete in itself in regard to its territory, population and culture.[6] It is questionable whether this is true of Limburg, the last province to join the state of the Netherlands. Politically, the territory of the Dutch province of Limburg had been fragmented since the end of the Middle Ages. During the period of the Republic of the United Provinces (1584-1795), only a few minuscule territories had ties with the Republic. The area did not achieve any political unity until the French occupation (1795-1813), which continued during the United Kingdom of the Netherlands.[7] When the Belgian revolution of 1830 broke up the kingdom, Limburg entered a new period of uncertainty regarding its

---

[4]   A. Doedens, *Nederland en de Frans-Duitse oorlog. Enige aspecten van de buitenlandse politiek en de binnenlandse verhoudingen van ons land omstreeks het jaar 1870.* (Zeist, 1973). For these statements see pp.31 and 142.

[5]   Doedens: *Nederland en de Frans-Duitse oorlog,* p.142.

[6]   J.C. Boogman, 'Kanttekeningen bij de geschiedenis van het nationalisme in Europa', in: *Nationalisme in de 3e wereld* (Assen, 1970), p.9, note 1.

[7]   For the main events in the history of Limburg see W.J. Alberts, *Geschiedenis van de beide Limburgen* (Assen, 1972/1983), and further A.J. Geurts, 'Historische aspecten van de provincie(s) Limburg 1815-1848', *Maasgouw* 105 (1986): 49-78.

national future. Between 1830 and 1839, the year of the final settlement of the Dutch-Belgian border dispute, Limburg was under Belgian rule, except for the city of Maastricht, which was held by a Dutch garrison. During the United Kingdom Limburg consisted of the combined territory of the present Dutch and Belgian provinces. In 1839 the area on the right bank of the Meuse and the eastern Peel-area were separated from the Belgian state of which they had been a part for nine years. This territory became a Dutch province, but it was also granted the status of duchy with the Dutch king William as duke, and as such Limburg joined the German League. The Limburgers, who had been de facto Belgian citizens for a decade, became inhabitants of two political units in one blow. This dual political situation was to last until 1866, when Prussia reorganized the German League after the wars against Denmark and Austria. Bismarck 'liberated' Limburg of all political ties with Germany, and Limburg finally attained an unambiguous political position.[8] From that moment on the Limburgers were able to focus on a single, unequivocal national perspective.

The attitude of the Limburgers toward the fatherland that they were more or less condemned to in 1839 was not marked by enthusiasm.[9] At first the feeling was anti-'Holland': the Limburgers wanted to be separated from the Netherlands and to be reunited with Belgium.[10] Economically, culturally, religiously and linguistically, Limburg had more in common with Belgium and the

---

8   Alberts *II*, p.199.

9   Alberts *II,* p.190f.

10   See L.J.Rogier, 'Nederlands Limburg 1813-1963', *Maasgouw* 84 (1965): 81ff.; J.P. van Banning, 'Honderd jaar "gewone" provincie', *Maasgouw* 86 (1967): 130; and M.G. Spiertz, 'Limburg uit de Duitse Bond', *Publications de la Société Historique et Archéologique dans le Limbourg* [PSHAL] (Maastricht, 1966) p.15. It should be borne in mind that these remarks only apply to the upper classes; the people with a lower status hardly took any notice of the nation at all. See e.g. I.M.H. Evers, 'Liever Turks dan Pruisisch. De publieke opinie in de provincie Limburg 1866-1867'. *Maasgouw* 100 (1981): 131 and 147.

German Rhineland than with the north of the Netherlands.[11] Circumstances which formed a part of everyday life prevented the rise of a more positive approach to the north of the country. Most important in this respect were the taxes, especially those on income derived from real estate.[12] Taxation in general was not only notably higher than the Belgian taxes had been during the eighteen-thirties, but the fact that the level of taxation was partly determined by the costs of the war that Holland had waged against Belgium stirred up bad feelings. Complaints about taxes were a constant characteristic of Limburg dissent throughout the nineteenth century.[13] A general dissatisfaction with the Dutch state was ventilated by a separatist movement. This movement, which was especially active during the eighteen-forties, agitated to detach Limburg form the Netherlands and to link the province to Belgium or Germany.[14] After the failure of the separatist movement in 1848, most Limburgers resigned themselves to membership of the Dutch state. However, the weak political position; the financial obligations to the state, which were regarded as onerous and unjust; the unprofitable position as an agricultural region within a trading state; and the scant attention paid by the government to the

---

[11]   See for instance Knippenberg and de Pater, *De eenwording van Nederland* (Nijmegen, 1988) pp. 26-28.

[12]   For this, and the impact of these and other taxes on different groups of the Limburg population see Nick Bos, Agitatie in Limburg, de verhoging van de grondbelasting in het hertogdom in 1865', *Maasgouw* 108 (1989): 79-95.

[13]   In 1866 the almanac of Maastricht, the *Oprechter Maastrichter Almanak*, contained the often quoted phrase 'We Limburgers know well, very well, financially well, that we are Dutchmen'.

[14]   For a brief and clear survey of the separatist movement in Limburg during these years see R. van der Heijden, 'Separatisme in Limburg 1840-1851' in: *Tussen twee Tricolores. Een Limburgse vestingstad onder Nederlands en Belgisch bestuur, Venlo 1815-1850*, (Venlo, 1990) pp.23-34.

infrastructure of Limburg created a public opinion in the province which remained unfavourable to the north of the country.[15]

Under these circumstances the growth of a Dutch national consciousness in Limburg between 1839 and 1870 was bound to be a difficult process. According to the historian Alberts, Bismarck's statement that Limburg would be free of all political ties with Germany from 1867 on was celebrated in the province as a liberation, which he considered to be 'a symptom of the growth of a Dutch national awareness that took place after the change of the constitution in 1848'.[16] Recent research, however, has shown that anti-Prussian feelings were much more important than profound Dutch national sentiments.[17] The historian Rogier considered the years after 1848 to be 'a period of national half-heartedness' for Limburg, and in connection with the tortuous political position of Limburg, he wondered 'whether one could think of anything less likely to encourage the expansion of a sound national idea among the population'.[18] According to Rogier, Dutch national consciousness could only have started to come into existence from 1866 onwards when 'the grotesque tie with the German League was cut'.[19]

---

[15]   This conclusion was already drawn by P. Orbons and L. Spronck in 'Limburgers worden Nederlanders. Een moeizaam integratieproces.', *PSHAL* 102 (Maastricht, 1966) p.43.
[16]   Alberts *II*, p.199. See also L.G.J. Verberne, *Van Gewest tot Provincie* (Amsterdam, 1947) p.110.
[17]   See in particular the article by Evers.
[18]   Rogier, p.82. The same judgements can be found in the articles by Spiertz, p.14 and Orbons and Spronck, pp. 41 and 48.
[19]   Rogier, p.83.

The image of the Dutch nation in the Limburg press during the Franco-German war

How did Limburg view the Dutch fatherland in the days of real or imaginary danger during the Franco-German war? Among the broad ranks of the Dutch population the response to the threat was unanimous: the Netherlands had to retain its political and cultural independence. This wish was supported by expressions of attachment to its freedom and the public institutions by which it was represented.[20] These statements reflected the lively existence of Dutch national feelings. The daily press mentioned 'loud national slogans' during a trip by King William the Third, and the British ambassador noticed an ebullition of 'national sentiments' throughout the country.[21]

Did Limburg share these feelings, and if so, how were they motivated? An indication can be found from an examination of four important newspapers that appeared in Limburg in this period. Two of them were liberal papers, the other two were Catholic and conservative.[22] These papers are a valuable source for what went

---

[20]   See Doedens: *Nederland en de Frans-Duitse oorlog*, pp.73-74 and 175.

[21]   Doedens: *Nederland en de Frans-Duitse oorlog*, p.74.

[22]   I examined four papers that all appeared in the south of Limburg. Newspapers issued in the middle and north of Limburg were traditionally more directed toward the Netherlands, and their inclusion in the sample might have resulted in distortion. The four papers were the relatively big ones which played an active role in forming public opinion in South Limburg. *Le Courier de la meuse. Journal du Limbourg* [CdlM] was published in the capital of the province, Maastricht. The Courier was set up in 1851 as a liberal newspaper, and after 1865 it was under the control of the liberal mayor of Maastricht, Pijls. The second liberal paper, *De Nieuwsbode. Weekblad van Sittard* [NB] was first published in Sittard in May 1869. *L'Ami de Limbourg. Journal Politique, Commercial, Artistique et Litéraire* [L'Ami] was founded in 1847 as a Catholic newspaper. Despite its liberal background, it was clearly conservative and Catholic in 1870-1871. Like the other Maas-

on in the minds of those Limburgers who participated in public life,[23] i.e. a small minority of the developed upper stratum of society, consisting of no more than 2 or 3 per cent of the total population.[24] Yet these were the people in charge of political, socio-economic and cultural developments in society, who thereby marked out the course which was to be followed by the mass of the population.

On the fifteenth of July 1870 a brief crisis connected with the vacancy of the Spanish throne ended unexpectedly when the French declared war on Prussia.[25] The Dutch government there-

---

tricht paper, the Courier, the Ami was in French. *De Limburger Courier* [LC], was published twice weekly in Heerlen, a city in the south-east corner of Limburg where German was an important language of the literate population as well as French. Founded as a Dutch-language weekly in 1845 (*De Limburger Koerier*) it was published in German from 1847 on. Dutch language was restored in 1868, but the following year a German-language supplement appeared (*Die Heerlener Zeitung*) at the request of the subscribers. *The Limburger Courier*, which had subscribers in Belgium and Prussia too, was a conservative Catholic newspaper. Information about the papers is taken from the papers themselves and from Evers.

[23]   There is hardly any detailed information on the circulation, historical evaluation and geographical distribution of newspapers before World War II, and what there is is often difficult to interpret. Every statement about the influence of these press organs on public opinion must be made with caution. All the same, the assumption that only the political and social élite saw its views reflected in the press seems to be beyond reproach. For this problematic issue see Evers, pp.135-136, Knippenberg and de Pater, pp.66-74 and Doedens, p.73.

[24]   See the diagrams in Knippenberg and de Pater, p69 and see Evers, p.147.

[25]   For this crisis and general information about the Franco-German war see e.g. J. Joll, *Europe since 1870* (Suffolk, 1982); or the more detailed account by A. Horne, *The Fall of Paris* (London, 1965).

upon decided to mobilize the armed forces.[26] In line with the strategic plans all troops were instantly withdrawn from Limburg and moved to the north. As a result of these measures the first consideration of the Limburgers shifted from international diplomacy to the Dutch fatherland. Differences between supporters of the activities of the liberal government and the critical conservative Catholics soon emerged. The irate Ami stated that the cabinet left Limburg completely to its fate. According to this paper, general opinion in Limburg required that the province should at least be given its own sons to defend the native soil if 'Holland' was not willing to defend its southernmost part itself.[27] The paper approvingly concluded that the Dutch population, unlike the government, viewed the Limburg soldiers as 'sons of one and the same family'.[28] The Courier de la Meuse, however, cheered at the military activities undertaken by the government, and defended the strategic value of the concentration of the troops in the north.[29] The Nieuwsbode joined these remarks with the statement that Limburg put its trust wholeheartedly in the north, 'where the flower of the population stood united behind the banner of Orange' and where the people could still breathe 'the pure air of civic virtue and religion. Therefore,' the Nieuwsbode continued, 'only one prayer was cherished by the Limburgers: God save the Netherlands!'[30] The Limburger Courier held itself aloof from the discussion on the defence of the country, but stressed that freedom of thought and speech was guaranteed in the Netherlands while it was still lacking in the belligerent countries.[31]

These discussions indicate the preference of the Limburgers for the liberal climate that existed in the Netherlands. This prefer-

---

[26]   For information about Dutch policy in general see Doedens: *Nederland en de Frans-Duitse oorlog.*
[27]   *L'Ami*, August 5 and 14, 1870.
[28]   *L'Ami*, August 5, 1870.
[29]   CdlM, July 20, 22 and 31, 1870.
[30]   NB, July 31 and August 13, 1870.
[31]   LC, August 13, 1870.

ence proved to be stronger than the dislike of the north based on religious motives. Limburg was homogeneously Catholic, and there was hardly any sympathy for Protestant Prussia. Nevertheless, public opinion among Dutch Protestants was pro-Prussian during the early days of the war.[32] Voices raised in favour of Prussia in the north were criticized in Limburg. The Ami's hackles in particular rose at the profit-seeking mentality of 'Protestant Dutchmen so eager to trade with Prussia'.[33] All of the Limburg newspapers showed more sympathy with France, particularly the Catholic ones, but this sympathy vanished in August when Napoleon III removed the French troops protecting the Papal State. But it was not religious preference which was decisive for public opinion. The startling successes gained by Prussia on the battlefield were soon to dominate the public mood completely.

When it became clear in the course of the autumn of 1870 that France had suffered crushing military blows, all the Limburg newspapers took a firm stand against victorious Prussia. The Ami put the blame for the war completely on Bismarck, while the Nieuwsbode portrayed King Wilhelm of Prussia with bitter mockery as 'the Traitor of the Peace'.[34] The Courier de la Meuse cherished the hope that the new administration in France would be able to fight the Prussian despotism with more success than its predecessor, and the Limburger Courier regularly reported the bad treatment that Catholics had to endure in areas occupied by Prussian forces.[35] It was probably no coincidence that the Limburger Courier stopped the publication of its German-language supplement on 13 November. At the same time, disappointment over the social and political developments in France was strongly expressed in the

---

[32]   Doedens: *Nederland en de Frans-Duitse oorlog*, p.74.
[33]   *L'Ami*, August 12, 1870.
[34]   *L'Ami*, September 12 and 13, 1870, NB, October 29, 1870.
[35]   CdlM, September 9 and 14, 1870; LC for a striking example see e.g. November 9, 1870.

Limburg press.[36] Thus the anti-Prussian attitude was not replaced by a pro-French one. The Limburgers only hoped that the fortunes of war would change in favour of France, so that the balance of power between France and Prussia would be restored. Limburg was primarily concerned with its own fate, and in this respect the Limburgers shared the anxiety of the Netherlands in general.[37] After the French military defeats, the Dutch government felt more at ease because German territorial objectives did not seem to include Holland. As a result, the government demobilised the Dutch army on 16 September.[38] However, the Limburg press revealed a growing fear of Prussia, and the demobilisation was received with disapproval. Under the headline 'Beware, Fatherland!' the Limburger Courier warned of the danger of German expansionism in the Netherlands after the final defeat of France.[39] Though it usually supported the government, the Nieuwsbode criticized the demobilisation too and regarded the structure of the Dutch army as 'an expensive guard duty'.[40] The Ami rejoiced at the homecoming of the Limburg militia, but it also recommended loans for the benefit of the country's defences.[41] With the advance of the Prussian troops towards Paris, the rumours of peace negotiations and above all the German demands gathered strength. The wish to stay Dutch was plainly expressed in the Limburg press. The Nieuwsbode tried to reassure its readers: 'Now the Prussians have won we will be Prussians. Wrong! We will remain Dutch, we will remain Limburgers'.[42] Nevertheless, the news was filled with the fear of the Prussian intention to annex Limburg

---

[36]   See e.g. *L'Ami*, September 9 and 19, 1870; CdlM, September 9 and 14, 1870; and LC, September 10, 12 and 17, 1870.

[37]   Doedens concluded this for the Netherlands in his *Nederland en de Frans-Duitse oorlog*, p.74.

[38]   See Doedens: *Nederland en de Frans-Duitse oorlog*, pp. 89ff.

[39]   LC, October 15, 1870.

[40]   NB, November 12, 1870.

[41]   *L'Ami*, October 1 and 3, 1870.

[42]   NB, September 10, 1870.

under cover of a claim to ancestral rights to all territory that had
once belonged to the former German League. The Ami viewed
Prussia's aim thus: 'After Alsace and Lorraine: Luxemburg and
Limburg'.[43] At the beginning of the new year, with Prussian
troops victorious in Paris and pending the final settlement, Limburg
was anxiously waiting to see whether the Prussian victory would
have bad consequences for the province, or perhaps even for the
entire Dutch state. The Nieuwsbode strikingly expressed this fear
in combination with its view of the independent Dutch fatherland:

> 'The Netherlands has erected a memorial to its glorious return to
> the ranks of peoples, and the Dutch are proud to be an indepen-
> dent nation. How much longer will this monument of the Dutch
> people stand, to show that the Netherlands is not part of the 'one
> and only Germany'? It is no exaggerated fear if we pose that
> question.....'[44]

On 28 January 1871 an armistice was concluded between France
and Prussia. At first the Limburg press adopted an attitude of wait-
and-see. The hope that France 'would soon rise again' was generally expressed, and news about the war-weariness of German solders
was received with satisfaction.[45] Several pleas for immediate
general conscription indicated that the Limburgers were not yet at
ease with the situation. The whole nation had to be enabled to bear
arms so that, in case of German aggression, that country would
meet more resistance than from 'some substitutes somewhere in
Holland alone', as the LC put it.[46]

But when it became obvious that the war really had ended,
the anxious tone in the Limburg press finally died down. A sense

---

43   *L'Ami*, February 1, 1871.
44   NB, February 4, 1871.
45   Cited from the LC, February 1, 1871. News about the war-
weariness of German soldiers appeared already on December 31, 1870
in the NB, and on February 8 in *L'Ami*.
46   LC, February 4, 1871.

of relief started to replace feelings of fear: Limburg, as well as Holland, had escaped only by the skin of its teeth![47] The conviction that Limburg would remain Dutch quickly made headway, and so did the feeling of satisfaction at this state of affairs. At the anniversary of the king at the end of February 1871, all the papers bore expressions of devotion to the Dutch fatherland, like the wish 'to continue to share in the prosperity of the Netherlands under the great privilege of the reign of William III'.[48] The Ami mentioned with satisfaction that in Amsterdam the king's anniversary was celebrated 'in a genuinely national manner'. The paper was also very pleased at the congratulations sent to the king by the inhabitants of Kerkrade, a village in the south-east corner of Limburg near the German border, which showed that the people of Kerkrade 'despite their German language do not wish to be part of the *Deutschen Vaterland'*.[49] The definitive peace treaty was not concluded until 18 May, but before that date Limburg was convinced that it would remain a part of the Netherlands. According to the Nieuwsbode, this meant that the province was guaranteed the blessings of 'education, labour, and tolerance' in the future, because 'a tree is known by its fruits. Don't ever forget that, free people of the Netherlands!'[50]

The reactions to the events of the Franco-German war in the Limburg press lead to an inescapable conclusion: the Limburg elite wanted Limburg to remain a part of the Dutch state. This attitude was strongly influenced by the fear of Prussian expansionism

---

[47] See e.g. the NB of March 18, 1871. *L'Ami* proposed an alliance between the countries that had been spared German aggression, like the Netherlands, Switzerland and the Scandinavian countries (March 5, 1871).

[48] This wish was expressed in the petition (mentioned below) presented by the inhabitants of Kerkrade to King William III, published in the LC of March 4, 1871.

[49] *L'Ami*, February 22, 1871.

[50] NB, April 1, 1871.

during the war. Though this fear existed before, it seemed much more real in the war situation. The fact that the fear of Prussian expansionism lasted longer in Limburg than in other parts of the Netherlands became clear after the military defeats of France in September 1870. The Limburgers' feelings of increased uncertainty and fear regarding the fate of the province and the Dutch state as a whole stood in contrast to the sense of assurance that was dominant in the north. This can be explained in terms of Limburg's historical relationship with Germany and the strategic position of the territory of Limburg beside the river Meuse, but there was more. There was no lack of protestations of devotion to the Dutch Royal House and the Dutch state in the Limburg press during the war in 1870 and 1871. *Vis-à vis* the belligerent countries, Limburg set itself off with the same moral codes that were stressed as basic elements of national identity in the north: freedom, tolerance, the love of peace and civic virtue. These ethics were expressed not only to motivate anti-Prussian opinion but particularly to stress the fact that, by sharing those ethics with their northern compatriots, the Limburgers were Dutch too. It is in this development that we can identify a sense of Dutch national consciousness among the Limburg elite.

Limburg seen through Dutch eyes

The image of the Dutch nation as revealed in the Limburg press during the Franco-German war of 1870-71 augured the growth of a Dutch national awareness in Limburg. In order to relate this conclusion to a general image of the Dutch nation, we must turn to the north of the country and examine its perception of Limburg within its view of the nation and national identity.

As we have seen, Limburg's attitude to the Dutch fatherland was not very positive during the first years of Dutch statehood. The

Dutch fatherland shared the same attitude to Limburg.[51] For some time Holland had had ties with the strategic cities of Maastricht and Venlo, but the territory of Limburg that was added to the Dutch state was for the most part strange to the north.[52] The complications brought about by the dual political status of Limburg caused uneasy feelings in the rest of the Netherlands. This clearly emerged during the forties. In 1848 *The Limburg Question* was published by J.G.H. Boissevain, editor of the *Arnhemsche Courant*. This book argued that the Dutch state should disown Limburg in order to prevent Prussia from ever wanting to start a war against the Netherlands because of that province.[53] Limburg was thereby qualified as 'a pitiful piece of land, an outgrowth of our country, that consumes our best juices' and which as such did not belong to the industrious Dutch nation but was no more than 'a strange appendix'.[54]. Voices were also raised in parliament calling for the separation of Limburg.[55] The Dutch government would probably have been prepared to make great concessions if the Germans had pushed through with the territorial acquisition of Limburg in 1848.[56] Public opinion in the north of the country remained reserved towards Limburg during the next decennia. In 1867 fear of Prussia once more led to anti-Limburg statements in the northern press,[57] and after the Franco-German war a Limburg newspaper

---

[51]   For the northern attitude to Limburg in general see Alberts *II*, Orbons and Spronck and Spiertz.

[52]   For the history of all the complicated pieces of territory in the future province of Limburg that had at some time belonged to the Dutch Republic see Alberts *II* especially chapters I and III.

[53]   See van Banning, p.132.

[54]   Cited by Alberts *II*, pp. 198 and 191.

[55]   Spiertz stated that Limburg did not belong 'to the fatherland as one-sided national feeling wanted it', p.15. Some politicians held the option that Limburg should form a new state together with Luxemburg, see p.15, note 19.

[56]   Spiertz, p.16.

[57]   See Evers, p.144.

complained that 'an inclination to look down on things in Limburg dominates all the press in the Netherlands.'[58] All the same, the political unification went some way toward creating a feeling of togetherness in the thirty years after 1839, even the northern provinces never came to display great interest in Limburg.[59]

Sources on feelings in the Netherlands toward Limburg are thin. The travelogues of Craandijk form a welcome exception in this respect. Craandijk travelled regularly through the Netherlands between 1873 and 1888 and provided many useful pieces of information as well as his own impressions. The information about Limburg recorded by this traveller of Dutch origin (he was a native of the province of Holland) gives us an indication of the place that Limburg occupied in the northern Dutch view of national identity.

J. Craandijk (1834-1912) was a Baptist vicar who lived and worked mainly in Rotterdam and Haarlem.[60] This 'nationally famous writer' of the *Wandelingen door Nederland* (Hikes through the Netherlands) was 'a Dutchman, and a Hollander, in his work as well as in his heart', and a 'vicar in heart and soul' whose 'religious moderation' enabled him to 'describe his country and people with love'.[61] His Protestantism was profoundly liberal, and his vision of the Dutch nation did not differ much from the civic nationalism of liberals like Tellegen. Craandijk wrote many works on the people and regions of the Netherlands (and also sometimes abroad) and their history. In 1873 he accepted a request to write

---

[58]   *Maastricht, Limburg en Nederland*. Weekblad gewijd aan de belangen van iedereen, number 1 (10-10-1872): 1-2.

[59]   The government's lack of interest in Limburg sometimes caused great frustration on the part of members of parliament who were Limburgers; see Evers, p.133. Spiertz, p.27 pointed out that the rule of Dutch law more or less forced Limburgers to orientate themselves on the north.

[60]   The information about Craandijk is drawn from an obituary by the later Professor of Ethnology J. de Vries in *Eigen Haard* (1912): 376-378.

[61]   De Vries: *Eigen Haard*, p.376.

illustrated works that would record the 'disappearing Netherlands' for posterity. Craandijk led his readers 'here and there' to make them familiar with 'characteristics of the landscape, nature, cities, tradition, morals and customs' of the country.[62] Craandijk crossed the Netherlands on foot with his friend P.A. Schipperus, a painter from Rotterdam. The *Wandelingen* earned Craandijk a degree of fame.[63] The detailed geographical and historical descriptions by this 'Hollander' even served as a source for the history of Limburg.[64]

Limburg in the travelogues of Craandijk.

During his first trip to Limburg, Craandijk noted the different use of language in this part of the Netherlands. As the train doors opened at the station in Valkenburg, he heard the guard shout: 'Fauquemont - Fauquemont'.[65] After staying a few days in Valkenburg and the neighbourhood, Craandijk concluded that

> 'French is the language that is mostly spoken. As a Dutchman from the North, you can walk around here under the impression

---

[62]   J. Craandijk, Introduction to volume I of the *Wandelingen* (Haarlem, 1874) p.I.

[63]   'Indispensable if one is to know one's country' was De Vries' assessment.

[64]   In his *Langs de Geul. Schetsen uit Limburg*, the writer of popular history J. Hobbel called Craandijk the most important source for the history of the city of Valkenburg (p.15). Accounts of Limburg were originally published in volumes 2 (1876), 3 (1877), 4 (1879), 5 (1880) and 6 (1882); all published by Tjeenk-Willink, Haarlem. The *Wandelingen* was re-issued in 1968, containing all the reports on Limburg in one volume (Zaltbommel, 1968). Following his earlier descriptions, Craandijk published the *Wandelgids door de schoonste streken van Nederland* (Hiker's Guide through the Loveliest Parts of the Netherlands) in 1892, in which some regions of Limburg regions were described again.

[65]   Craandijk: *Wandelingen 2*, p.313.

that you are in some foreign country, and from time to time you must do force yourself to remember that you are among fellow countrymen'.[66]

Although Craandijk knew by experience that each part of the country had its own dialect, in Limburg 'it easily happens that your Dutch will not be understood, just as you cannot understand a word of the language that you hear'.[67]

For Craandijk language was an important index by which a nation could distinguish itself from others. This becomes very clear in the description of his first impressions upon arriving in the city of Venlo:

'He who enters the city of Venlo hardly knows in what country he finds himself. He is reminded of his fatherland only by some signs written in his own language. But even the orthography of those words and names is mostly Flemish. German and French have the upper hand and on countless pubs you can read higgledy-piggledy *Schenkwirtschaft*, *Estaminet* and *Tapperij*. The appearance of the city is entirely outlandish.'[68]

Craandijk clearly noticed the difference between this city and those in the north, and he repeated these remarks as he visited other cities in Limburg.[69]

---

[66]   Craandijk: *Wandelingen 2*, p.314. French seems to have been omnipresent in those days among the upper classes of Limburg. The Limburg aristocrat and author Frans Erens, who grew up in Schaesberg near Heerlen in the 1960s and 1970s, later wrote: 'Because of my education I was at an early stage familiar with the tones of the French language. Limburg was more imbued with French culture in my youth than it is now'. In: Frans Erens, *Vervlogen jaren* (Bygone Years), published by H.G.M. Prick (Amsterdam, 1989) p.175.

[67]   Craandijk: *Wandelingen 2*, p.315.

[68]   Craandijk: *Wandelingen 6*, pp.3-4.

[69]   See e.g. *Wandelingen 4*, p.91: reflections on Roermond, and *Wandelingen 2*, p.322: reflections on Valkenburg.

Like the general appearance of the province, the 'mountainous landscape' and the strange-looking cities, the people of Limburg differed from the Dutch in the north too. For Craandijk this was logical in view of the frequent contacts between the Limburgers and their close neighbours in Belgium, Germany and even France:

> 'No wonder that the appearance of the cities and the peculiar character of the people are not of the pure Dutch type. (...) The Dutch blood in their veins is not completely free of foreign stains. Here it flows perhaps with more liveliness than in the northern regions.'[70]

Craandijk defined the people's character as 'Belgian, like the character of the landscape, the style of building, the dress and the life-style', but added that the population was 'not Belgian-minded and even less Prussian-minded.'[71] This was not to say that the Limburgers were taken by the Dutch:

> 'Although you will meet benevolence and a obligingness everywhere, not seldom you will get the impression that the Limburger considers himself only half a Dutchman, and holds you for only half a brother.'[72]

The explanation for the deviant character of the Limburgers and the existence of certain negative attitudes toward the north of the Netherlands could only be found in history.

> 'What makes some individuals a nation is their history, their common past, a certain amount of congeniality of mind which is the fruit of their common sympathies',

---

[70]   Craandijk: *Wandelingen* 4, pp.84-85.
[71]   Craandijk: *Wandelingen* 2, p.315 and Wandelingen 4, p.85.
[72]   Craandijk: *Wandelingen* 2, p.315.

and in this respect

> 'the history of Limburg differs from the history shared by the northern provinces.'[73]

Craandijk realised that Limburg had always had been a toy of international diplomacy, and so 'no natural ties with the Republic of the United Provinces had been able to grow.'[74] It was quite understandable that Limburg had its grievances, for the ties with the Dutch Republic had only been a burden.[75] To the north Limburg had been a remote region until late in the nineteenth century. Thus:

> 'It stands to reason that travel in the times before the railways was not such that a lively traffic took place between Limburg and the rest of the Netherlands, while on the other hand the intercourse with Germany and Belgium, easy accessible from almost everywhere, was maintained continuously. So it is not at all strange that North and South view one another somewhat strangely'.[76]

However, Craandijk stated, the continuation of history would make Limburg an undeniable part of the Dutch state and the Dutch nation:

---

[73]   Idem.
[74]   Craandijk: *Wandelingen* 2, pp.316-317.
[75]   Craandijk: *Wandelingen* 2, p.316.
[76]   Craandijk: *Wandelingen* 2, pp.317-318. In 1865 there was a rail link connecting Maastricht, Heerlen, Sittard, Roermond with Venlo. The link with Dutch cities outside Limburg was realised between 1865 and 1885, while Maastricht already had connections abroad with Aachen (1853), Hasselt (1853) and Liège (1864). See Knippenberg and de Pater, p.49, and M. Kemp, *Geschiedenis van Limburg* (Maastricht, 1934) pp.94-95.

'Though we are still strangers to each other in some ways, in the course of time intensified traffic will forge the relationship that was laid down by diplomacy and fulfil what no statesmanship is ever able to do. A nation is never produced in the Cabinets of Ministers or by the authoritative utterance of a king: it is formed by history alone. Now Limburg belongs to the Netherlands. May it not only be Dutch, but wanting to be Dutch as well, and may it be proud of being Dutch. (...) Then the Netherlands will really have *won* a beautiful province.'[77]

Craandijk's analysis of the place of Limburg within the Dutch nation is ambiguous. On the one hand, since he considers that a nation is based on the common history of its people, Limburg differed from the rest of the Netherlands, as appears from specific features such as the people's character, life-style and language, and the appearance of the landscape and the cities. On the other hand, history had decided that Limburg *was* a part of the Netherlands, and hence it had to have its share of the Dutch nation. From his 'northern Dutch' point of view, Craandijk pointed out that the north of the Netherlands shared a longer common history, and Limburg still had to accommodate to the north. The Limburgers had to *desire* to be Dutch. In the short term this would mean 'placing less emphasis on old grievances than often happens at present'.[78] In the long term, Limburg would naturally come to share the appearance, language and people's character of the Dutch nation that already existed elsewhere in the Netherlands. The fact that in some respects this process had only just begun did not elude the attention of this observant Dutch wanderer.

---

[77] Craandijk, *Wandelingen* 2, p.366.
[78] Idem.

Limburg and Dutch national feelings during the 1870s

In an article on the relationship between the Netherlands and Limburg in the past and present published in 1872, the weekly paper *Maastricht, Limburg en Nederland* (Maastricht, Limburg and the Netherlands) noticed:

> 'It is undeniable that Limburg does not have a great respect for the present situation in the Netherlands. But is Limburg in the wrong there? Lay your hands on your hearts, you people of Friesland, Groningen, Holland and Zeeland: is Limburg in the wrong there?'[79]

This quotation shows that critical commentary on the Dutch fatherland did not fall silent in Limburg after 1870-71. At the same time, however, there was a reference to the inhabitants of other regions of the Netherlands, so that Limburg was emphatically placed within a Dutch context. This is yet another sign of the growth of a Dutch national consciousness in Limburg in the course of the nineteenth century, but it also throws light on *what* that national consciousness consisted of. This newspaper appeals to people in other regions of the country besides Holland, which suggests that the Netherlands were seen as a kind of federation of (provincial) identities. Furthermore, it assumes that Limburg does have its place among the other regions that together form the Netherlands, even though it should be a better place. This is an essential point, which is also to be found in the reactions of the Limburg press to the events of the Franco-German war. During that war the members of the Limburg elite which participated in public life had to account for their own nationality because of the threat to their state- and nationhood posed by Prussia. They clearly refused the Prussian option of a centralised and culturally regimented state. As the Nieuwsbode stated during the climax of the war:

---

[79]   *Maastricht, Limburg and Nederland* 1, (10-10-1872): 2.

'As for those two eagles, fighting themselves like birds of prey, in our eyes neither of them can be the soil where true illumination is declared for all people. Therefore we cannot be and are not French or German, but Dutch.'[80]

Certain cultural factors such as Catholicism - a minority religion in the north -, the use of non-Dutch languages for everyday purposes among the Limburg elite, and the close connections with their counterparts in neighbouring countries initially distinguished the upper class Limburgers from the Netherlands. By the time of 1870-71, however, it was clear that these Limburgers had come to realise that they would be best off within the Dutch state with its tradition of toleration of cultural difference. If this toleration of cultural difference enabled the Limburg elite to identify itself, with all its peculiarities, with the Dutch state and the Dutch nation, it might be regarded as a key feature to the Dutch national formation. The literate Limburgers found identification with the Netherlands by associating themselves with ethics that were viewed as characteristic of the Dutch nation. So the Dutch national consciousness that is found to have been taking shape in Limburg during the 1870s consisted merely of an attachment to presumed key features of the Dutch nation by the Limburg elite *without* the existence of an emotionally felt historical, religious or cultural alliance to it.

Craandijk's observations offer an affirmation of those presumed key features. Limburg was a special case within the Dutch nation. In the eyes of this Hollander, Limburg was a part of the Dutch *state*, but the region and its inhabitants still displayed many exotic, un-Dutch traits of character. What the province needed was a shared history with the north before it could truly be called a part of the Dutch *nation*. The conditions were laid down, and, as Craandijk stated, 'now it is up to individuals whether the fusion into one nation, in a short or longer period of time, will take

---

[80]   NB, August 13, 1870.

place more or less to the full.'[81] With this quotation Craandijk clearly laid down the ability and willingness of the north to assimilate Limburg within its national character. This suggests an interaction of northern and Limburg influences in the further creation of what was to be a Dutch national identity. The fact that the north was open to the incorporation of Limburg into the Dutch nation, as well as the evident willingness of the Limburgian elite to become enveloped in the Dutch nation, gives reason to suggest that Dutch national feelings were in a formative phase in the 1870s. They were not laid down as the obvious result of an already formed nation state. What feelings of national consciousness existed, if any, on the part of the mass of the Limburg population is a matter for further inquiry. At all events, the Limburg elite was obviously aware of its place within a cultural framework already accepted as being that of its own nation.

---

[81] Craandijk: *Wandelingen* 2, p.318.

'NOW I WILL WRITE YOU SOMETHING ABOUT AMERICA...': DUTCH MIGRANTS' VIEWS OF THE UNITED STATES AROUND THE TURN OF THE CENTURY.[1]

Annemieke Galema

Introduction

A century ago Frederick Jackson Turner tried to explain the character of America and the American people by the frontier experience. In 1893 this young scholar of the University of Wisconsin gave a lecture at the American Historical Association in Chicago about 'The significance of the Frontier in American History'.[2] Turner argued that the country had a frontier with uninhabited lands behind it until 1890. Pioneer settlers had moved westward across the American continent, creating all kinds of characteristic institutions. The first settlers symbolized opportunity

[1]   This publication is possible with financial support of the Netherlands Organization of Scientific Research (NWO). I wish to thank Prof. R.P. Swierenga of Kent State University, Ohio, for his comments with great expertise.
[2]   Frederick Jackson Turner, *The Frontier in American History* (New York, 1920).

and opportunism, individualism and democracy, as well as social upward mobility. According to Turner, after 1890 it was no longer possible to talk about the United States as if there was a frontier line: Turner's thesis emphasized the fact that the American frontier constantly expanded westward until four centuries after the discovery of America. Turner concluded in his 1893 lecture that the first period of American history was closed and that the frontier had disappeared.[3]

The distinguishing feature of American history, Turner argued, had been the lure of the open frontier. By giving every person a chance to own property, he stated, and by rewarding the democratic virtues of individualism, self-reliance, optimism and resourcefulness, the western frontier had turned Europeans into Americans. This frontier had determined the American character. At this frontier, an ordinary people had met an extraordinary land. The American institutions were not just a copy of the Old World; the years of pioneering had changed America radically into a country with a national character of its own, a country that was different from Europe.[4]

According to Turner's thesis, immigrants became Americanized and turned into people with very specific characteristics that were recognizable and unique. The frontier was the key to understand American history and identity, the key to understand America! The frontier thesis meshed perfectly in 1893 with the confident, nationalistic mood of a young country that was just starting to flex its muscles in the global arena. Turner became a national figure and his theory launched a new academic discipline: the history of the American West. Turner and his supporters were

---

[3]   David W. Noble, 'The American West: Refuges from European Power of Frontiers of European Expansions?' in *The American West as seen by Europeans and Americans*, ed. R. Kroes (Amsterdam, 1989), pp. 20.

[4]   Michael P. Malone, 'The West in American Historiography', in: R. Kroes (ed.), *The American West as seen by Europeans and Americans* (Amsterdam, 1989), pp.1-19.

characterized as environmental determinists because they held that in the struggle of human beings against nature, the wilderness overwhelmed the pioneer. For their own purpose, frontiersmen abandoned the civilized life and institutions they had known. It was only later that they discovered the opportunity and ability to build their own society with distinguishable features. In fact, according to Turner and his followers, the frontier people went back to the roots of mankind for a while, and built their own new environment afterwards.

In the decades following Turner's key essay, there were many critics who were convinced that his view was at least half myth. They argued that Turner was ruled by patriotic passions instead of intellectual impulses. In his romantic nationalism, Turner forgot the wild land speculation, the destruction of natural wilderness, the arrogance of American expansionism and the tragedy of the Indians.   All the same, the frontier thesis displayed remarkable resilience, and is still taught in colleges from coast to coast, although not without criticism.[5] The prominent Dutch journalist and historian Ben Knapen described the influence of the Turner thesis as follows: the frontier thesis did not survive as a scientific concept, but it did survive as a creative metaphor, an American identity, and also as a tribute to American values and uniqueness.[6] The frontier thesis functioned as a specific American introspection, as the image of a nation that was cherished most by the American people. In a way it still functions like that today. Every year thousands of Mexican immigrants illegally cross the border into the

---

[5]   *The Washington Post*, (October 10, 1989) pp. A3.
[6]   Ben Knapen, 'De veroveringssdrang van het goede Amerika' in *NRC Handelsblad*, December 23, 1989. Knapen also describes Turner's thesis in the book *De grenzen van Amerika* (Amsterdam, 1990), which includes essays based on earlier newspaper articles. See also William Everson's foreword of the book about the western American experience in the live theatre by D.H. Ogden, D. McDermott and R.K. Sarlós (eds.), *Theatre West: Image and Impact* (Amsterdam, Rodopi, 1990), pp. 1-4.

United States, the land of wealth and freedom of their dreams. This American myth still serves the American people in composing its specific identity.

Observation and Analysis

The study of the process of image-building between nations is a complex task. The Dutch sociologist A.N.J. den Hollander is convinced that there are various obstacles that hamper an accurate perception. He believes that one can only observe another society by breaking through certain barriers, and by realizing that the view is always wrapped in a veil of secrecy.[7] There is always a discrepancy between reality and the muddled perception. Autonomous mental processes are an illusion, since they are always influenced by the surrounding culture. Den Hollander argues that values, institutions, preoccupations, and taboos of the national culture and subculture to which we belong always form some kind of screen through which we judge both ourselves and others.

However, it is not only (sub)national values and preferences that influence the human mind. There are other important aspects that shape a person's way of thinking, preferences, and presuppositions: the specific personality and characteristics of the observer, his/her social position and education.[8] The 'real' America is tucked away behind *a prioris* and prejudices.

Den Hollander regarded the veil of secrecy and the screen that surrounded the observer as a serious obstacle to the study of foreign people. He used a distortion model in which pre-

---

[7]   A.N.J. den Hollander, *Americana. Studies over mensen, dieren en een kaktus tussen Rio Grande en Potomac* (Meppel, 1970), p. 7.

[8]   Marianne Mooijweer, 'Waarnemen vanuit de verte', *Intermediair* (June 20, 1986): p. 11. See also: A. Lammers, 'Amerikanist van het eerste uur: A.N.J. den Hollander' in *Amerika in Europese ogen*, ed. K.van Berkel ('s-Gravenhage, 1990), pp. 181-193.

suppositions about 'Self' and 'Other' bias true observations. In my opinion, however, we need versions of 'Others' to construct an account of ourselves. Of course, these versions may be more or less faulty recognitions in terms of the version that the other produces of itself, but Den Hollander's view suggests a radical subjectivism and individualism that cannot be true in a qualified sense. The *quality* of knowledge about the other will certainly make a difference to subordinated or colonised people, for example, as is shown by the variation on the topic of American Indians riding around in the wilderness, scalping 'white men', and imprisoning their women.

The Dutch historian K. van Berkel argues that the prejudices that we have in our observations of foreign cultures should be the objects of our studies. Very often the prejudices concerning a foreign nation operate as judgments on our own country and culture. Whether images of other nations are right or wrong is more or less irrelevant. The existence of these images is important enough for the historian to pay attention to them, he claims.[9] Besides, it is also worth asking how the images change over time. In this perspective it is not enough to study the changes in American reality. If we follow Van Berkel, it is more interesting to study the changes in the imagination of the European observer. It might be the right move to take the frameworks or structures of feeling themselves as the object of study. All the same, is it really evident that the perception of the accuracy or inaccuracy of images of other nations is irrelevant? Is not an image (the term is wide enough to include discourse and fantasy) a particular force directed gainst other aspects of reality? When we speak of the image of America, we are referring to a psychologically complex group of associations, phrases, ideas, fantasies and attitudes in varying forms and combinations, that the name of America evoked in European minds.

---

[9]   K. van Berkel, *Denken over cultuur* (Groningen, 1990), pp. 29-30.

Against the background of Turner's romantic nationalism and Den Hollander's and Van Berkel's ideas about observing and interpreting other nations, one might ask why so many Dutch decided to emigrate to the United States in the second half of the nineteenth century. What was their perception of the New World, and how did the process of image-building develop? Why did they abandon the security of their homeland to risk their lives amid uncertainty and sometimes even violence? After all, they came from a small, relatively well-organized, conveniently arranged country. The fact that thousands upon thousands did migrate is indisputable. Almost 20 million people migrated to the United States in the nineteenth century, including 200,000 Dutch.

It is only recently that students of migration patterns have begun to pay attention to how emigrants imagined their future homeland before they left. Even fewer studies have been made of their image of the 'old fatherland' after they had settled in the United States. However, once the image of other nations became a hot issue in research on nationalism, scholars started to shed some light on matters related to the process of migration.[10] In 1990 the historian and migration expert John Bodnar put it thus: 'The missing dimension of current immigration historiography lies not in the realm of economic detail but in the realm of cultural construction. The predominant scholarly need today is not so much the generation of more social and economic data, although that is needed, but it is the penetration of the structures of meaning or interpretations that immigrants gave to the economic and political systems in which they moved and lived'.[11]

---

[10]   The Tenth International Economic History Congress in Louvain, Belgium (August, 1990) had a specific session on 'Emigration from Northern, Central and Southern Europe, 1880-1939'. A number of papers dealt with illusion and reality in the expectations of migrants.

[11]   John Bodnar, 'Reworking Reality: Polish Immigrants and the Meaning of the Immigrant Experience'. Paper presented to the *Tenth Economic History Congress*, Louvain, August 20-24, 1990.

The present article focuses on the realm of cultural construction. It deals with the image that prevailed of America among the communities which supplied migrants from the province of Friesland, and how this image was shaped.

Home and Future Domicile

More than ten thousand migrants left for America from the northern area of the province of Friesland between 1880 and 1914.[12] They came from an agricultural region with fertile clay soil, which had been hard hit by the agricultural depression. What made these migrants leave the Netherlands? Did they consider the United States as the land of milk and honey? How did they adopt or embrace certain views, and what kind of process created their image?

There are not many sources for an investigation of the migrants' images of their future country, nor of their former homeland as they looked back. Almost all the members of the group that left the northern Netherlands around the turn of the century were from the lower classes.[13] They were mostly agricultural labourers and their families. The sources are therefore scanty. At the level of private sources, direct personal information about

---

[12]   A.J.B.E. Galema, *Computer Compilation: Frisians to the U.S.A.*, Revised Edition (Groningen, 1992) Unpublished.

[13]   Annemieke Galema, ''Se binne nei Amearika tein'. Aspekten van Friese landverhuizing naar de Verenigde Staten rond de eeuwwisseling', *It Beaken*, 52, II (1990): pp. 45-58. See also ibid., 'Transplanted Network, a Case Study of Frisian Migration to Whitinsville, Mass., 1880-1914' in *The Dutch in North-America. Their Immigration and Cultural Continuity*, ed. R. Kroes (Amsterdam, 1991), pp. 174-188; A. Holtmann and A. Galema, 'Aus den nördlichen Niederlanden und dem deutschen Nordwesten nach Nordamerika. Motive und Reiseerfahrungen der Auswanderer im 19. Jahrhundert' in *Rondom Eems en Dollard/Rund um Ems und Dollart* (Groningen/Leer, 1992), pp. 433-449.

images and image-building of the 'new' and 'old' nations is mainly found in letters, which went back and forth over the ocean. These letters represent private views or views that circulated within a domestic or personal context. Their special interest for this study is the glimpse they provide of personal opinions.

At the level of public sources, there was activity by what we will call the image-makers, i.e. means travellers, promoters and novelists. The investigation of these image-makers is valuable because it gives an indication of the huge impact they had on the image-building of America among the emigrants. Of course, private and public sources interacted; they cannot be separated in the study of the process of image-building.

The group of image-makers consisted of agents of steamships and immigration companies, real estate speculators, and employees of immigration agencies. There were also reformers who sought a better future for their fellow countrymen; travellers who described their own experiences; and successful immigrants whose letters home sometimes glowed with exciting tales of their own prosperity and happiness.

Although travel accounts and novels enable us to understand a bit more of what the emigrants felt toward the United States around the turn of the century, I shall concentrate on the role of the promoters of emigration in the process of image-building rather than on the travellers' and novelists' views.[14]

---

[14]   See for example the article of J.W. Schulte Nordholt, 'Dutch Travelers in the United States. A Tale of Energy and Ambivalence' in *A Bilateral Bicentennial. A History of Dutch-American Relations 1782-1982*, eds. J.W. Schulte Nordholt and Robert P. Swierenga (Amsterdam, 1982), pp. 251-265. Also A. Lammers, *Uncle Sam and Jan Salie* (Amsterdam, 1989).

Promoters of the 'Go!!'

The Prins & Zwanenburg company tried to recruit emigrants for America in the city of Harlingen in the 1880s. They dealt with the Koninklijke Nederlandsche Stoomvaart Maatschappij (Royal Dutch Steamship Company) and also promoted their services as a land agent. Prins & Zwanenburg used glossy brochures and advertisements in local newspapers like *Het Weekblad voor het Kanton Bergum* to promote land that they had bought in different states. These areas were selected for Frisian settlement, and the emigrants were encouraged to leave for the cheap plots of land, especially in the West.

At the same time the well-known Frisian poet and writer Tjibbe Gearts van der Meulen became an immigration agent. After a visit to his brother in Iowa (who had emigrated in 1853), he promoted the New World, but not at the expense of everything. Van der Meulen castigated the land speculators and exposed their nefarious practices. In 1882 he wrote in *Het Weekblad voor het Kanton Bergum*:

> 'America is the land of Cockaigne, a Wonderland, but before one arrives there, one has to eat one's way through the mountain of pulp and there many perish. Many swindling agents are active; they stir in this pulp and many newcomers have their eyes smeared shut. Many weep when they finally realize where they have actually landed: oh, oh, that pulp mountain'.[15]

This article in *Het Weekblad* had a very pointed title: 'Whoever wants to earn a lot of money should become a recruiter'. In this essay he mercilessly exposed the activities of the land sharks.

The newspapers also published articles in which future emigrants could read about the burdens and hazards of settling in

---

[15]   T.G. van der Meulen, 'Wie veel geld wil verdienen worde werver', *Weekblad voor het Kanton Bergum*, (February 25, 1882).

America, but the Frisian newspapers like *Het Weekblad* and *Het Nieuw Advertentieblad* always carried an article or letter that emphasized the positive aspects of settlement in the United States. The pros and cons were discussed very often in almost every newspaper in Friesland. The phenomenon of Frisian migration to the New World was by no means ignored by the local press. The image of America painted in newspapers and letters was positive on the whole.

Besides the steamship companies and the land agents, other image-makers were active too. In the 1880s and 1890s the agents of the Northern Pacific Railroad, carefully selected from the ranks of successful immigrants willing to return to their homelands for a fat fee, were advertising in local newspapers and brochures. They pictured the northern Great Plains as the Garden of the World, a land with a favourable combination of circumstances unmatched in all the world.[16] Even the smaller railroad lines, unable to afford separate European agencies, tried to secure their share by creating combined immigration companies.

Of course, negative propaganda was spread by people who felt mistreated by the land agents. But it is generally the case that this negative image did not keep people from emigrating to America. It had less influence and was less common than the positive image. According to the Frisian newspapers of the last decennia of the nineteenth century, people were very well aware of the fact that the purpose of these railroad agents was to sell land, and that their advertisements were suspect. Still, an unemployed

---

[16]   For example, the agent J. Wijkstra in the village of EE in Friesland operated for the agency of Prins & Zwanenburg with a glossy brochure in which he painted the advantages of the railway land in glowing colours. Wijkstra told his readers something about the climate, tourism and the city and villages alongside the Northern Pacific Railway. A huge map of the Northern Pacific Railway completed the brochure. See 'Informatie voor ontginners van de landerijen langs den Noordelijken Pacific Spoorweg', *Rijksarchief Leeuwarden*, collection immigrant letters P.Y. Groustra 1881-1941.

and landless Frisian labourer could be tempted by headlines in the local newspaper proclaiming: 'LAND FOR SALE! 60 MILLION BUSHELS GRAIN IN MINNESOTA AND NORTH DAKOTA IN 1882! MONEY TO EARN!'[17]
Besides, the agents' main trick was to print the life stories of the most successful emigrants as if they were typical. This can be illustrated by many published letters, such as one from W. Nauta in Howell County, Missouri. In 1909 he wrote in the newspaper *Het Nieuwsblad van Friesland*:

'After a stay of 28 years in America, I have now returned to the fatherland for a while. I think I will go back to America early next spring. I would like to tell you something about the land over there, especially about Howell county. The capital city of Howell county is West Plains, with a population of 4500. One lives right in the middle of the United States. Howell county is crossed from north-west to south-east by the Frisco Railway, which makes the transport of fruit, grain, cattle etc. to big cities like St. Louis, Kansas City, Memphis, New York, etc. very easy...
They have planted a lot of peach trees over the last few years. This year about 800 railway wagons with peaches were exported from this area alone, as well as 500 wagons with strawberries...
The climate is very healthy. Enough rainfall; the maximum temperature is 95 degrees, and the nights are always cool. Winters are short and mild; there is no need to stable the cattle for more than three months. I never heard of foot-and-mouth disease of the cattle, nor of any sheep diseases or swine plagues. Cattle-breeding and horse-breeding are very profitable. Chicken-farming is also big business. The waters are full of fish, the forests crowded with wild animals, mostly deer, hares, partridges and wild turkeys.
It is possible to buy farms here for the price you pay for rent in Holland, and taxes are very low because the coun-

---

[17]   'Informatie voor ontginners...'

ty did not get into debt. We also have Catholic as well as Protestant schools here, as well as churches.

Potential emigrants can ask for further information at the American Consulate in Amsterdam.

The undersigned is also very willing to provide information on travel, costs of travel, the money you need to take with you, settlement, etc...'[18]

The author came from a small village in the north of Friesland where he had a cattle farm. He and his wife left the province of Friesland in 1882. It is easy to conclude that this letter was deliberately written for a larger public. As a matter of fact, this letter can be seen as a semi-private, semi-public source. The writer's account was certainly influenced by the fact that he knew it would serve as a source of information source for a larger audience than his own family. The information in the letter indicates that the writer was well aware of its informative character. The content is full of references to mainly economic perspectives, while hardly any comments concern social circumstances. The account is obviously gendered, giving away nothing on the prospects for women and children there. The economic dimension receives far more attention than other aspects of immigrant family life, such as school and education. However, the focus on the determination of jobs or labour environment may well be connected with the complexity of migrant motivation. Generally speaking, the economic background of potential Frisian emigrants was an important factor in the decision to change their surroundings.

Nauta's letter supports the conclusion that the impact of promotional agents was dwarfed by that of the 'America Letters' which crossed the Atlantic in the thousands. It is not known how many letters arrived in Friesland between 1880 and 1914, but in Denmark nearly half a million were received in 1883.[19]

---

18   Letter of W. Nauta in *Nieuwsblad van Friesland*, (15-9-1909).

19   K. Hvidt, *Flight to America* (New York, 1975), p. 186.

That thousands were written to Friesland too can be deduced from the many letters published in contemporary newspapers and those uncovered in a recent natural search.[20] The private letters are important for several reasons. They give us some insight into the personal lives of people who are otherwise poorly represented in the documents and who were not very ready to write accounts of their daily experiences. America letters also contain information about the multi-ethnic social life and assimilation and acculturation in the New World. We can learn about the immigrants' views and ideas on schools, churches, neighbours and factories. They also tell us about the discrepancy between norms and values in the 'Old' and in the 'New' world. Immigrants made the comparison of both sides of the ocean and in that way they show us the image of a nation. In general we can obtain psychological information about the immigrants' experience: their loneliness, hardships, despair and sometimes tragedies, but also their courage, optimism, sense of adventure, hopes and hard work.

The fact that the letters were written in large numbers is a reflection of the psychological needs of the emigrants. They must have feared exile from Friesland. O.H.de Vries from San Francisco, for example, writes a phrase in 1889 that could have been written by many other immigrants:

> 'Since February this year I have been receiving the "Workumer Courant" (The Journal of the city of Workum) and that was it! I expected you to write something with it, but no letter appeared to be enclosed.... I

---

[20]   In the autumn of 1990 I coordinated a national campaign to find letters of Dutch immigrants to America in the nineteenth and twentieth century. A few thousand letters were collected within a period of three months, mostly donated by private individuals who had relatives oversees. A large number of these letters were written in the nineteenth century, and on many occasions it was possible to obtain series of letters written by one and the same person or family.

think it's stupid that we haven't written to each other for
such a long time....'[21]

Other immigrants felt that they had to justify their move. Many
letters give the impression that immigrants experienced a compelling urge to appear better than those left behind, and they were
often incapable of admitting error or lack of success. Th.M. Oostenbrug writes in 1882 from the town of Hospers in Iowa:

> 'I had better tell you how things really are in America.
> The farmers here are all Dutch and Frisian, the same as in
> your area. Labour is done by horses and machines. So
> there is no place here for the day labourer. Everyone here
> is a farmer, or shoemaker.... The soil is in perfect con-
> dition, because the manure is burned instead of used. One
> sees beautiful grain fields...hay can be mowed as much as
> you want and it's of better quality than can ever be found
> in Friesland....'[22]

These kind of exaggerations might have easily influenced the
actual lives of the immigrants in their new place of settlement. The
fact that they were trying to justify their move and their new way
of life in America possibly *made* them look back without sorrow
or nostalgia. In a way, a bright and positive judgment of the future
was the key to survival.

The arrival of a letter from America in a north Frisian
village could be a major event. The correspondence shows that
many people were readers; the letters circulated among family and
friends, and were sometimes read in church. In his book on Dutch
emigration to North America, the Dutch historian Bertus Wabeke
even claimed that each fresh batch of America letters in a village

---

[21]   Letter from O.H. de Vries from San Francisco, November 17,
1889 to Friesland.
[22]   Letter of Th.M. Oostenbrug from Hospers, Iowa June 11, 1882
to the town of Roodkerk near Leeuwarden.

was responsible for a general exodus.[23] In view of the complexity of the motivation to migrate, it is hard to agree with Wabeke. His statement is an exaggeration of one undeniably important piece of the migration motivation puzzle.

Immigrants wrote to the old country, and that was the moment when the image-building started to brim over into the efforts of the image-builders. Most immigrant letters provided basic and essential information: the cost of land, nature of soils, wages and labour conditions. Most of them narrated the writer's success in simple prose: 'I am earning enough money to return to Holland, if I wanted to. And you cannot imagine what good food I get here', Ulbe Eringa wrote in 1892 from Iowa to his sister in Friesland.[24] Or, a few years later from Runningwater, South Dakota: 'Yesterday when I rode to town with my two horses hitched to our buggy, I wished that my wife and I could ride over to your place that way - that would give you a better idea of our life here in America'. These success stories were mixed with descriptions of opportunities for those who were thinking of following the migratory pattern: Eringa writes: 'Our brother-in-law, Gerlof, has got work with our neighbour and is earning good money and his board. These people are very happy to be here. They didn't realize how good it could be - there is plenty of work and the food is so cheap. In comparison, the poor day labourer in Holland has a pitiful, poverty-stricken and sorrowful existence'.[25] Another immigrant from Pennsylvania concluded his long letter in *Nieuwsblad van Friesland* in 1911 with the words: 'In my area, about three hours

---

[23]   B. Wabeke, *Dutch emigration to North America 1624-1860* (Amsterdam, 1970), p. 98.

[24]   Letter of Ulbe Eringa from Hull, Iowa to Friesland July 4, 1892. Letters available in *The Archives*, Calvin College Grand Rapids. Some of the letters of Ulbe Eringa are published in the book: *Emanual Reformed Church, Springfield South Dakota 1888-1988* (Freeman, 1988). Also in *Ons Friese Platteland* (July 4, 1981 etc.).

[25]   Letter of Ulbe Eringa from Runningwater, South Dakota to Sneek in Friesland April 8, 1894.

by train from New York, more than a hundred farms are for sale. Prices are very low, about 70 to 80 dollars per acre. In Iowa that kind of land is sold at least for 150 to 200 dollars per acre. There are good reasons for telling you this, for I know what I am talking about!'[26]

The experience of Aukje Pruiksma from Paterson, New Jersey in 1895 shows that the image of America was not always very precise or easy to construct. She wrote about her new environment: 'the surroundings here are somewhat mountainous and it seems to be a steep climb'.[27] Mrs Pruiksma had to get used to the hills of New Jersey; probably she had previously seen nothing but the flat countryside of Friesland. Many, many more such examples could be quoted; the new country proved to be a visual collision as well as a culture shock.

Once again the gendered nature of the letters should be stressed. As a result of their different experience of immigrant life, men and women often wrote about different subjects. Most Dutch immigrant women did not have a job outside the home; some of them never learned to speak the new language; and immigrant women sometimes felt themselves in a more isolated position than the men, which is reflected in their written accounts to the old country.[28]

---

[26] Letter from an immigrant in Pennsylvania to *Nieuwsblad van Friesland* (August 5, 1911).

[27] Letter of Mrs Aukje Pruiksma from Paterson, N.J. to Friesland May 16, 1895. *The Archives*, Calvin College Grand Rapids.

[28] For more information concerning Dutch immigrant women see: S. Sinke, 'Home is Where You Build It: Dutch Immigrant Women and Social Reproduction' in *The Dutch in North-America. Their immigration and cultural continuity*, ed. R. Kroes (Amsterdam, 1991), pp. 410-421. Also Annemieke Galema and Suzanne Sinke, 'Paradijs der Vrouwen? Overzeese migratie naar de Verenigde Staten van Friese vrouwen rond de eeuwwisseling' in *Vrouwen en Migratie* (Walburg Pers, 1993 forthcoming).

Disappointment faded by bacon letters

Although most of the immigrant letters consulted give a positive impression of America, more balanced or even negative accounts are available too. Some immigrants were not afraid to tell the people of the old village that migrating to America was not a blue-print for success. Some could not hide their feelings of homesickness. In 1911 a woman wrote from Iowa City that she had a carefree life, but she did not enjoy it at all because she was not able to understand anybody. Although she knew that very many Dutchmen lived in the city, she never met one because the city was so huge and filled with people of many different nationalities![29]

Or take J.G Boekhout from Paterson city in 1882:

'Now I will write you something about America, because if many people really knew about America, they would decide to stay where they are. Lots of those who live here want to return because it's a strange world here: parents can't boss their own children here, because if the young-sters tell the police that Mum or Dad don't treat them well enough, the parents have to pay 5 dollars. That's how things work here....'[30]

---

[29]   Letter of Mrs Duba from Iowa City, 1911 to The Netherlands. Published in: H.J. Brinks, *Schrijf spoedig terug* ('s-Gravenhage, 1978), p 139.
[30]   Letter of J. Boekhout from Paterson, N.J. August 22, 1882 to J.J. Hoogland in St. Anna Parochie. Collection *Rijksarchief Leeuwarden*. The literal text of the fragment in Dutch is as follows:
'nu zal ik u ook nog eenige leteren schrijfen van amerika
want als de meest minsen wisten hoe het in Amerika was
dan bleefen zij daar zij waren want hier zijn een boel die
wel weer te rug willen want het is hier een nuvere weerelt
want den ouders zijn hier geen baas van hun eigen kin-
ders want als die tegen den pliesj zege dat moeder of
vader behandelt mij niet goed dan moeten zij weer 5
dalders be talen zoo gaat het hier...'

According to Boekhout, parental influence in America was not far-reaching enough or independent enough by Dutch standards.

Negative experiences were also reported, though on a far smaller scale. Two themes stand out: the description of social freedom and equality, and the reports of economic success.

During the 1880-1914 period, the Frisian immigrant letters echoed in chorus: 'America is a great country for those who want to work with their hands'. People in Friesland knew from immigrant letters that more could be earned in the silk industry in the city of Paterson than what an agricultural labourer could earn in the old country. In America one could expect immediate rewards and a long-term potential for economic and social progress. It is certainly true that many landless emigrants did become farmers and that wages in the USA were higher than in the Netherlands. The letters therefore exaggerated the fact that there was always plenty to eat, particularly meat. The 'spekbrieven' ['bacon letters'], in which the great quantities of inexpensive meat were extolled, helped many future emigrants over the Atlantic.[31]

According to many writers, the supposed scenario for emigrants ran as follows: leave your impoverished homeland, modify your culture, work diligently, and the fruits of prosperity will be within easy reach.[32] Social mobility could be achieved by anyone in America. The fact this was not true for many ethnic groups in the late nineteenth century is not important in the context of this article. More important is the fact that the image of America appeared to contain elements of *possible* future social mobility.[33]

---

[31]   J. van Hinte, *Nederlanders in Amerika* (Groningen, 1928), I, p. 166.

[32]   John Bodnar, *The Transplanted* (Bloomington, 1985), p. 169.

[33]   Examples of important mobility studies are: Stephan Thernstrom, *The other Bostonians: Poverty and Progress in the American Metropolis, 1880-1970* (Cambridge, Mass., 1973); Richard L. Doyle, 'Wealth Mobility in Pella, Iowa 1847-1925' in *The Dutch in America, Immigration, Settlement and Cultural Change*, ed. R.P.

Dutch folkloristic dances are taught every year to students in Holland, Michigan.
They show their skills during tulip time.
(1991; private collection Annemieke Galema)

The Tulip Time Festival in different settlements recalls and commercial-
izes the origins of its inhabitants.
(1991; private collection Annemieke Galema)

If any phrase appeared more often in America letters than 'we eat meat three times a day', it was 'here we tip our hats to no one'! The immigrant as an image-maker painted America not only as a land of opportunity, but also as the land of equality, where every man considered himself as good as his fellow townsmen. An emigrant who settled in South Dakota writes in a Frisian newspaper in 1911 about travelling by rail in the United States:

> 'Our wagon was full of Dutchmen. You could walk all the wagons, because there are no separate classes! It should be like that in the Netherlands. But over there are 'classes' (*standen*); here we have rich and poor people but 'classes'?. If a rich person passes with his car or buggy he will stop and ask if you want to come along. Here, the millionaire is sitting next to the labourer and very often they look alike'.[34]

W.J. van den Bosch writes from Indiana about an American 'foreman' in the factory where he works in 1893:

> 'This foreman is the boss of about 50 people. He earns 1100 dollars or 2750 guilders a year. In Holland someone like him would have been properly dressed, giving himself airs and graces, proudly commanding those under him. The man in question, the foreman, walks around with a chew of tobacco in his mouth, in the thick of it all. He even helps with the loading if necessary, and there's no difference between him and his men...'.[35]

Swierenga (New Brunswick, 1985), pp. 156-171; and Gordon W. Kirk Jr., *The Promise of American Life: Social Mobility in a Nineteenth-Century Immigrant Community, Holland, Michigan, 1847-1894* (Philadelphia, 1978).

[34] *Nieuwsblad van Friesland*, (August 27, 1911) No. 77.

[35] *Nieuw Advertentieblad*, (July 8, 1893). The literal text of the fragment is:

> 'Die 'foreman' of chef heeft p.m. 50 lui onder zich... ja zoo'n man die een 1100 dollar of een f2750 per jaar verdient, zou in Holland netjes gekleed, met een 'schut-

This must have been a startling and appealing prospect to Frisian agricultural labourers. It was the desire to achieve social status, rather than money alone, that was attractive to many potential emigrants and that developed an image of America as the land of democracy in the European mind. People longed for independence from the landlord. In Friesland the emigrants had been accustomed to a life where authority was concentrated in the landed class and where any bridging of the gap between those with and those without land was almost unthinkable. Social status was closely connected with the possession of land. The democratic nature of the American way of life was not lost on the Frisian immigrants. Whether the 'egalitarian rhetoric', as the historian Walter Kamphoefner calls it, really proved to be a positive immigrant experience, is not a question that can be answered here.[36]

Their correspondence shows that the emigrants did not decide to move to the United States because their appetite for adventure had been whetted, but because they believed that America offered them a better opportunity for economic and social mobility than the old country. As we have seen, they came from a region that had been hit by depression. Many of the land labourers were unemployed or only worked seasonal jobs. The crisis had extreme consequences not only for the agricultural population, but also for the people who were directly linked to that sector of the labour market, such as butchers, bakers and carpenters. There was also disappointment among the land labourers because of the absence of ideas of social freedom and social equivalence.

---

tersmaaltijd' in 't hoofd, met gekozen trots zijn ondergeschikten commanderen. De persoon in kwestie hier, die chef, wel, hij loopt ook met een pruim in den mond, tusschen alle goederen door, helpt zelfs mede te laden als er handen te kort zijn en tusschen zijn werklui en hem bestaat geen afstand...'

[36] Walter D. Kamphoefner, *The Westfalians. From Germany to Missouri* (Princeton, 1987), p. 135.

It was therefore by no means surprising that people hoped for a better future for themselves and their children. They had been taught this lesson by the group of image-makers mentioned before, in the province of Friesland, but also in other parts of the Netherlands, who propagated America as the land of promise. The propaganda was credible and acceptable.

The reports from the New World were often difficult to interpret in Friesland, and some news was too good to be true. In general, however, we may assume that the impact of the America letters was phenomenal. Guide books or immigration brochures might stretch the truth now and then, but who could doubt the word of friends and relatives? Until the letter arrived, Iowa and South Dakota had been distant mirages, mere names on a map; now Ulbe and Maaike were there and the vision cleared to reveal a village, a farm, a family. The people learned about America from those who came from their own milieu, from the ones they trusted, in their own language and according to their own way of thinking.

Images of the 'Old World'

After these reflections on the images of America among (prospective) Frisian emigrants, and how this image-building took place, I shall present some brief impressions of the immigrants' image of the Old World.

In 1897 members of the Dutch community in Holland, Michigan drew the following conclusions on their migration history: 'A peculiar feature of many of these (Dutch) colonists has been that they preserved their identity, and retained many of their national characteristics without refusing to become fully incorporated with our body politic, preserving their individuality without refusing to be absorbed into the national life'[37]

---

[37]   Henry S. Lucas, *Dutch Immigrant Memoirs and Related Writings* (Assen, 1955), p. 5.

It is very important to realize that the immigrants' image of their home country was not static. The longer they had settled in the United States, the more their view of the old country became influenced by impressions of the New World. Of course, the image was also affected by whether the immigrants settled in a Dutch community or in one without other Dutch immigrants and with a lot of ethnic diversity. Furthermore, the image of the old country does not seem to be a very independent one. In the Netherlands the emigrants held a different view of their native country than in the United States. Actually, the image of the home country was not very real before they left; it came to the fore after the migrants settled in America.

The American historian Herbert J. Brinks argues that in common American usage 'Old Country' often means an immigrant's land of birth or ancestry, but 'Old' can also embody a more literal meaning, such as the country of the old folks. I would like to add the sense of 'Old Country' as 'worn out' or 'depreciated'. Some people believed that Europe had lost its vitality and that progress, prospects and a future were reserved for the New World of America.

As he examined letters to America written from all parts of the Netherlands around the turn of the century, Brinks discovered that the second, more literal meaning is often highlighted, 'because the Dutch reported more steadily on the vicissitudes of the aged - their ailments, their progressive diminution of powers, and death, - than on the prospects of youthful expectation'.[38]

This general characteristic is hardly surprising, since a study of Frisian migration patterns reveals that the immigrants came largely from the younger ranks of the population. As Brinks points out, the older family members stayed in the Netherlands.

---

[38]   Herbert J. Brinks, 'Impressions of the 'Old' World 1848-1940' in *The Dutch in North-America, Their Immigration and Cultural Continuity*, eds. R. Kroes and H.O. Neuschäfer (Amsterdam, 1991), pp. 34-48.

Without a doubt the Frisian correspondents often provided the immigrants with a very unpleasant picture of everyday life in Friesland. Although I have not yet been able to trace many Friesland letters to America, and despite the fact that those I have managed to trace may well be unrepresentative, much of the news from the area which the emigrants left behind did not paint a very rosy picture of the old country of Friesland. This impression corresponds to Brinks' findings for the Netherlands as a whole.[39] In the wake of the agrarian crisis which preceded the turn of the century, the information was dominated by generally unstable or uninviting economic prospects. To cite again, R.J. Algra from EE in Friesland writes to Iowa in 1892:

> 'Because my income is rather slender, I don't have much money to spend. Yes, dear friends, wouldn't it be wonderful if you sent me some of your abundance...'[40]

Or take E.J. Brouwer to his family in Iowa in 1881:

> 'The situation is very sorrowful. No one can ever be successful here. It is really sad and this is not the case in your country, at least that's what they say around here'[41]

In 1899 Rev. T. Dalhuijsen is concerned about the future of his children:

> 'Our son Hans studies for his teacher's degree, he doesn't like it, is well able, but refuses; he prefers birds, rabbits, fights etc. What shall I say? Hendrik is 13 years old and

---

[39] H.J. Brinks, 'Impressions', 35.

[40] Letter of R.J. Algra from Ee to J.D. Douma in Pella, Iowa, January 3, 1892. Collection *The Archives*, Calvin College Grand Rapids, Michigan.

[41] Letter of E.J. Brouwer from Ee to D.J. Douma in Pella, Iowa, April 8, 1881. Collection *The Archives*, Calvin College, Grand Rapids, Michigan.

wants to become a farmer; as a hobby he learned how to
milk cows and earns a quarter a week for that; he would
rather be dead than go for an education. So what shall I
do with these boys in our poor and miserable and hungry
fatherland? To America! There they should go. There
they will be able (if they use common sense) to get a
farm or so. Here normally nothing else except sand potatoes and grease.'[42]

Dutch immigrants' views of the Netherlands must have been
influenced by this kind of correspondence from the old
country. Contemporary immigrant newspapers in Dutch-American
communities, like 'De Volksvriend', often contained letters from
the Frisian homeland.

Other impressions of the immigrants' view can be gleaned
from their own letters home. They wrote to Friesland, often comparing their new environment with the situation that they left
behind. This comparison functioned as their justification for the
move.

This explains part of the criticism of Friesland that the
immigrants had. Once again, the key word is 'equality':

'Isn't it required in Holland for example for a person A.
to have a certain status and income to associate with
some person B.? Isn't it true that there is a horrible class
distinction? Nobody can deny these distinctions in class!
That's why I can breathe in America, thinking how
people in Holland have to distinguish themselves in their
neighbours' views, with a medal of "class and
position"!'[43]

This perception of Holland is representative. The burdens of class
conflicts and class distinctions could not be forgotten. As for the

---

[42]   Letter of Rev. T. Dalhuijsen from Wanswerd April 5, 1899 to
America. Collection *The Archives* Calvin College, Grand Rapids.
[43]   *Nieuw Advertentieblad*, (July 8, 1893).

economic situation in Friesland, the American Frisians held a poor view of it, as we have already seen.

The immigrants had a more positive view of Friesland once they turned to social and religious life. They generally considered American church life to be superficial, and they missed the cosy social life of the old village.

According to Brinks, the most obvious counter-perception to unpleasant memories lies in fond romanticization of closely-knit families in the old country, - the proximity of grandparents, uncles, aunts, and village companions.[44]

These perceptions of The Netherlands are limited to the province or origin. The immigrants in America considered themselves as natives of Groningen, Friesland or Brabant rather than of the Netherlands. Dutch Americans derived their identity not from a national horizon, but more or less from a sub-national, provincial horizon.

Images and migrants reconsidered

At the turn of the century, the exodus of thousands of able-bodied young men and women and their families, convinced that a better life awaited them beyond the seas was a fact. It is very plausible that a connection existed between the better life promised to emigrants by the image-makers and the rate of flow of the emigrant tide. This, in turn was linked to conditions in the Netherlands. The more alluring the promises, the less attractive the Frisian homeland appeared during periods of economic stagnation.[45] The agrarian crisis was such a period of stagnation in

---

44   Herbert J. Brinks, 'Impressions', 2.
45   Franco Ramella found the same for Italian workers who went to New Jersey at the turn of the century. America seemed to offer what potential emigrants were looking for: 'jobs in abundance, good pay and

the province of Friesland. In general there was little opportunity for upward social mobility in the prevailing social order and daily life was difficult. The written accounts by the immigrants give the impression that the negative voices found their motivation in the difference of culture. The positive sounds, however, originated mainly in a more promising material perspective; once in the new country, the immigrants found it harder to embrace the new cultural values than to adjust to the new laborious life. We may conclude that the perception of America of the late nineteenth-century emigrants was defined by their socio-economic background.[46]

Against this background, the lure of America is understandable. Turner's thesis that the American frontier was unlimited also became part of the imagination of the Frisian emigrants. The contrast between the old, crumbling Europe and the new, promising America was getting stronger and stronger.[47] The American example made clear what was needed: widened franchise, weakened class barriers, proper assurances of respect by the elite, and a certain opportunity for self-improvement and upward social mobility. If America at a certain time or place did not meet these demands, prospective emigrants created the America that did.

---

freedom to express themselves politically'. See Franco Ramella, 'Across the Ocean or over the Border: Experiences and Expectations of Italians from Piedmont in New Jersey and Southern France', in *Distant Magnets: Migrants' Views of Opportunities in Industrializing Areas in Europe and America* (New York, Holmes & Meier. Forthcoming).

[46]   This is in contrast to the group of emigrants who left for America with their leader Rev. H.P. Scholte in the middle of the nineteenth century. Their nation image of America was defined by their religious concept. See the article by R. Kuiper in the present collection.

[47]   For a beautifully written reflection on images of America of Dutch Calvinist immigrants in the middle of the nineteenth century see J.W. Schulte Nordholt, 'Perceived in Poetry. Poetical Images of America for Dutch Immigrants' in eds. R. Kroes and H.O. Neuschäfer, *The Dutch*, pp. 3-15.

To return Den Hollander's reflections on the discrepancy between real society and muddled observations: 'With some exaggeration one can say: Every human being creates his own outside world'. Den Hollander's vision implies that one does not give the other world a value of its own, but reduces it to a function of our own world, our self. Images, according to Den Hollander, are clear in the mind: something that strikes the imagination is not easily forgotten, despite the fact that it may no longer correspond to reality. Fantasy is often richer, more colourful and more emotional than reality can ever be. It often seems that we allow ourselves to be confronted by the satisfying myth rather than by tedious and dreary reality.

Den Hollander makes a clear distinction between fantasy and reality, but where does the distinction actually lie? Is it not true that myth and fantasy often create reality, and that myth and fantasy are part of reality? This is also the reason why it is important to study the changes in the imagination of the European observer. As Van Berkel claims, the prejudices that we entertain in our observations of foreign cultures should be object of our studies. However, Van Berkel's assertion also raises the thorny issue of the power of the image, or of myth and fantasy as against other aspects of reality. Is it inevitable to accept fantasies as 'unreal'? I do not think so; Van Berkel and Den Hollander go too far in making the implicit distinction between reality and fantasy. Fantasy is as much a part of everyday life as, for example, the 'fact' of travel abroad. Images and myth certainly have real effects, but only within a ready-made context. Den Hollander exaggerates in saying that every human being creates his own outside world, since such a view also entails acceptance of a radical subjectivism and individualism. This is only true in a very qualified sense. The image of America that affected the potential emigrant was not necessarily the main reason for leaving. All the same, we may assume that without this image most emigrants would not have left for that faraway land.

GERMAN MAIDS IN PROSPEROUS 'GULDENLAND' (GUILDERLAND) AND THE LAND OF MORAL THREAT: NATION IMAGES AND NATIONAL IDENTITY DURING THE INTERBELLUM PERIOD.

Barbara Henkes

'I went to Holland with the idea that Holland was a paradise, at least according to the stories told by a friend, who could do "miracles" in Germany with every guilder earned in Holland', Mrs. Akkerman remembers. She is one of the women who came to the Netherlands during the interwar years as German maids and have remained ever since.[1]

---

[1]   Questionnaire Mrs Akkerman.
I have contacted more than a hundred former German domestic servants in the Netherlands to date for my research on 'German Domestic Servants: Significance and Images of Female Migrant Workers in the Netherlands, 1920-1950'. Ninety-three of them filled in a questionnaire; twenty-two of them told me their life histories. The investigation includes women who returned to Germany after a temporary stay in the Netherlands as maidservants; so far conversations have been held with 12 women in Northern Germany and 9 women from Nordrhein-Westphalen.

The migration of German workers to the Netherlands was nothing new. For centuries German labourers had been going to the Low Countries to earn a wage on the land or in the mines and the building trade. German women had also been looking for positions in the Dutch cities, though only in modest numbers.[2] However, their numbers increased dramatically after the First World War. During the interwar years tens of thousands of young, unmarried women left their war-torn native soil to try their luck in the undamaged neighbouring country. In 1920, only 9,100 foreign female workers were registered in the Netherlands; by 1930, however, their numbers had increased to 30,500, more than 24,000 of whom were German. This figure continued to rise until it stood at about 40,000 in 1934. From then on it fell: at the end of 1936 the number of foreign female servants was estimated at 22,000, and when the Germans invaded the Netherlands in May 1940, there were only about 3,500 German maids left.[3]

Because of the supposed shortage of Dutch female domestics, they were at first received with open arms. Their industriousness (*Tüchtigkeit*) and gift for 'accommodating themselves quickly to their circumstances' were generally praised, and a number of women's organisations soon set up agencies 'for the recruitment of German domestic servants'.[4] The ties between Germany and the Netherlands that had existed from earlier days presented a helpful starting-point. The Dreesman, Kloppenburg, Hirsch and other families of German

---

[2]   J. Lucassen, *Naar de kusten van de Noordzee; trekarbeid in Europees perspektief, 1600-1900* (Gouda, 1984). J. Lucassen en R. Penninx, *Nieuwkomers. Immigranten en hun nakomelingen in Nederland, 1500-1985* (Amsterdam, 1985).

[3]   Statistics from the Dutch Central Statistic Office (*Centraal Bureau voor de Statistiek*), published in C. Haitsma-Mulier, *Hulp in de Huishouding gevraagd* (Amsterdam, 1947) pp. 77-78.

[4]   B. Henkes, 'Changing images of German maids during the inter-war period in the Netherlands; from trusted help to traitor in the nest', in *The Myths We Live By*, ed. R. Samuel and P. Thompson (London, 1990) pp. 225-239.

origin from the substantial business community were - like their Dutch neighbours - in need of cheap and conscientious domestic servants. Thus a chain migration of unmarried female workers started, whereby the first German maids helped their sisters, girls next door or friends to obtain positions with their mistresses' sisters, neighbours and friends. Many a Dutch guilder found its way to Germany to support the relatives that had stayed behind and to save for a fine trousseau. Apart from that, Dutch relief actions[5] on behalf of the German population who had been hit by runaway inflation reinforced the image of the Netherlands as 'the land of milk and honey'.

The present article is intended to confront the changing images of a nation expressed at an organised, institutional level with those images expressed at an individual level. The first part draws attention to German institutions in the Netherlands and the way in which the migration of German maidservants gave rise to organised images of the Netherlands and - inextricably linked to them - of Germany. The second part pursues those less articulate images of a nation which could be found among the German maids themselves with regard to their national identity. In this way I propose to examine what influence organised images at the institutional level could exert on the individual experience of migration. The intention is not to look for the disciplinary effect of the German institutions on their young countrywomen, but to pay attention to different ways in which German maids dealt with these collective images within their individual lives. Since the influence of the organised images on an

---

[5]   The Committee *Ruhrhilfe aus den Niederlanden* was set up in February 1923 in The Hague to help the distressed population in the Ruhr district. The Committee raised a total sum of f13,336 and clothes worth about f30,000. The Dutch Red Cross followed with a relief action at the end of February. All over the country there were initiatives to get German children from the occupied Ruhr district to the Netherlands to catch up (*zur Erholung*). (Sources: Municipal Archives The Hague: archives Committee *Ruhrhilfe aus den Niederlanden*; Municipal Archives Amsterdam: *Guldenfonds voor Duitse kinderopvang* (Guilder Fund for the Reception of German Children).

individual life cannot be traced when different fragments of life
stories are selected and connected outside their own dynamics, the
focus is on the individual life story of one former German maidservant.

Land of milk, honey and moral threats

The image of the Netherlands as the land of milk and honey played
an important role in the - permanent or temporary - migration of
German women to the Netherlands. Their departure to the guilder-
paradise (*Guldenparadis*), however, evoked another image as well:
the image of moral decay that threatened these young, single women
in their new and unfamiliar surroundings. This potential moral decay
was seen as a threat not only to the prestige of the German girls
themselves, but also to the prestige of the German nation. The young
women's wanderlust was accompanied by warnings against the
'increased moral and physical dangers' that the girls' stay abroad
involved. Even before they left, the ignorant women were said to be
already in imminent danger of falling into the wrong hands through
unverifiable newspaper advertisements or shady intermediaries.
During the journey they would run the risk of coming into touch with
ruthless white slave-traders, and once they had arrived at the place of
destination misfortune still lay in wait, as the religious women's
organizations in particular emphasized.

   The German National Union of Catholic Societies for the
Protection of Girls (*der Deutsche nationale Verband der katholische
Mädchenschutzvereine*) and its Evangelical counterpart, der *Deutscher
Verband der Freundinnen junger Mädchen*, saw an important task
reserved for themselves in this respect. At a national and international
level they were working on the extension of an interdenominational
network of Station care (*Bahnhofsmission*), to assist the travelling
girls in word and deed. Through their contacts with sister organizations in the Netherlands and with the support of the German
authorities, they advanced the care for German girls at their places of

destination in so-called *Mädchenvereine*. These girls' societies served to offer the young women a safe home base (*ein Stück Heimat*) in the unfamiliar Dutch surroundings. The societies could be found in large cities like The Hague, Rotterdam, Amsterdam and Utrecht; in Haarlem and the surrounding area, in the Gooi, in Twente and in other places where many German maidservants worked. They often met more than once a week under the leadership of a German clergyman (*Seelsorger*), a sister or a lay woman (*Fürsorgerin*). During the winter their numbers could rise to 150 in the big cities, while in the smaller places they involved about 10 to 15 girls at a time. There was generally an employment agency which could help the domestic servants to find a 'decent' situation connected with the girls' societies.[6] All the same, these activities could not prevent a lot of German maids from getting into trouble. The anxious *Fürsorgerin*, Johanna Schwer, wrote from Amsterdam: 'many of them have lost their faith and good morals, have spent their money on worthless trash and cinema, and have lost their fancy and love for their work. How many girls are not here nowadays, who not only have to look after themselves, but also after their child!'[7]

The German Catholic clergyman, rector Heinemann in The Hague, also expressed his anxiety in a widespread pamphlet on 'German Catholic girls in Holland': 'Whoever is working in the German girls' care (*Fürsorge*) as a foreign clergyman (*Auslandsee-lsorger*) is confronted with the religious, moral and social distress in which a large part of the girls find themselves almost daily. In Germany itself they mostly see only the bright side, especially the

---

[6] The data of the first Annual Report (1927) of the St Elisabeth foundation for Catholic German girls (*St Elisabethstiftung für katholische deutsche Mädchen*) in The Hague may serve as an illustration of the extent that the activities of some of these societies could assume: the visitors totalled 15,000. Sometimes more than 150 girls came in one evening during the winter months. Their own agency succeeded in finding 240 jobs.

[7] J. Schwer, 'Die deutschen Mädchen in Amsterdam', *Mädchenschutz* 1/2 (1925): 8-13.

economic advantages of the migration.'[8] Heinemann pointed out that
the dangers for German girls abroad did not differ much from those
in their native country in the first instance. Denominational relations
in the Netherlands, however, would involve a large part of German
Catholic maidservants accepting situations with non-Catholics or non-
believers. This did not further the ties with the church among the
girls, to whom the different customs and different language used in
the Dutch church were unfamiliar anyway. The clergyman saw the
moral dangers as being closely interwoven with religious alienation.
The religious indifference which easily arose would decrease their
resistance, which was slight anyway due to the absence of parents or
relatives.

Holland was not only the country of the solid guilder for the
hard-working German girl, but it was also the country of moral threat
to the single German girl.

'Deutschtum' in danger

The German domestic servants were in danger, not only because of
the unfamiliar Dutch environment with its large ports, fashionable
seaside resorts and different morals and customs.[9] The threat to their
pure morals, against which religious circles warned so intensively,
came from 'bad' girls within the Germany community itself as well.
Whereas it was mostly well-educated (gebildete) girls from the
middle classes - in reduced circumstances due to the inflation - who
went to the Netherlands in the early twenties, this was supposed to
have changed after the stabilization of the mark in 1924. It was said

---

8   C. Heineman, *Deutsche katholische Mädchen in Holland*, s.d.
[1928]. I came across this special issue (*Sonderndruck*) not only in the
archives of the Cologne Archbishopric, but also in the archives of the
German Evangelical Community in The Hague and in the archives of the
German Department of Foreign Affairs in Bonn.
9   C. Heinemann, *Deutsche katholische Mädchen*, p.4.

that from then on it was mainly girls from the industrial region - which had been hit by unemployment most severely - who were crossing the border.[10] It was especially among these girls that 'immature elements' could be found, who 'did not do honour to Germanness' (*den Deutschtum keine Ehre machen*), as representatives of German religious organizations in the Netherlands put it.[11] After her visit to a German-Dutch conference in 1929 on the care of German girls in the Netherlands, Käthe Kuhlenbäumer of the National Union of Catholic German Societies for the Protection of Girls wondered: 'Is it not a threat to the prestige of our German civilization abroad, if, for example, 132 German girls were expelled by the Dutch police from The Hague only during the past year, 55 of them for immoral behaviour, 55 of them for theft and the rest of them because they were without means of support or without papers?'[12]

In the interest of the German girls, but certainly also in 'the interest of the German nation', measures were taken to restrict the free passage of young German women across the border. Emigration Consultancies (*Auswandererberatungsstelle*) were enlisted to prevent unplanned departures of German girls and to prepare them better for their migration. Free advice was given to those who planned to leave the country by the passport bureaus (*Passantragstelle*), employment exchanges, women's organizations and in pamphlets. Special questionnaires 'for young girls who wish to accept positions abroad' were implemented in 1927, including questions about their background and forthcoming employment in the Netherlands.[13] Enquiries

---

[10]   Annual Report for 1927 of the *Deutsch Evangelische Gemeinde* in The Hague.

[11]   Among others: P. Louis, 'Die deutschen Katholiken in Holland', *Caritas* 31 (November 1926) pp. 342-347; and E. Winkel, 'Mädchenschutzsorge in Holland', *Mädchenschutz*, 7/8 (1930) pp.54-57.

[12]   K. Kuhlenbäumer, 'Deutsche Mädchen in Holland', *Mädchenschutz*, nr 11/12 (1929) pp. 89-93.

[13]   Quaterly report of the public Emigration Consultancy (*öffentliche Auswandererberatungsstelle*) Düsseldorf, dated 31-3-27 (Nordrhein-Westfälisches Hauptstaatsarchiv, Düsseldorf).

about the employers were made by women advisers (*Vertrauens-damen*), mainly German *Fürsorgerinnen* or women from Dutch Societies for the Protection of Girls. Was the employer's family known to be decent (*einwandfrei*)? Could the girl fulfil her religious duties? Was there separate sleeping accommodation for the maid, and was the work not too heavy? These were the points by which the situation in the Netherlands was judged. If the prospective household received a negative evaluation, the informant was given addresses of the local German girls' societies in the Netherlands which could help her to find a more suitable situation. On the other hand, the emigration consultancies made enquiries about the girls who wanted to leave as well. Did they really have an irreproachable character? Would they be able to cope with the work? Were they not too young?[14] If a young woman was found to be unsuitable, she and her parents would be put under great pressure to retract the migration plans.

Many girls were given advice by such consultancies[15]; many more girls went across the border on their own, without consulting the agencies, and looked for work with the help of family and friends. Efforts to protect German girls in the Netherlands continued without abatement. Catholic and Evangelical circles wholeheartedly agreed that this work had top priority. Mr Kösters, a German priest in Amsterdam, wrote to the Bishop of Cologne in 1930: 'In this way, with the help of God, we hope to extend and deepen our social charitable activities for the German girls more and more, so that they will bear fruit for every single one of them and not least for our German fatherland.'[16]

---

[14]   Archive of the *Auswandererberatungsstelle Münster* (Nordrhein-westfälisches Staatsarchive in Münster).

[15]   The number of questionnaires of the *Auswandererberatungsstelle Münster* for the years 1929 -1936 that has been preserved shows that at the peak period in 1932 at least 880 girls from this area wanted to go to the Netherlands as domestic servants through this institution alone.

[16]   Letter dated 21-5-1931 (Historical Archive Archbishopric Cologne, Generalia XXIII, 53, vol.1.).

Depression in the Netherlands

The Netherlands still had something to offer, but 'we entered the year 1931 with a certain anxiety', to quote the annual report of the German Catholic *Elisabethstiftung* in The Hague. 'Should we have to fear that the ghost of unemployment, which was wandering about in Germany devastatingly and which kept its hold on more and more layers of society, would also call on its neighbouring countries? Or might we hope that Holland, the country with the stable gold standard and the rich colonies, would offer security and jobs for the time being?'

The Netherlands did not escape the economic crisis of the thirties. Trade slackened and unemployment increased. At first the position of domestic servants remained unaffected by this decline. That is why the eyes of many German girls in the early thirties increasingly turned towards the Netherlands, the country which was still known as a *Guldenparadis*.[17] It did not take long, however, before the depression in the Netherlands became perceptible to the German maidservants too. Wages decreased and many a Dutch housewife saw herself forced to dismiss her domestic staff partly or completely. The milk had been skimmed and there was no more honey left. The Netherlands no longer represented the rich country with the coveted guilder which received the German girls with open arms. On the contrary, the maidservants who used to be so popular now met with restrictive measures. As unemployment grew, people were urged - especially by the government - to replace their foreign servants by Dutch maids. In spite of objections by Dutch employers, the Foreign Workers' Act of 1934 also became applicable to foreign domestic servants in October 1936. If they did not have labour permits, German girls could be expelled from the country without appeal; and without proof of a permanent situation they were no longer allowed to enter the Netherlands.

---

[17]   Annual Report *St Elisabethstiftung* for 1931.

While measures were taken in the Netherlands to prevent German maids from entering the country, the German authorities took action to stop the women from migrating and to make them return if they were already abroad. The law on employment agencies (*Gesetz über Arbeitsvermittlung, Berufsberatung und Lehrstellenvermittlung*) of November 1935 imposed severe restraints on activities other than those of the federal employment bureaus, and from 1939 on the latter were confronted with a prohibition on the placement of German domestic servants abroad too.[18] Still, by then few young women - at least 'Aryan' women - were inclined to leave their native country. The 'depreciation' of the Netherlands in the course of the thirties seemed to be to the advantage of Germany. After Hitler's rise to power in 1933, preparations for war in Germany boosted the labour market. Once again the homeland opened up new perspectives. The flow was reversed as fewer girls were inclined to go to the Netherlands[19] and more of them returned to the *Heimat* for good.

Fatherland calling

German domestic servants who stayed in the Netherlands often had good situations, serious lovers or had become anchored in Dutch

---

[18]   Report for October, November and December 1939 of the *öffentliche Auswandererberatungsstelle* Cologne.(Nordrhein-Westfälisches Hauptstaatsarchiv, Düsseldorf)

[19]   Naturally, this does not apply to the Jewish and political refugees. After the Dutch Minister for Social Affairs' initial refusal, the Jewish Women's Council (*Joodsche Vrouwenraad*) in the Netherlands appealed to the existing need for domestic servants and succeeded in opening the border for only sixty Jewish girls to work in Dutch households in 1939. (Source: *Het Vaderland*, 15-12-'38; letter dated 14-10-1939 from the Jewish Women's Council in the Netherlands in the archive of the Union of Domestic Servants (*Bond van Huispersoneel*) at the International Institute of Social History; Els Blok, *Uit de schaduw van de mannen. Vrouwenverzet 1930-1940* (Amsterdam, 1985) p.256.

society in some other way. They did not have the slightest intention of returning to the German Reich. If they had not exchanged their German nationalities for Dutch ones by marrying Dutchmen, they were confronted in December 1938 with a summons by the German authorities to return to Germany. The fatherland was calling.

In a way, the fatherland had been calling more often: a sick mother that had to be cared for, the desire for the German mountain scenery, or the misery of homesickness at Christmas. The *Heimat* always exerted a certain pull, but on the other hand there were the ties the German girls had established with their new surroundings. Each one of them had to decide which had the stronger attraction, but now others decided for them. The fatherland, represented by the National Socialist authorities, made a collective appeal to the German girls to return. If they refused, they would lose their citizenship.

The Action for the Collective Return of German Maidservants (*Hausmädchenheimschaffungsaktion*) aimed at taking in more women for the German labour market, but it was thought just as important to save the native women outside Germany for the German national community (*Das deutsche Volkstum*). That concerned first of all the girls who worked in the households of Jews, German political refugees or Dutch people who displayed a negative attitude toward the Third Reich.[20] They had to go back as soon as possible to be committed to National Socialist charge. But all the others had to return as well, unless they worked with Reich Germans or were members of the Reich German Community (*Reichsdeutsche Gemeinschaft*) or other National Socialist organizations in the Netherlands.

Butting, leader of the Reich German Community, wrote to his Department of Foreign Affairs in February 1939: 'Since, considering

---

[20]   Letter dated 6-12-1938 from the German Department of Foreign Affairs (*Auswärtiges Amt*) to the German Legation in The Hague. The Legation in its turn sent copies of this letter to the German consulates in Amsterdam, Rotterdam and Maastricht on 16-12-1939 (Politisches Archiv des Auswärtigen Amtes in Bonn - from now on referred to as AA - Rotterdam, AZ II A1, volume 22).

the population policy, it will be unbearable if a large number of German girls stays in the Netherlands, I have proposed to call back all the girls who would not be burdensome to German prosperity because of their old age, or do not work with political personalities that are of great importance to Germany.'[21] In the same letter he gave a numerical survey of the German domestic servants in the Netherlands: one-third of the 3,800 German maidservants could not be contacted because they had changed jobs without reporting it to the authorities. About 10% of them had returned to Germany on their own initiative, according to Butting's information. Some 25% of the group that could be traced did not respond to the summons. This meant that apart from the 1,150 German maids who could not be traced, 650 kept quiet. Among the 1900 or so who did react were many who tried to back out of the forced repatriation, for example by adducing their forthcoming marriage with a Dutchman. These girls in particular received no mercy from Butting and his companions: 'Because it runs strongly counter to the importance of the German national community (*Volksgemeinschaft*) if German girls marry into another people and are thereby lost as mothers of the German Nation.'[22]

The large amount of written requests from German maids and Dutch mistresses for dispensation[23], as well as the news in the Dutch press[24] about the 'run on the town halls'[25] and the painful farewell scenes at the Dutch railway stations indicate that there was not much

---

[21]   Letter dated 2-2-1939 (AA, Den Haag, R4,2).
[22]   Letter from Butting to the German Consulate in Rotterdam dated 2-2-1939 (AA, Rotterdam, AZIII a6, volume 95).
[23]   AA, Den Haag, AZ R4,2.
[24]   Sources: collection of newspaper cuttings on German domestic servants in the Netherlands of the *Nederlands Bureau voor Vrouwenarbeid* (Dutch Women's Labour Agency) at the International Archives of the Women's Movement in Amsterdam (IIAV), newspaper documentation of the Amsterdam and Rotterdam Municipal Archives and the documentation in the archives of the AA.
[25]   Headline of an article in *De Rotterdammer*, 16-12-1938.

enthusiasm for returning. The German authorities' populist and patriotic language apparently did not appeal to the German maids who had not left the Netherlands by 1939, and those who eventually did decide to leave the Netherlands did so out of fear of the threat of a new war.

This political crisis made their anchorage in Dutch society unsettled. Under these circumstances their German identity, which had played a social role at most until then, and had often been valued positively, acquired a political dimension with a negative character. This applied not only to the unmarried German maids in the Netherlands, but also to the married women of German origin who had adopted Dutch nationality. Only a few managed to withdraw from this polarization under the impending doom of the Second World War.[26]

Nation image and national identity

In this outline of the images of the Dutch nation produced at the level of the German institutions involved in the migration of German domestic servants during the inter-war years, we have seen how the attractive image of the Netherlands as 'the land of milk and honey' changed as a result of a shift in the socio-economic climate, while the image of pauperized Germany was also subject to changes under the influence of National Socialism. As the migration movement involved single girls at a time when the independent mobility of unmarried women was not a matter of course, it is not surprising that the image of the Netherlands as a land as sweet as honey was linked to the image of the dangerous child-molester: Holland as the land of slack morals, to which the order and discipline of the parental home in Prussian Germany could be contrasted. This image was especially promoted by German religious circles, not least to justify (and to

---

[26]   This appears from the interviews.

raise funds for) their presence in the Netherlands as a substitute and disciplining fatherland.

At the end of the thirties the National Socialist authorities were bent on taking over this organising, protecting and educating task from religious and other independent German societies in the Netherlands.[27] At first they tried to catch the German domestic servants under the umbrella of the local *Reichsdeutsche Gemeinschaft* or the *Deutsche Kolonie*. When this failed and as war was approaching, the girls were more useful at home.[28] The severe measures by which the maids were forced to return found their justification in the reference to the moral decay among German girls in the Netherlands 'that was overrun by jews' (*das verjudete Holland*)[29], not to mention the importance of future mothers for the German nation.

To what extent did these changes in the collective image of both nations impinge on the German girls living in the Netherlands? What had made them cross the border in the first place? How did they experience their position as German maidservants in the Netherlands at the time? And under what circumstances did they feel an appeal to their national identity? In their writings, German institutions emphasized the importance of national identity as a mainstay for the German girls in a foreign country. From interviews

---

[27]   Note (*Aufzeignung*) dated 1-12-1936 (AA, Rotterdam, AZ II A1, volume 22); Letter from Machensen to the German Department of Foreign Affairs dated 26-10-1937 (AA, R V, band 8); Letter from Butting, The Hague to the head of the *Ausland Organization* dated 1-12-1937 (AA, Den Haag, AZ R 4,2).

[28]   Correspondence, beginning of 1939, between various local *Reichsdeutsche* communities and the German consulate in Rotterdam concerning the *Heimschaffungsfrage* (AA, Rotterdam AZ II A6, volume 95).

[29]   Report by Emil Maier-Dorn of the NSBDT to the *Auswärtige Amt* dated 8-12-1938 as a result of his stay in the Nederlands. (AA, R V, volume 9) and a letter of Butting to the head of the *Ausland Organization* in Berlin dated 2-2-1939. (AA, Den Haag, R4,2).

Gretchen in Holland: the photographer's romantic offer.
Proud greetings in Dutch national costume were often sent home.
(Scheveningen, 1927 - private collection Mrs A. Kroese-Leonard)

Anna Haye, 20 years old.
(1919; private collection Mrs A. van Vliet-Haye)

with former German domestic servants, however, a much more differentiated image emerges. The significance they attach to a national identity strongly depends on their specific background. (How strong were the ties with the people and the surroundings they left behind?) Besides, the situations in which they found themselves in the Netherlands were determinant (How were they taken care of and by whom?) Moreover, the experiences played a role later on, especially in their confrontation with the outbreak of the Second World War.

In the present article the image of the Netherlands at an institutional level is related to the German female migrants' own images of their national identity. In exploring the significance of a national identity. I will focus on the life story of Mrs Anna Johanna van Vliet-Haye.[30] Her account may provide insight into one of the many ways in which the women involved could give expression to their personal identity in relation to the collective image that existed of the group of German maids at the time.

---

[30]   The basic material for the life story of Mrs Anna Van Vliet-Haye consists of the biography of her husband, written by herself; her own autobiography; and three conversations we had for the purposes of my research at the end of 1986. Her unpublished autobiography consists of two volumes of 76 and 46 typewritten pages respectively. In 1977 she wrote the first part of her life story, called *De jonge jaren van een Plattelands-meisje in het Groothertogdom Oldenburg* (A country girl's youth in the Grand Duchy of Oldenburg). Two years later she completed part two: *Een gastarbeidster in de Twintiger jaren* (A Female Migrant Worker in the Twenties). For the sequel to her life story, she refers at the end of this volume to the story of *Het leven en de tijd van Meester-Loodgieter Cornelis Franciscus van Vliet* (The Life and Times of Master-Plumber Cornelis Franciscus van Vliet). This unpublished biography of her husband, consisting of 121 pages, preceded the other volumes.

Quotations from the written life story of Mrs Van Vliet are indicated by M1 if they are taken from the first volume, and by M2 if they are taken from the second volume. I indicate fragments from our conversations as G1, G2, G3, referring the interviews held in September, November and December 1986.

Merits and self-confidence

Hardly twenty-one years old in 1920, Anna Haye was one of the first group of young German women to work in the Netherlands after the end of the First World War: 'In those days you could find a lot of advertisements in the papers from Dutch housewives looking for household help. A few girls I knew had already left in order to earn their trousseau in a short time. In Germany the financial situation had become pretty miserable in the meantime and the guilder was worth a lot. I rather liked that and answered some advertisements. My decision was further strengthened when my father became un-employed because of the end of wartime production. For me, being a burden to my parents was out of the question'.

This is how Mrs Van Vliet motivates her decision to go to the Netherlands [M1,p.74]. The mere prospect of good earnings, however, does not explain enough, for a lot of German girls did not leave their homeland, despite the poor circumstances in which they and their relatives lived. A certain desire to see more of the world, in com-bination with a degree of self-confidence and self-esteem, played a role for the pioneers of this migration movement. The collective image of the immensely rich Netherlands had to be supplemented with a self-image that gave them sufficient confidence to cross the border.[31] In order to acquire more insight into this question, I shall concentrate on Mrs Van Vliet's story of the period before her departure to the Netherlands.

Born in 1899 as the eldest of three daughters, Anna grew up in the grand duchy of Oldenburg. In *De jonge jaren van een plattelandsmeisje* (A Country Girl's Youth), the first part of her unpublished autobiography, Mrs Van Vliet gives a detailed account

---

[31]   This pioneer mentality among German girls played a minor role at a later stage of this migration movement, because many of the girls, who arrived later, could expect some relief from relatives, friends or acquaintan-ces who had smoothed the way for them.

of a harmonious childhood in the Northern German countryside. The family lived on a small farm, which was mainly run by her mother, while her father worked in the nearby shipyard. 'Not poor and not rich' [G1,p.2] is how Mrs Van Vliet describes the circumstances in which the family lived during her younger years. To Anna, at least, this meant that there was not enough money to let her continue her education after primary school (*Volksschule*). As a *Stütze der Hausfrau* she was taken into a farmer's household for a period of training with board and lodging. In practice the long and the short of it was that she had to work hard without getting paid. The war that had begun in 1914 did not pass the farm unnoticed: the day-labourer joined the colours, and with the motto 'there is a war going on' [M1,p.53], Anna had to take over the heavy men's work. 'You were not allowed to complain, for you did everything for the fatherland' [M1,p.51], Mrs Van Vliet writes. During one of our conversations she adds: 'Because there were no men left, I had to do a lot of things, also at home, wearing boots, all of the men's work. We weren't men, were we! But if you grumbled and protested they immediately said: 'I can't believe that you won't do that for the fatherland.' I heard that many a time. And all those things annoyed me. I was fifteen when I left school and twenty when I came over here and all those years I - and not only I - had to drudge for the fatherland. But in reality we did all this for other people, of course. But they used it as a stick, to make us just do everything, to make up for the shortage of male workers' [G1,p.8].

From that moment on patriotism was viewed with due scepticism. When we follow the description of her first situation with the farming couple, a different aspect of her social position that may have played a role in her decision to leave is revealed: 'In the evening, before dinner, I rushed upstairs to put on a good dress hastily. When we had finished eating and had washed up the dishes, we sat in the living-room with some mending or a piece of fancy-work. Embroidering complex monograms on linen for one's trousseau (...) For the whole training was based on a future marriage, wasn't it! I didn't fancy this prospect at all. A girl who married a small farmer could expect nothing but toiling on the land for the rest of her life. Well-to-do farmers' sons liked having their eyes on the pretty daughters from the middle class or from farmers beneath their own station; but marrying them was another thing' [M1, p.54].

Anna soon became aware of her position within the agrarian community, which offered her few prospects. In spite of the sweet memories of her younger days, a life in the country did not much appeal to her. This was accompanied by an increasing desire for urban surroundings and a plain aversion to the farm work. In one of our conversations she illustrates this: '... if you had to work in summer, you couldn't help perspiring terribly. There was an awful lot of dust and you got horribly dirty. And I never liked that. I could do any kind of work I wanted, but I disliked getting dirty. Ruining my finger nails, having my hair all knots and tangles, and getting a colour, such a farmer's colour, well, I just didn't like that at all.' *Could one say, then, that you were a 'little lady'?* 'I don't know what to call it, but my mother didn't like it either.(...) my mother had an aversion to farm work all her life and she always wanted to live in town, but my father never wanted to. She never got him to do that.' [G3,p.6-7]

Due to her repugnance to country life and farm work, she creates a large distance from her parental home and her mother who was especially responsible for the farm work. At the same time, she tries to bridge this gap by referring to the fact that her mother disliked the country too, and had always wanted to live in the city. She is going to do all the things her mother did not manage to do. An advertisement by Frau S. in Oldenburg, who was looking for a *Stütze der Hausfrau*, offered the opportunity. City life brought 'culture' and variety, and rescued her from 'that dirty agricultural labour' [M2,p.3]. Because of her work in the city, Anna became emancipated from country life. An unfortunate love-affair, combined with the deteriorating economic situation in Germany, provided the impulse to explore other possibilities. She successfully answered an advertisement by a German professor's family in Utrecht (the Netherlands).

Determined, decent and distant

The 'feeling of sensational expectation' with which Anna crossed the border met with a damper in her first situation. She did not have enough to eat in the country of abundance, and her lodging consisted of 'a poor bare den' [M2,p.3], which she had to share with the kitchen-maid. Her expectation of making a lot of money was disappointed too, particularly as her relatives in Germany expected to get their share [M2,p.3].

All the same, this was no reason to return to Germany. She was striving to improve her position and for that purpose Dutch surroundings offered better opportunities than Germany at the time. Earnings were important - as the series of ever better-paid situations proves - but Anna Haye realized only too well that social contacts were also part of the capital with which she could secure, if not improve, her position. Looking for 'people of quality' (*mensen van niveau*), she carefully tested her contacts one by one against her own values and standards of taste and good manners. She kept the necessary distance from those she thought 'too common' [G1,p.13]. Thus a meeting with the brother of the Dutch kitchen-maid with whom she worked was doomed to failure: 'At the first glance I already regretted our date. He was wearing a far too blue suit, mucky yellow shoes and a hat had been stuck upright on top of his round noddle.' [G2,p.8]

However, making the acquaintance of German girls ended in disappointment quite a few times too. By way of explanation she quotes an old lady who once told her 'that I should always be careful with them. Because there might be a lot of chaff among the wheat with people who leave their country' [M2,p.13; G2,p.9]. Naturally there were exceptions to this rule, but it shows that Anna did not necessarily view a shared nationality as a basis for friendship. On the contrary, she avoided those German girls whom she regarded as too loud and conspicuous. 'They weren't my type really' [G2,p.1] and she associates such group behaviour with impudence and loose morals of girls from 'working-class quarters' from whom she wanted to stay clear.

This did not always prevent others from tackling her on her national identity. During her stay in a doctor's practice in Amsterdam, the foreign police came round to inspect her passport. 'This was connected with that business in the Doelen hotel, all of them got syphilis there. Those were big-city girls who had quite something behind them, you see. They were from Frankfurt and Munich...well, that's saying something, isn't it? .... These girls, they were quite ordinary girls from the working-class quarters .... of course, some respectable girls may have come as well from Frankfurt, but this lot had ended up as chambermaids in the Doelen Hotel, so that was their profession and they were used to going out with the gentlemen for a night or so. To them it was nothing to write home about. They thought it was quite normal. But we - not only I, there were more of us - we didn't want that, it wasn't proper. We had learned at home that we shouldn't do that. And it didn't suit us either' [G1,p.21-22]. The inspector of the foreign police assured her that there was nothing wrong with her passport and that she would never get into trouble. 'I was simply proud of it, I dare say! That I was respected and was, what they call, a respectable girl. Well, perhaps that's my own attitude to life, but I've always set a high value on that' [G1, p.21-22].

Mrs Van Vliet uses this occurrence[32] to stress an essential difference between the various German girls. Just as the mouthpieces from German circles did at the time, she draws a distinction between the 'respectable' middle-class girls of the first migration wave and the less educated working-class girls of the second wave. Of course, she

---

[32]   This occurrence, which appears twice in our conversation, is not in her written life story. So far I have not succeeded in finding written sources confirming her recollections. It may be that this came to her notice by way of the informal circuit of medical practitioners she worked with at the time.

rates herself among the girls of the first group. In the second part of her autobiography, *Een Gastarbeidster in Nederland* (A Female Migrant Worker in the Netherlands), she writes: 'There were still few German girls in the Netherlands at the time, and those who were there came from decent middle-class families and had, as a rule, been well educated.' 'Respectable' is the term Anna Haye wished to be judged by, and this encouraged her to set herself off against the German national identity rather than to feel connected with it.

The cautiousness with which she watched over her bourgeois respectability was no hindrance to making contacts with men. In the various chapters of *Een gastarbeidster in Nederland*, Mrs Van Vliet passes in review a large number of potential suitors. Eventually she married the self-employed plumber Nelis Van Vliet (1895). The description of their first meeting concentrates on a detailed dialogue, from which it emerges that Nelis only accidentally found out that Anna was of German origin.[33] Her very command of the Dutch language proved her ability to adjust to Dutch society and made her unrecognisable as a German maid. It was not the fact that she was a German woman, but that she was a respectable one - before Nelis addressed her, he witnessed her turn down a strange man's offer to accompany her to the cinema - that attracted the young plumber. They were married within a year. The story might have ended at this point. Mrs Van Vliet's autobiography, indeed, ends in November 1924, but not without referring to 'my late husband's biography' for 'what happened afterwards.'

Caught between two national fires?

The minutely described events in Nelis Van Vliet's work and life show to what extent Anna Haye, by now Anna Van Vliet-Haye, took root in the Amsterdam tradespeople as his wife, as assistant in his

---

[33]   A. van Vliet-Haye, *Het Leven en de Tijd van Meester-Loodgieter Cornelis Franciscus van Vliet*, (unpublished), p.35.

business and as mother of his children. Was sixteen years' naturalization in Amsterdam society enough to prevent her from being tackled on her German background when the Germans invaded the Netherlands? Or could she not avoid a confrontation with her former German nationality under these circumstances?

10 May 1940, the day on which the Germans invaded the Netherlands, is described by Mrs Van Vliet as part of her husband's life story in the third - detached - person in a slightly ironic tone: 'Nelis tore open the front door and cried: 'They have come!' His wife immediately understood what he meant and answered: 'So they have come after me after all'' [p.68].

The personal and political events - and their interaction - in which the Van Vliet family were involved during the war are described by her in detail. There is, however, no reference at all to the relatives in Germany, nor to the German background of Nelis' wife. A confrontation with her former German nationality did not crop up in our conversations either. To my provocative question of whether she was ever ashamed of her German background, she therefore answers impatiently: 'No, no. I think that's foolish, but still I know a lot about it. There were no Nazis in my own family, except for one. I know exactly what happened, they told me everything. It would have happened here in exactly the same way, for don't tell me they were all patriots here, nonsense. They wouldn't have been a whit better here. Those people had to live, they were afraid, they had no other choice and it was always relatives' lives that were at stake...it isn't that simple, for that matter.' [G1,p.29] By pointing out the fact that Dutch people would have been as 'bad' as the Germans in these circumstances, she again emphasizes that neither 'the' Germans nor 'the' Dutch exist. She herself is the living evidence for this.

Mrs Van Vliet-Haye's life story shows that national identity is only one of the many ways in which women can create a sense of themselves.[34] Her aversion to the rural setting - strengthened by the events during the First World War - created a distance with regard to her *Heimat* in both the material and the ideological sense of the word. First she distanced herself from the agrarian environment of her parental home by going to the city. Next she distanced herself from her national origin - the fatherland which was used to make her toil 'like a man' - by going to the Netherlands.

National identity did not offer her anything to hang on to in the new surroundings, but bourgeois respectability did. This forms the guide-line according to which she behaved and determined her choices. Even the outbreak of the Second World War and the concomitant mobilization of national sentiments did not seem to change this. Influenced by the political and moral crisis that the German occupation in the Netherlands brought about, and the sharp contrast between those 'on the right side' and those 'on the wrong side', 'The Dutch' and 'The Germans' respectively, which this period entailed[35], most of the former German maidservants whom I talked to in the Netherlands regard their German descent as much more ambivalent. They often tend to mobilize their Dutch nationality - which they obtained after their marriage - in order to be able to range themselves 'on the right side'. Mrs Van Vliet, on the other hand, kept this ambivalence at a distance.

This contribution to 'Images of the Nation' is intended to confront the significance given to the concept of a nation at an institutional level with that at the less articulate level of individual experience. After tracing the ideas that German organisations held with regard to the position of German maids in the Netherlands during the inter-war

---

[34]   R. Samuel, 'Introduction: The 'Little Platoons', in *Patriotism: The Making and Unmaking of British National Identity, volume II*, ed. R. Samuel (London/New York, 1989) pp.ix-xxxx.

[35]   J.C.H. Blom, 'In de ban van goed en fout? Wetenschappelijke geschiedschrijving over de bezettingstijd in Nederland', in Id., *Crisis, bezetting en herstel. Tien studies over Nederland 1930-1950* (Universitaire Pers Rotterdam, 1989) pp. 102-121.

period, I have tried to relate these ideas to the ideas of one former German maidservant about her own place in Dutch society.

In this context I did not choose the life story of Mrs Anna van Vliet-Haye because it is representative for most of her fellow maidservants who migrated to the Netherlands. On the contrary, her story forms more of an extreme on the line between identifying with and distancing oneself from a nation, with the accent on distancing. However, for that reason her story may provide more insight in the problematic relationship of nation images at the institutionalised level and national identity as expressed by individuals. The migration of Mrs van Vliet involved not only physically turning her back on her fatherland, but also an emotional detachment. A key to this double distance is offered by her notion of bourgeois respectability.

The German organisations in the Netherlands expressed a concept of the fatherland that was heavily steeped in moral notions. The idea of respectability linked with patriotism was a potential force behind the efforts to organise German maids under the care of German institutions in the Netherlands. The girls were supposed to honour the good name of the German nation by their decent conduct as women and subordinates. The German institutions were meant to control this, although they were not always successful. In so far as the German institutions referred to 'immature elements' coming from Germany to the Netherlands, Anna Haye subscribed to this image of the indecent behaviour of German maids, but she detached the notion of respectability from the notion of patriotism. She already did so when she was still in Germany, where she had to do the kind of work that - in her eyes - hardly suited a decent girl. In the Netherlands she linked respectable behaviour to a far-reaching adjustment to the new surroundings that seemed to offer her much more opportunity.

In the face of the efforts from the German side to bring together the German maids in the Netherlands in order to protect their decency, Anna Haye posed an individualising attitude. The bringing together of German maids made them recognisable as 'outsiders' in Dutch society, while Anna Haye above all wanted to be part of Dutch society, and to be accepted as such. By reacting against her 'unrespectable' countrywomen, she emphasised her own decency and capacity to adjust. This form of inclusion and exclusion is part of the building of a personal identity that exceeds the national boundaries.

As pointed out earlier, it was not national identity that offered a guide-line in the life of Mrs Anna van Vliet-Haye. For this former German maid, the concept of respectability is the connecting thread running through her life story. In this way she remained impervious to national appeals, whether from the German or the Dutch side.

TOWARDS A CULTURAL THEORY OF THE NATION:
A BRITISH-DUTCH DIALOGUE

Richard Johnson

I have been involved in research and in teaching on national identity in Britain since the early 1980s. Our first project took shape under the pressures of the resurgent nationalism of the Falklands/Malvinas War though my interest in national identity has continued beyond the fall of Mrs Thatcher.[1] In the later 1980s, however, these interests were revitalized and refocussed by a dialogue with the authors of this volume. In our conversations and in their studies of Dutch history, I encountered a very different national formation from that in Britain; but one which, I was sure, could be analyzed in similar ways.[2] In this paper, I have tried to

---

[1]   Many ideas in this piece began life in the work of the Popular Memory Group in the Centre for Contemporary Cultural Studies, University of Birmingham [hereafter CCCS] from 1982 onwards. They have been further developed with the help of the students who took my course on *Nationalism and National Identity* in the same department from 1985 to 1991.

[2]   I am particularly grateful to the editors for their detailed, perceptive and helpful comments, for their encouragement, and warm engage-

bring these two phases of work together. Although I find the comparisons intriguing, I have not really aimed at comparative insights. Perhaps I am too suspicious of what is normally involved in such cross-national transactions. Rather I have sought to abstract from our knowledge of the two countries an 'approach' or framework of analysis for understanding national identity more generally. I have also tried to illustrate the usefulness of this approach by applying it back to the studies themselves, sometimes extending their theses, sometimes rephrasing them in terms I find more helpful. The studies therefore figure twice in my argument: as the *source* of many insights; and as *illustrations* of the value (I hope) of a particular approach. Beyond these intellectual considerations, the original political problem informing the work since 1982 remains. It is even more urgent, perhaps, in contemporary Europe. How can we have a politics of the nation, which is not, however, a nationalism, and which is not articulated to the sustaining of social inequalities in different ways?

I should stress the 'cultural' in the title. I do not pretend to deal with the larger formation of nations, a many-sided process, involving, for instance, both the nationalisation and the globalisation of economic life in an uneven and not-so-orderly capitalist world. Some features of the history of economic power - Britain's 'early start' or the rival imperialisms of Europe - are decisive for domestic social structures and cultural formations.[3] Indeed, nationality or

---

ment with the project. I have also learned much from other contributors too, especially about Dutch history - and from comments on my comments!

[3]   See, for example, E. J. Hobsbawm's discussion of the consequences of the 'early start' in *Industry and Empire* (London, 1968) and the discussion of the domestic ramifications of different phases of empire in P. J. Cain and A. J. Hopkins, 'Gentlemanly Capitalism and British Expansion Overseas I: the Old Colonial System, 1688-1850', *Economic History Review*, 2nd Series, Vol.39, No.4, (1986): 501-25, 'II: New Imperialism, 1850-1945', *Eonomic History Review*, 2nd Series, Vol.40 ,

national identity is inconceivable without international relationships of all kinds. These involve meanings, symbols and psychic relations as much as wars, diplomacy, and economic power. If I prioritise culture here, it is simply because I am as interested in 'image' as I am in the nation.

I have, however, some quarrels with 'image' as a key word. Used metaphorically it implies reflection and sometimes distortion (e.g. inversion), therefore a view of culture as either mechanically mirroring a pregiven, known reality, or as a kind of false consciousness.[4] The most interesting thinkers on culture have been in flight from such conceptions for thirty years or more, sometimes, perhaps, too readily.[5] Most students of culture today see language, discourse or image (the means of representation themselves) as constitutive, to some extent, of reality, as we know it. Culture has a hardness and determinacy of its own; it is not secondary or derivative merely. Cultural analysis also foregrounds the *activity* of representation and the *production* of culture, formulations which

---

No.1, (1987): 1-26.

[4]   This is especially the case in Marxist versions of reflection theory.

[5]   This flight has been associated, especially, with two 'generations' of critics of orthodox marxist conceptions: those connected with early New Left movements in Britain especially Raymond Williams and E.P.Thompson; and later critics influenced by structuralist and post-structuralist theories. For accounts of these movements in connection with cultural studies see Patrick Brantlinger, *Crusoe's Footsteps: Cultural Studies in Britain and America* (London, New York, 1990) and Graeme Turner, *British Cultural Studies: An Introduction* (Boston, 1990). For a defence of some elements of classic Marxist theories see Jorge Larrain, *Marxism and Ideology*, (London, 1983). Many of the positions in cultural theory argued for in this essay have been developed, often in collective projects, with colleagues and students in CCCS from the mid 1970s and in the Department of Cultural Studies from 1988.

imply more of human practice than the passivity of 'image' allows.[6] Used less metaphorically, 'image' denotes a visual dimension, hardly stressed in this volume. Yet, in other ways, 'image' is distinctly interesting. Rendered as 'self-image', it has connotations of 'style' and self-presentation which link it to questions of identity and its construction. From these perspectives, 'image' indicates the theoretical problem of cultural representation; but also implies the imaginary nature of all identities.

These issues are especially alive today in relation to the nation. If struggles over gender raised new questions in the 1970s and early 1980s, the most urgent agenda for cultural study today come from critiques of Western ethnocentrism, including that articulation of race-and-nation-and-culture so characteristic of European nationalisms.[7] National identity has also assumed a new importance because of the massive, geo-political rearrangements in Europe, in 'East-West relations' and along the axis of 'North' and 'South'.

The nation has been a central focus too in a more diffused concern with so-called 'identity politics'. The Nation has often functioned as the Conservative rival to more radical political identities, from various forms of socialism and populism to the

---

[6]   The emphasis on practice comes from early Marx, but via early New Left theorists. See the discussion in Raymond Williams, *The Long Revolution* (Harmondsworth, 1965). Williams' 'culture' is a translation of 'praxis'.

[7]   There is a substantial literature deconstructing these connections, often from the point of view of intellectuals with Third World links living in the West. See, especially, Edward Said, *Orientalism*, (Harmondsworth, 1985); Homi K. Bhabha ed., *Nation and Narration*, (London,1990); Louis Henry Gates ed., *'Race', Writing and Difference*, (Chicago, 1986); Paul Gilroy, *There Ain't No Black in the Union Jack*, (London, 1986); Gayatry Spivak, *In Other Worlds* (London, 1987) and Stuart Hall, 'Cultural Identity and the Diaspora' in Jonathan Rutherford ed., *Identity, Community, Culture, Difference* (London, 1990).

new social movements of the later twentieth century.[8] In the era which some call 'postmodern' all these political identities have tended to fall apart. This disaggregation has been accompanied by philosophical clashes on both Right and Left: between a revived Neo-Conservatism and Neo-Liberalism for example; and between the humanism of a first radical wave and the anti-essentialism of a second.[9] I have written this essay with these contemporary transformations in mind.

Approaches to Nationality: From Nationalism to National Identity

The six essays in this volume approach these questions from different directions. Four of the essays start from attempts to define and propagate 'images' of the Dutch nation in political campaigns or public debates. Roel Kuiper discusses the version of the nation propagated by theorists and statesmen of a particular religious-

---

[8]   This is not to deny that in some circumstances, especially in struggles against imperial domination and powerful neighbours, nationalism may be articulated to an egalitarian and democratic politics. In Britain since the later nineteenth century notions of nation and empire have been strongly linked to the Right. See Hugh Cunningham, 'The Language of Patriotism', *History Workshop Journal*, No.12, (Autumn, 1981): 8-33.

[9]   The shift from one framework to another can be traced across the concerns of all the new social movements. For feminist 'anti-essentialism' see, for example, Denise Riley, *Am I that Name? Feminism and the Category of 'Women' in History* (London, 1988); Diana Fuss, *Essentially Speaking: Feminism, Nature and Difference* (New York, 1989). For debates around lesbian and gay sexualities see, for example, Jeffrey Weeks, *Sexuality and Its Discontents: Meanings, Myths and Modern Sexualities* (London, 1985) and Martin B. Duberman, Martha Vicinus and George Chauncey ed., *Hidden From History: Reclaiming the Gay and Lesbian Past*, (Harmondsworth,1991); on race and ethnictity, see Rutherford, *Identity* and Gates, *'Race'* (both cited above, note 7).

political tendency (later a party) - the Dutch Orthodox Protestants (later the Anti-Revolutionary Party) - from the 1840s to the early twentieth century. Abraham Kuyper and his predecessors defined the nation in terms of its Calvinist history; but had to modify this conception to come to terms, if only pragmatically, with the actual diversity of the nation. The Orthodox Protestant version of the Dutch is an especially interesting example of the uses of history in images of the nation and, contradictorily it seems, of belief in an abiding national character or essence.

In Wim Klinkert's essay, army officers take centre stage as would-be makers of the nation. Less directly 'political', the debate over the appropriate kind of army for Dutch circumstances and character is rich, nonetheless, in socio-political themes. This suggests that in pre-World War I Netherlands, as in other European countries, questions of military organisation (especially conscription) were vehicles for campaigning around the nature and future of the nation as a whole, especially via the moral and physical state of 'youth'. They were also a main site for elaborating new masculinities.[10]

If Abraham Kuyper's nation was essentially a band of calvinists and the van Dam van Isselts' essentially an army of citizens, then Huizinga's Dutchman was more a cultural type - the burgher. Henk te Velde pursues suggestions from his 1934 essay 'The Spirit of the Netherlands' in a wide-ranging exploration of modern definitions of Dutchness. He analyses discourses produced not by party men nor by state professionals (e.g. professional soldiers), but by academic intellectuals, often by historians. In its

---

[10]   For Britain see M. D. Blanch, 'Imperalism, Nationalism and Organised Youth' in Richard Johnson, Chas Critcher and John Clarke (eds.), *Working Class Culture: Studies in History and Theory* (London, 1979); John Springhall, *Youth, Empire and Society*, (London, 1977); Graham Dawson, 'Soldier Heroes and Adventure Narratives: Case Studies in English Masculine Identities from the Victorian Empire to Post-Imperial Britain' (Unpublished Ph.D thesis, University of Birmingham, 1991).

agents and themes this debate seems more 'cultural' than 'political', more about identity, apparently, than power. Like the other debates, however, it was conducted in public: in this case especially in books and reviews. As Henk te Velde shows, however, these descriptions of the Dutch as 'burgerlijk' were varied in their social standpoint and historical context, and were always associated with a political project of some kind.

Rico op den Camp's essay is concerned with the national-political consciousness of Limburgers, but covers other themes as well. Two contrasted sources are used - the local newspaper press and the writings of the Hollander J. Craandijk, especially his travelogue *Wandelingen door Nederland*. These sources give us access to two rather different aspects of national identity. Just as Benedict Anderson has argued that the development of printing generally was a cultural precondition for the nation as an 'imagined community', so the newspaper press, in its historical forms, became a key means of this imagining.[11] In Britain, after the demise of the popular radical 'unstamped' press of the early nineteenth century, a central role was played by those mainly Liberal provincial newspapers (like the original *Manchester Guardian*) whose editors had social links with the Liberal and Dissenting bourgeoisie in the cities, but included among their preferred readers respectable Liberal working men.[12] Such newspapers were a crucial part of the classic bourgeois public sphere.[13] Without knowing more of the Limburger press, it seems there was a similar formation there. The local press gives us access to the political

---

[11]   Benedict Anderson, *Imagined Communities: Reflections on the Origins and Spread of Nationalism* (London, 1983).

[12]   For the British press in this phase see Alan Lee, *The Origins of the Popular Press, 1855-1914* (London, 1976). For the larger political context see John Vincent, *The Formation of the British Liberal Party, 1857-68* (Harmondsworth, 1972).

[13]   As defined in Jurgen Habermas, 'The Public Sphere' (trans. Sarah Lennox and Frank Lennox), *New German Critique*, Vol.3, (Fall, 1974).

ideas of the Limburger elites, especially as these were organised
around the newspapers' political commentaries on such themes as
war, diplomacy and invasion fears.

The travelogue on the other hand links public affairs with
private lives and feelings. In England too it became a key form of
reflection on national character. Polemic on the state of the nation
could, as in William Cobbett's *Rural Rides*, be allied to thoughtful
observations on the lives of the people and the display of the
writer's own feelings of anger or nostalgia. It has been argued
indeed that reflections on the country side became one permissable
form in which men, as public beings, could express their private
feelings.[14] In the case of *Wandelingen*, Craandijk, who was clearly
a considerable theorist of cultural nationality, was concerned not
only with formal political allegiances, but with everyday differences too.

The two remaining studies extend our understandings more
decisively in these directions. Both use public sources (commercial,
philanthropic, or official) but find ways to explore private or local
meanings too. Side by side with the versions of 'image-makers',
Annemieke Galema uses letters written to friends and relatives by
Dutch immigrants to America in the period 1880-1914. Letters are,
aside from inner speech, diaries and face-to-face conversation, the
most private of communicative forms, which is not to say they are
immune, in any way, to publicly circulating meanings. Here,
however, images of America were produced in Holland, not only
by public media but through personal communications. In these
letters, typically, national difference is understood less through
categories like national character or religious essence, more
through differences of daily life, and the realisability or otherwise

---

[14]   For discussions of the gendered nature of ruralism see Robert
West, 'English Ruralism and Nationalism in Britain 1920-1945' (Unpublished Ph.D Dissertation, University of Birmingham, 1987). For the
classic discussion of ruralism see Raymond Williams, *The Country and
City* (St. Albans, 1975).

of ordinary ambitions. From the same sources, it is also possible to say something about how Friesland in the 'Old World' was retrospectively viewed by settlers in the New.

Barbara Henkes' study is also concerned with the way national meanings relate to personal lives. She explores the history of young German women who crossed over the border to become domestic servants in Holland in the period before World War II. This study, which pursues national and other identifications at the 'micro' level of the individual life history, is made possible through the techniques of the oral history interview and through the survival of Anna Haye's written autobiographies. This combination of sources offers unique insights into the motives that impelled one woman to move and to settle. Her life choices and aspirations were rooted in everyday life experiences but necessarily involved negotiating her relationships with publicly-circulating versions of two nations. On the one side there were early images of Holland as a land of milk and honey, a 'Guldenparadis', but also a place of 'moral danger'; on the other, calls to self-sacrifice in the cause of the Fatherland in two Wars, and the philanthropic discourse of the Girls Societies on how to be a respectable young German woman.

Our first cluster of studies show us much about the forms of publicly circulating national images, and of the contexts and agents which produce them. Our second set of studies add to this a crucial insight: that orientations towards the nation, like other identifications and disidentifications, are rooted in local, ordinary, necessary and specific practices, which acquire personal and group meanings. The meanings of the nation - in all its competing versions - rest on a basis of mundane and common practices: the experience of waged and domestic labour, the preparation and consumption of food and drink, the forms of intimacy, leisure and sociability in family, community and region. Under certain circumstances, these practices, or some of them, are made to mean a nation and come to be evaluated in positive and negative ways; they are culturally nationalised. Thus eating meat three times a day and not doffing your cap to anyone comes to mean America and to signify abundance and hope; while despair in the Old Country is handled in a striking everyday image of 'sand and potatoes and greese'.[15] In these everyday accounts of nations, images of food (milk, honey, bacon, potatoes, peaches, strawberries) and money (guilders, dollars) are everywhere. Similarly in the migrations of (some) German maids, aspirations and fantasies of respectability come to be associated with living in a Dutch city. For all of them, perhaps, national identity works or fails to work through many other identifications.

Most studies of national identity privilege the political or the public world.[16] They focus on nationalism as a political ideology or as an aspect of the nation state, or on the historical role and nature of nationalist movements in nation formation in the West[17]

---

[15]   Quoted in Annemieke Galema's essay above.

[16]   For useful recent reviews of the literature see Peter Alter, *Nationalism* (London, 1989) and E. J. Hobsbawm, *Nations and Nationalism since 1780* (Cambridge, 1990). Two writers have been especially influential in debates on nationalism in Britain: Anderson, *Imagined Communities* (see note 11 above) and Tom Nairn in *The Break-Up of Britain* (London, 1977) and *The Enchanted Glass: Britain and Its Monarchy* (London, 1988). Social historians have also contributed: Raphael Samuel ed., *Patriotism: The Making and Unmaking of British National Identity* (3 vols, London, 1989); Robert Colls and Philip Dodd ed., *Englishness: Politics and Culture 1880-1920* (Beckenham, 1986) and the debates on national history in *History Workshop Journal*, esp. Nos. 29 and 30. Of earlier studies, Karl W. Deutsch, *Nationalism and Social Communication: An Inquiry into the Foundations of Nationality* (Cambridge Mass., 1953) was concerned with cultural themes but limited by some premises of the study of 'Communications', in particular a relentless positivism.

[17]   For a review which defines nationalism 'as a distinct ideological variety of social and political movement' see Anthony D. Smith, *Theories of Nationalism* (London, 1971). Smith sees the nation state as 'the chief definer of a man's identity' (ibid., p. 2). Much of this essay is concerned with the (rather limited?) sense in which this is true.

or in the process of decolonialisation.[18] Until lately, the topic has
been dominated by political scientists and political historians rather
than by students of culture or by social historians. In this, academic studies have mimicked the nation-state itself, which, however, is only one form of existence of the nation. This dominant
framework privileges the public sphere as the site of subjective
significance and powerful action. There has been much less study
of the 'private' face of the nation - of nationalism as a form of
subjectivity or of individual and group identity, though this work is
now beginning. The popular 'roots' of national feeling have been
much invoked, but little studied. Accounts of the Henkes-Galema
kind are unusual, commoner in literary or filmic representations
than in academic studies.[19] Preoccupations with the nation in
literature, however, have produced rich veins of commentary which
touch on many of our themes.[20] On its side, Cultural Studies was
slow to problematise its own national frameworks and make a
topic of cultural nationality.[21] Where a more cultural approach has

---

[18]   Timothy Brennan argues that critics of nationalism in the West
have ignored its role in decolonialisation: Timothy Brennan, *Salman
Rushdie and the Third World: Myths of the Nation* (Basingstoke, 1989),
esp. pp. 1-31. My own essay is certainly limited in this way, but I
wonder if it is not possible to support liberation struggles but take a
distance from their nationalist forms? Is Brennan right to read Rushdie's
novels as so very clearly about the nation? I argue here that the associations between national and other popular identifications are contin-
gent and constructed, and not necessary at all.

[19]   Britishness has been one main theme, for instance, in 1980s
films from the many nostalgic treatments of the British Raj to the
interventions of Black-British and Asian-British film makers like Isaac
Julien and Hanif Kureishi.

[20]   The debates around colonial and post-colonial literature are
especially pertinent. See the sources cited in note 7 above, Brennan,
Rushdie, and Bill Ashcroft, Gareth Griffiths and Helen Tiffin, *The
Empire Writes Back: Theory and Practice in Post-Colonial Literatures*
(London, 1989).

[21]   An important starting point was Paul Gilroy's critique of older
styles of cultural studies in *There Ain't No Black in the Union Jack*.

been taken, there has been a tendency to simplified or essentialist accounts which stress the homogeneity of the nation at the expense of recognising internal differences.[22]

In historical studies, the neglect of popular and private points of view is connected to the problem of sources. The official archive has certainly been shaped by the historical construction of public life as a masculine and middle-class domain. But historians' own perspectives matter too. It is possible to compensate for the official archive by reading it critically, with an eye on margins and for absences especially. We can also, as our second set of studies show, actively seek new sources. It is not the new sources or even a new methodology, however, which is decisive here. They will not deliver new insights on their own. A critical theory or framework is crucial too.

---

[22]   The classic instances here are theories of the nation as a 'whole way of life', indeed as a unified 'soul' bound for self-realisation, associated with German Romanticism. The classic modern critique of this view, which, however, overestimates the influence of 'doctrine', is Elie Kedourie, *Nationalism*, (London, 1960). For a modern defence of a cultural or 'ethnic' conception, see the work of Anthony D. Smith in *Nationalism in the Twentieth Century* (Oxford 1979) and *The Ethnic Origins of Nations* (Oxford, 1986). For the espousal of a specifically socio-biological underpinning for 'ethnocentrism' see James G. Kellas, *The Politics of Nationalism and Ethnicity* (Basingstoke, 1991). It is important not to overstate the cultural homogeneity of nations, but also not to reduce all differences to 'ethnicity'; social identifications also arise in relation to class, gender, region, religion, age group for instance. Ernest Gellner, in the most complex account of nationalism as cultural cohesion, disregards these differences and conflicts. He sees nationalism as a form of modernisation involving a standardised 'high' culture promoted by the state. See Ernest Gellner, *Nations and Nationalism* (Oxford, 1983). The British and Dutch cases lend little credence to the stress on institutionalised cultural homogeneity: cultural heterogenity in Britain often arises *in opposition to* official cultures; in the Netherlands cultural *differences* have often been institutionalised.

The Two Sides of Cultural Nationality

In what follows I want to adopt the distinction between more public and more private forms, derived from comparing our essays, and elaborate it a little. This distinction is far from new in the writing on nationalism. As one of the most interesting recent commentaries puts it:

> '[Nations]...are in my view, dual phenomena, constructed essentially from above, but which cannot be understood unless also analysed from below, that is in terms of the assumptions, hopes, needs, longings and interests of ordinary people, which are not necessarily national or still less nationalist.'[23]

I want first to clarify these aspects of cultural nationality by making some disavowals. Then I will use the elaborated version of the distinction to discuss two common and unhelpful reductions in the theory of the nation. Later, however, I will suggest that the distinction between public and local forms may itself prove unhelpful and I will try to reformulate it. I will suggest our distinction is better seen as two moments in a process or a circuit.

Older critical theories, often worked with a distinction between ideology (understood as false consciousness) on one side, and an authentic 'reality' or 'culture' on the other.[24] Against this, it is important to insist that versions of the nation produced by political parties or even by immigration agents are as much a part of social reality as the most practically-anchored everyday beliefs.[25] There is no way either that popular, communal or private forms are closer to some authentic expression than are

---

[23]   Hobsbawm, *Nations and Nationalism*, p. 10. I agree with Hobsbawm that Gellner does not pay 'adequate attention to the view from below'.
[24]   This argument spans versions of Marxist, feminist, populist and, of course, nationalist accounts.
[25]   See the discussion in Annemieke Galema's essay above.

public representations, or any less a matter of representation itself. Each is equally conventional: structured by language and generic rules, whether of journalism, political rhetoric, letter-writing, or the conversational rules of a particular social *milieu* or group. Even the most private form of all - our inner speech which is so important an arena for individual identifications - has, as Volosinov put it, its own 'genres', 'social orientations', and imaginary addressees.[26] The notion of an authentic popular expression is not, in the end, a viable one, though it rises, comprehensibly enough, in the course of cultural resistance.

The distinction I have in mind, then, is not primarily an epistemological or a moral/political one (though it may acquire these dimensions). Public forms are not *a priori* superior or inferior to local or private forms either as knowledge or as forms of evaluation. Nor is it useful to see one as the product of fantasy and the other of 'experience'; or indeed to make too sharp a general distinction between these two terms. In public representations *and* in everyday lived culture, we find a mix of 'realist' and fantasy elements, of discursive construction and emotional investment, of 'interest' and imagination, of plan and wish. As we have seen, common experiences, in their good or bad sides, can come to typify a homeland; just as desire for a better future can come to mean another country: a 'wonderland', a 'Holland' or an 'America.' As Annemieke Galema argues against Den Hollander, it is not so much that our view of other nations is a distorting screen we must penetrate or correct for; more that the screen itself is a part of our object, an aspect of the process of cross-national identification itself and therefore of the cultural construction of nations. From this point of view the elements of fantasy are just as real as 'economic conditions', and quite as much a social presence or force in the world. They need to be documented (specified textually) and understood ('read') with equal care.

---

[26]   V.N. Volosinov, *Marxism and the Philosophy of Language* (New York and London, 1973), esp. pp. 85 - 89 and pp. 117 - 20.

The distinction between public representations and lived cultures is not exactly a distinction between the cultures of different social groups either, though it is certainly linked to questions of power and inequality. If we can speak of 'ruling ideas', I doubt if we should see them as a kind of property of the ruling class.[27] Rather dominant ideas - in the sense of those with access to the public sphere - are unequally negotiated. They therefore express the dominant *relationships*.[28] They must always involve elements which speak to different social groups, including those that are economically and culturally subordinated. To ascribe ruling ideas to dominant social groups alone is to forget that everyone is a philosopher and also that the dominant or publicly-articulate groups have their own implicit and private knowledges too. Indeed, though there are certainly inequalities of access to the public forums, each of us may, as individuals, inhabit both modes of cultural being.

Rather the distinction is primarily a cultural one: between *modalities* of culture, *forms* of consciousness and their social *locations* or *sites*. The notion of 'articulation' is useful in speci-fying what is involved here. 'Articulation' combines two ideas - the making explicit of an idea or experience; and a partial separa-tion of two discursive elements, which may remain, however, conjoined.[29] According to the first idea we may refer to 'highly-articulated' (relatively explicit) or 'under-articulated' (relatively implicit) cultural forms; according to the second idea we

---

[27]   Compare Karl Marx and Frederick Engels, 'The German Ideolo-gy', *Collected Works*, (London,1976), Vol. 5, esp. pp. 59-60.

[28]   This formulation is *also* to be found in 'The German Ideology', *ibid.*, p. 59.

[29]   A useful (if mechanical) visualisation is an articulated lorry! The analysis of 'articulations' has been important in post-structuralist (espe-cially post-Althusserian) approaches to political discourse. Key texts include   Ernesto Laclau, *Politics and Ideology in Marxist Theory* (London, 1977) and Chantal Mouffe, 'Hegemony and Ideology in Gramsci' in Chantal Mouffe ed., *Gramsci and Marxist Theory*, (London, 1979).

may envisage processes of *dis*-articulation and *re*-articulation, by which discursive elements are uncoupled and then recombined.

Highly articulated forms are produced within institutions and practices where the pressure is towards coherence and social reach, especially the power to represent groups other than your own. One example might be the law; another the academic disciplines, especially those that make claims to 'science'. Such forms tend to be abstract in at least two senses. First, they are produced through relatively separated or abstracted *institutions* (law courts, the academy), to which the majority of people have, as primary producers, little access. This process of the real abstraction of culture is a marked historical tendency of modern times. It can be seen not only in legal codes and academic knowledges but in the growth of public media, education systems, state apparatuses and in artistic and professional knowledges of all kinds. Second, however, this separation into institutions is accompanied by changes in the *forms* and the *framing* of such knowledges. Knowledges become abstract in the sense of generalising or universalising: they are made to speak on behalf of others, even of all of us, as legal judgements do; or neutrally, apparently, without a point of view, as do 'sciences' and other kinds of expertise.[30]

Other versions are relatively implicit. They are often under-articulated in comparison with the grand public narratives. They are also more modest in address and more local (geographically and socially) in scope. I have in mind face-to-face forms like shop-floor cultures, or conversations in supermarkets, or the private, sub-cultural forms of all kinds of social groups. These forms are more concrete, more connected with daily living, and therefore

---

[30]   These formulations are influenced by Antonio Gramsci's distinction between 'common sense' and 'philosophy', his re-conceptualisation of the old Marxist idea of 'superstructures' and his account of hegemony. See Quintin Hoare and Geoffrey Nowell Smith (ed. and trans.), *Selections from the Prison Notebooks of Antonio Gramsci* (London, 1971).

share its contradictory character, with less philosophical smoothing out. In a striking passage Gramsci described the 'strangely composite' 'personality' which he associated with these 'common sense' forms:

> 'It contains Stone Age elements and principles of a more advanced science, prejudices from all past phases of history at the local level, and intuitions of a future philosophy which will be that of a human race united the world over.'[31]

This distinction between modes of consciousness or subjectivity may itself seem abstract; but it may be amply illustrated from personal experiences of nationality today; and from the historical essays in this volume. Two examples must suffice: first my own experiences of being British or English through the 1980s; second Craandijk's reflections on the peculiarities of the Limburgers.

I was at best a reluctant Briton throughout the 1980s. I could not recognise myself in either of the dominant repertoires of the 1980s. I could not see myself as a subject in the Neo-Conservative story of the nation, in the story of 'our national heritage', as some pugnaciously resurgent 'Brit'. Nor could I see myself as a Thatcherite entrepreneur.[32] Even if I had wished to conform (which I did not) I would have found it hard. Like so many radical professionals of the 1960s and 1970s, I had made the 'wrong' career choices. Brought up in a small-business family, I had deliberately opted for a profession· as against commerce, for public institutions, for cultural studies and social history not for economics or management studies. So in the 1980s we were not

---

[31]   *ibid*, p. 324.

[32]   For a useful account of these figures see John Corner and Sylvia Harvey, 'Mediating Tradition and Modernity: The Heritage/Enterprise Couplet' in Corner and Harvey ed., *Enterprise and Heritage: Crosscurrents of National Culture*, (London 1991), pp. 45-92. See also Patrick Wright, *On Living in an Old Country: The National Past in Contemporary Britain* (London, 1985).

Thatcher's children but her 'folk devils', in a front line of New Right attacks whether we liked it or not. At the same time, there was no attractive, alternative Britain publicly in place, except sub-culturally. At this level, however, alternatives abounded; there was an immense and exciting cultural diversity indeed, but no publicly articulated strategy for change and no movement of a more inclusive kind to rally around. Even radical professional groups - an important constituency in left, feminist, black and gay and lesbian movements - were very fragmented, and not only between the movements. How could you belong to a country in which the people and ways of life you warmed to (including whole groups and regions) were continuously misrecognised and de-valued? So in my own most reflective or 'philosophical' moments I thought of myself as an anti-nationalist or internationalist of some kind. I found it hard to rescue elements of worth from the recent and most public versions of who the British were. Drastic recon-structions seemed to be required.

Yet at another level, I am 'English' (not British) through and through. My nationality is imposed or 'given', even where not consciously affirmed. Sometimes it is legally enforced, as in the regulation of migration or citizenship; always it is a strong cultural pressure around my appearance in the world, a pressure which is hard to evade, since cultural nationality is an important means to social recognition. Internationalist I may be, but I am necessarily implicated in national identities through my 'built-in' cultural Englishness. This includes forms of language and accent (mono-lingually English, with northern 'a-s' compromised by southern schooling); tastes in food (cosmopolitan/vegetarian but with a nostalgic Yorkshire undertow); ruralist pleasures like coun-tryside walks and gardening. Apparently innocent pleasures like these are often connected up to deeply naturalised 'Stone-age elements' of racist, sexist and homophobic kinds. I have also retained resistances (unreasonable in 1980s circumstances?) to emigration, and used to resent my siblings' international choices in these matters. This *version* of Englishness is connected with my other half-conscious cultural conformities: my Anglo-ethnicity (as opposed to other ethnicities in Britain like Black-British, Jewish-British, Northern-Irish-Protestant, South-Asian-British, or South-Walesian for instance) my professional middle classness, and my ways of being a man. I hope these features do not describe me too exhaustively; nor need they be named as English. Made conscious they may be changed. But they do also acquire a kind of (social) objectivity. They make me recognisable to others 'at home' where I can be 'placed' in a socio-cultural landscape with some exactness; and 'overseas' where I appear, I assume, 'an Englishman'.

Vicar Craandijk's encounters with Limburg involved a similar distinction. He noticed how the Limburgers were not really Dutch in their 'character': they were more Belgian perhaps, certainly 'outlandish' or strangely hybrid in their ways. Yet they were not 'Belgian- and even less Prussian-minded', rather Dutch, if 'only half a Dutchman'. More interesting still than these puzzles, Craandijk saw these two aspects of cultural nationality, conscious national affiliation or disaffilation, and everyday cultural implication, as related in some way. Maybe, as the Limburgers became more 'Dutch' culturally by sharing connections with the other provinces, they might 'desire to be Dutch as well' and even become proud of this identity. This account of cultural interactions seems interestingly thoughtful and complex, even today.

Engaging though his account may be, Craandijk, the Protestant vicar, was also wielding a kind of power over the Limburgers, assessing their place in the nation. The connection between national identity and power will be a major preoccupation of this essay. What kind of power is involved in the public construction of versions of the nation? What resistances does such a power create? At this stage in the argument two preliminary points can be made: the often hidden nature of these processes, which reinforce their power; and the way in which nationality works on and through other forms of social identification.

A rich example of both these aspects is Huizinga's project of defining Dutch character.[33] His account seems mere description, an evocation of national characteristics, given or already in place. It is the 'common sense' of Dutchness. All Huizinga appears to do is to generalise what everyone already knows ('our national culture... in every sense'). As Henk te Velde shows, however, his calm account was driven by an urgent political project: his defence of quiet virtues in the face of the 'heroisms' of fascism and the class struggle of the Left. It must also be read in the context of a whole historical repertoire of rival versions of burgerlijk, clearly a highly contested category which could be given different inflections. Huizinga's description, in other words, was an intervention, a bid to define the nation in a particular way.

This combination - actively intervening in forms that are supposed to be already fully formed, even essential or natural - is a particularly potent rhetorical move, the theoretical features of which we will return to later. It is characteristic of certain kinds of nationalist discourse. One main effect is to disguise or hide the cultural work which the speaker has just performed, to win consent by stating the obvious. As Gramsci and Foucault have shown us, in different theoretical vocabularies, power is likely to be most effective when it works not only by domination or coercion but by exercising leadership, winning some measure of consent, or by inciting us to take up a particular identity.[34] Defining the nation is

---

[33]   I am grateful to Henk te Velde for a detailed discussion of this and other readings of Huizinga's project. He helped greatly to clarify my own position here.

[34]   As Foucault puts it: 'If power were never anything but repressive, if it never did anything but to say no, do you really think one would be brought to obey it? ... it doesn't only weigh on us as a force that says no, but ... traverses and produces things, it induces pleasure, forms knowledge, produces discourse.' 'Truth and Power' in   Colin Gordon ed., *Knowledge/Power: Selected Interviews and Other Writings, 1972-77* (New York, 1980). And compare Gramsci on 'the ethical state', *Selections from the Prison Notebooks*, esp. pp. 258-59.

a work of 'education' or 'civilisation' in this larger sense. Images or versions of the nation are not merely reflections; they also 'produce' or 'construct' the nation in a particular form, elaborating in Barthes' term, a national 'mythology'.[35]

These specifically cultural forms of power are linked - but often not transparently - to larger social asymetries like gender, class, race and age. Versions of the nation have a key role, indeed, in helping to transform and reproduce these differences and inequalities, in ways to be explored. Huizinga's sign 'burgerlijk' provides examples of the connections between nationality and other social identifications too, in this case connections with social class. As a sign whose meanings have been naturalised in a culture, 'burgerlijk' must sound more neutral than 'bourgeois' with its Marxist resonances.[36] Its references to respectability and other virtues may outweigh its other meanings. Huizinga can therefore claim that we are all 'burgerlijk' now in a specifically cultural or metaphorical sense. But he cannot altogether efface the social associations of the term. His chosen national sign (it is *chosen*) therefore continues to privilege not only certain virtues but also the social groups which are held quintessentially to be their bearer - that is various fractions of the middle class. After all, if large sections of the working-class are also 'burgerlijk' or 'respectable', why not change the keyword altogether? Why retain the social connotation? Or why not invert it - being Dutch is to be a really good 'worker' or 'workmanlike' after all? As Henk te Velde also shows, the cultural migrations of 'burgerlijk' and similar terms in other languages have much to do with the vicissitudes of mid-

---

[35] Roland Barthes, *Mythologies* (London, 1973).

[36] Ingrid Mittenzwei, an historian working at the Institut fur Sozial- und Geisteswissenschaften in Berlin, notes a contemporary instance of the same euphemism in the advice given her by her publisher to substitute 'Burgertum' for 'Bourgeoisie' in her own text. See Jan Blokker, 'De Olle DDR is voorbij, voorgoed verleden tijd', *De Volkskrant*, 9 November 1991. Thanks to Barbara Henkes for the reference and a translation.

dle-class power of different kinds, and the challenges of more popular forces. It is therefore of some consequence that the term employed to describe the Dutch nation also connotes a leading social group.

This articulation of national to class identities is only one instance of a general feature of discourses of the nation - the referencing of other social identities too. More generally, we may say that at both everyday and more public levels (and especially in the relations between them) representations of the nation are formed in relations of domination and resistance: they are connected to other forms of social power. They also act back on these relationships in different ways. This goes for the accounts of historians as well of course. In my own autobiographical sketch, for example, I found it impossible to talk about my Englishness except through my other identifications, especially those of class, gender and ethnicity. To bring the matter still closer to home, it was disconcerting for me as a man to realise how strikingly gendered were the essays in this volume in their topics, in their approaches to nationalism, and especially in their handling of the public-private divide.

The Nation as Construction and as Essence

The terms 'construction' and 'essence' are borrowed from general debates in cultural theory, especially on the politics of identity.[37] They are relevant here because they name some common and problematic reductions which our earlier distinction may help to illuminate. In summary, constructivist accounts stress the power of particular discourses or institutions to 'construct' the nation. Essentialist accounts take national identity or character as given, all-of-a-piece, and therefore not 'constructed' at all.

---

[37]   For uses of these terms see sources cited above, note 9.

More fully, then, 'constructivism' is the tendency to overestimate the power of discursive or institutional construction in general or even of some singular version of the nation, a single nation-text.[38] The indispensable insight here is that cultural forms, when read as 'texts' position or put pressure on their readers in particular ways. This pressure can be understood semiotically in terms of meaning,[39] psychoanalytically in terms of psychic investments[40] or discursively as the power of certain knowledges to construct us as 'subjects'.[41] The purpose of such an analysis in critical versions of constructivism is to reveal the unconscious processes at work, and to de-construct them.

Constructivism is not necessarily critical however. Constructivist features are also found in accounts which stress the role of the nation-state and its forms of citizenship, or of nationalism as an ideology, or the role of formal political society in general. These accounts have in common that privileging of the public sphere and that 'top-down' approach which is so familiar. Indeed, the idea of the nation as a political construction or as 'citizenship' has been used to classify whole forms of nationalism. The split-off Other to this 'constructed' nation is the nation of implicit knowledges, of involuntary membership, of 'culture'. Friedrich Meinecke's celebrated distinction between 'Staatsnation' (a nation constructed through political citizenship) and 'Kulturnation' (a nation resting, involuntarily so to speak, on a common culture) is an elaborated

---

[38] This tendency is most systematically pursued in linguistic and para-linguistic approaches; in the debates about identity politics it is often associated with post-structuralist critiques of essentialism. But it is a more general feature in approaches which stress the constitutive force of political instititions or movements, e.g. of the 'state' aspect which, in fact, is a by no means invariable feature of nationhood.

[39] As in Barthes earlier work e.g. *Mythologies* and *Image - Music - Text* (Glasgow, 1977).

[40] As in the influential strand of film analysis associated with the journal *Screen*.

[41] As in Michel Foucault's work.

version of this split[42]; Hans Kohn's distinction between 'subjective' (Western European) and 'objective' (East-Central European) modes of nationhood is a (somewhat occidentalist) deployment of it to explain cross-national difference.[43]

Such accounts exaggerate the importance of the most public (and historically best documented) forms. Like public discourse itself they abstract from the more complex process. Such a method may usefully uncover the productivity of a particular apparatus or text; but it cannot properly weigh its power and limits in the social world. Yet the reduction is tempting for anyone who studies the most highly articulated forms. Positively, it has lead to a large body of critical work which deconstructs nationalisms and other leading discourses by revealing their conventionality.[44] Negatively, it offers tempting shortcuts round researching more diffused and composite social phenomena, encourages a disregard of popular forms, and allows uncomplicated theorisation in the form of ideal types. How far students of public texts depend upon constructivist assumptions depends, in part, on the academic discipline they work with. The more formal kind of literary scholarship, which seizes on the exemplary text, and the more philosophical types of political theory are liable to this reduction.[45]

---

[42]   Friedrich Meinecke, *Cosmopolitanism and the Nation State* (Princeton 1970; Ist pub. in German 1907), summarised, for example, in Alter, *Nationalism*, pp. 14-23.

[43]   Hans Kohn, *The Idea of Nationalism* (New York, 1961) pp. 455-576.

[44]   See for example many of the essays in Gates, *'Race', Writing and Difference* and Bhabha, *Nation and Narration*.

[45]   Both approaches to the nation are very influential just now, in and around cultural studies. Good examples are to be found in the work of Homi Bhabha and Slavoj Zizek. The link between literary and philosophical approaches is often the adoption of Derridean ideas of deconstruction. I am grateful to Stuart Hall for suggesting connections here.

It is hard to describe the wider 'social world' which is so reduced in such accounts without fixing its features in advance of empirical investigation. But there are moments in which meanings are not so readily separable as texts because they are so closely connected with other practices. The reading of relatively abstracted discursive forms cannot be a sufficient method even for a cultural study. To retain something of older conceptions of culture - culture as meanings held or sedimented in whole ways of living - is to stay sensitive to such connections. From this point of view national identity cannot be reduced to discourse or narrative, especially not to a singular discourse or narration. Any cultural product only acquires weight and a long life by activating a complex moving web of discourses and narratives, already in process in many different public and private spaces. In these spaces the combinations of meaning are always closely connected to the histories, memories and psychic and other investments of individuals and social groups. These associations occur in 'biographical' clusters, hard to predict in advance, and with presences and absences as singular as any literary text.[46] They depend on linguistic and other conventions of their own (they are not outside discourse in this sense); but they are also anchored in repeated practices which constrain the formal fluidity of symbols and signs. Certain versions of Britishness or Dutchness, for example, will be woven tightly into the more entrenched defences and resistances (I use these terms in both their social and psychoanalytic meanings) of individuals and groups. Other versions will be reproduced and transformed in the repeated strategies of power-holders in the key

---

[46]   For a fine analysis of such clusters and absences in material produced in oral history interviews see Louisa Passerini, *Fascism in Popular Memory: The Cultural Experience of the Turin Working Class* (Cambridge, 1987), esp. pp. 19-63; for arguments in relation to material produced in contemporary group discussions see Wendy Hollway, *Subjectivity and Method in Psychology: Gender, Meaning and Science* (London, 1989) especially Ch.4.

institutions, or incorporated in 'selective traditions'.[47] In short though culture always has a formal or conventional dimension, the model of culture as subject-producing textuality has definite limits.

It also follows that an adequate strategy of interventions in the politics of national identity cannot be limited to putting new meanings into circulation, or even disarticulating old meanings and rearticulating them.[48] Nor can it successfully rest on a grasp of the publicly available meanings alone. We need knowledges too of the patterns of daily living of individuals and groups, of the power relations so produced and of the meanings by which these relations are lived, subjectively, in the many sites of existence. We need to learn to read the public versions themselves as attempts to secure some advantages in these complex, diffused and many-sided relations of force.

What, then, of essentialist thinking? What are the difficulties here, especially in studying nationalism? Here the focus is less on the constructive power of public discourse, more on the everyday 'ways of life', the implicit forms, the nation of culture. It is *this* moment in cultural forms which lends itself to essentialist interpretations. Again, however, theoretical choices always accompany an empirical focus. They may reinforce appearances or help us question them. Essentialist theories encourage us to represent ways of life and their more naturalised meanings as given; we lose sight of the fact that they have been produced. Since essentialism is such a familar tendency on Left and Right, we need to look at it more closely.

---

[47]   For the notion of 'selective tradition' see Williams, *The Long Revolution*, pp. 66-70; for the role of tradition in nationalism more generally see Eric Hobsbawm and Terence Ranger ed., *The Invention of Tradition* (Cambridge, 1983).

[48]   Compare the view of articulation implied in poststructuralist theorisations of politics: e.g. Ernesto Laclau and Chantal Mouffe, *Hegemony and Socialist Strategy: Towards a Radical Democratic Politics* (London, 1985).

Difficulties arise whenever some open or 'chaotic' conception like 'everyday life' or 'way of life' is specified tightly, ascribed to a nation and presented as the whole cultural process.[49] We then slip from phrases like 'cultures or ways of life in Britain' to 'British culture' or 'the British way of life' or even 'British character'. The same can happen in 'critical' discourse but with evaluations reversed. A notion like 'peculiarities among the English' or 'ideologies in England' quickly hardens into 'the Peculiarities of the English' or 'the English ideology' without us noticing the difference.[50] As constructivist analysis speedily grasps, there has been a massive discursive intervention between the first and the second sets of terms. There has been a work of selection and of evaluation. This renders the second set of terms normative, politically compelling and psychically compulsive, in ways that the first set of terms were not. Whenever national characteristics are specified in this way I start to feel uncomfortable - especially if the character in question is mine.

Against this we might argue that there are 'peculiar' or particular formations in any territory or among any people - as well as many features shared with geographic or demographic others. It may be that we can reach some historical conception of national particularities by using a careful comparative method, by being aware of global dimensions, and by being alive to the different kinds of cross national exchange, including psychic projections and ambivalences. But I am struck by the ease of the slip from an apparently rational conception of this kind to some frankly metaphysical, stereotypical or wish-fulfilling 'image'. There are, it

---

[49]   'Chaotic' in the sense of describing many complexities, contradictions and determinations which are not untangled, however, in the category itself; so 'chaotic' as opposed to analytic or explanatory.

[50]   As in the debate following the publication of Perry Anderson's influential essay, 'Origins of the Present Crisis' in *New Left Review*, No. 23 (1964). See especially, E. P. Thompson, 'The Peculiarities of the English' in *The Poverty of Theory and Other Essays* (London, 1978; first published 1965).

seems, strong pressures to state national characteristics in simple terms, suitable for moral evaluations. The studies in this volume, for instance, include the following vignettes of the Dutch over about a hundred years: essentially Calvinist; basically healthy, but weakened by commerce, cosmopolitanism, booklearning and anti-national attitudes; rich but corrupting (in comparison with Germany); 'poor miserable and hungry' (in comparison with the United States); neat, proper, stingy and rude; reliable, conventional and unoriginal; and tolerant, respectable and unheroic. It is not difficult, of course, to supply similar vignettes for the English, Scottish, Welsh and Irish and perhaps for the British as a whole. Some of these images are of a comfortably self-identifying kind; others present a stigmatised self or Other. The English, for instance, are hypocritical, pathologically reserved and incurably class-ridden; the British, so the story goes, are a peaceful and freedom-loving people, slow to anger, but formidable when roused...

The Forms and Uses of Essentialism

Like constructivist accounts national essences take many forms and appear in different combinations. They may be biological, as in racist notions of fatherland and folk, pervasive in European nationalisms. Even a predominantly cultural theorist like Craandijk can also refer to 'pure Dutch type'... 'Dutch blood in their veins'... 'not the pure strain' etc. It seems to have been hard for nineteenth-century Europeans to conceive of implicit or sedimented cultural forms, historically laid down but of long duration, aside from the language of biology and race.

National essences, however, can also be religious or metaphysical as in notions of a chosen people.[51] Or they can take a cultural form, centred on language, religious allegiance or some

---

[51]   e.g. 'the Dutch Isreal' in Orthodox Protestantism.

cultural 'common denominator', core value or 'basic' belief.[52] Or
the essence of the nation may be a single geographical feature, as
in Turner's romantic nationalism of the American frontier;[53] or a
single exemplary group, as in the self-image of the Dutch liberal
bourgeoisie[54] or of the City of London. We can even speak, paradoxically, of 'historical' forms of essentialism, the belief, for
instance, in a singular founding moment or tradition.[55]

In practice these forms are found in combinations. The
Orthodox Protestant belief in the Dutch as a Calvinist nation
clearly combined religious, cultural and historical elements. A
modern instance is the widespread idea of a homogeneous and
distinctive culture which is the 'heritage' of each European nation.
This idea has been marshalled politically in a variety of contexts:
debates about European unity; criticism of multi-cultural or anti-racist programmes; right-wing populist attacks on migrants,
refugees and settlers, especially from the Third World. Clearly
there are convergences here between cultural and biological theories. Particular cultures seem to adhere to persons with the tenacity
of skin colour, and according to all-too-familiar racial
categories.[56] In this respect conservative cultural theories and

---

[52] e.g. the 'burgerlijk' character of the Dutch.
[53] As discussed by Annemieke Galema above; or the essentially
Dutch stubborn 'peasant' defence of the polders discussed by Wim
Klinkert above.
[54] As discussed by Henk te Velde above.
[55] e.g. in the case of the Dutch Revolt, discussed by Roel Kuiper
above.
[56] For this cultural formation in Britain, variously decribed as 'the
new racism', 'ethnic absolutism', or as an aspect of 'the New Right' or
of 'Neo-Conservatism' see Martin Barker, *The New Racism: Conservatives and the Ideology of the Tribe* (London, 1981); Stuart Hall *et al.*,
Policing the Crisis: Mugging, the State and Law and Order (London,
1978); Paul Gilroy, *There Ain't No Black in the Union Jack*; Gill Seidel,
'Culture, Nation and "Race" in the British and French New Right' in
Ruth Levitas ed., *The Ideology of the New Right* (Cambridge, 1986), pp.
107-135.

contemporary socio-biology have a similar function today as did 'scientific racism' and social darwinism a century ago.[57]

Essentialism is not necessarily combined, however, with like features: accounts may be essentialist in some respects but constructivist in others.. My favourite example is taken from an interview with Mrs Thatcher on the subject of British morals and manners:

> 'The culture of courtesy could be reintroduced, and it should begin in the homes and go on through the schools and into university life and then business. It could become ingrained and there are still plenty of societies in the world where it was. And, she repeated, it was natural to the British.'[58]

Even the massive deletion of agents in this passage ('could be introduced' ... 'go on through' ... 'become engrained') and the final naturalisation ('natural to the British') cannot disguise Mrs Thatcher's 'great crusade': the fact that she is strenuously prescribing, even to the point of indoctrination, what is supposed to come naturally anyway. Such naturalising moves are crucial in nation construction, since they tend to disguise (usually much better than here) all the hard labour that goes into the launching of a version. If we return now to Huizinga's 1930s intervention, we can define the move more clearly: he presents a construction as an essence.

Even more interesting are those combinations of essences and histories which have been a stock-in-trade of nationalisms. The historic nation of orthodox Dutch Protestantism, the 'Dutch Isreal', is an example for which 1980s British nationalism provides many

---

[57]   See Douglas A. Lorimer, *Colour, Class and the Victorians* (Leicester, 1978) and Jan Breman, *Imperial Monkey Business: Racial Superiority in Social-Darwinist Theory and Colonial Practice* (Amsterdam, 1990). Thanks to Barbara Henkes for this reference.

[58]   'This is My New Crusade', Interview with Mrs Thatcher, *The Daily Mail*, 29 April 1988.

parallels and comparisons. Roel Kuiper's study provides an intriguing instance of the vicissitudes of such a conception under the pressures of further historical change - here secularisation, democratisation and increasing religious and cultural pluralism. Kuiper shows how, in the face of political defeats, the close relation between the Dutch reformed church and the state loosened, and Orthodox Protestantism retreated to the conception of the denomination as the nation's conscience. Even on the retreat, however, this idea could support an activist political stance: not merely the preservation of an ideal, but its revival. In Abraham Kuyper's populism a version of the old Calvinist essence was relocated in the Dutch people or their 'true' spirit or character. Whatever their faiths, they displayed their Calvinistic inheritance in their ways of living, civic virtues and historical sense. In a similar way, Mrs Thatcher can argue, rather as Kuyper did for 'the baptised nations' of Europe, that the British, whatever the actual diversity of their beliefs, are a fundamentally 'Christian' people.[59]

Interesting comparisons can be made between the Orthodox Protestant conceptions and the 'Whig' history which has attached itself so tenaciously not to the culture of the people in Britain but to parliamentary (including monarchical) institutions. Here again we begin with historical construction but end by defying historical change in the present. Once 'the Mother of Parliaments' has evolved, it remains a salutary lesson for the world, even when contemporary constitutional development becomes illiberal.[60] The

---

[59]   See for example her series of speeches on politics and religion in Margaret Thatcher, *The Revival of Britain: Speeches on Home and European Affairs 1975-1988* (Compiled by Alistair B. Cooke, London, 1989) esp. pp. 62-70, 122-32 and 249-55.

[60]   For 'Whig History' see Herbert Butterfield, *The Whig Interpretation of History* (Harmondsworth, 1973). Illiberal British trends include the untrammelled sovereignty of parliamentary majorities (however narrowly based electorally), the erosion of civil rights, and the loss of public confidence in police and judiciary. These have featured in a decade dominated by politicians who have not spared the world (and

Orthodox Protestant essence was located in heaven, or perhaps in the people. Though historically realised once upon a time, it also stood against historical realities in some sense. It was 'a historical truth stronger than the constitution', 'a reality which could not be established or repudiated by a mere act of the state'.[61] In the case of Whig history the essence is not in tension with realities; it is located in actually existing institutions. These are conceived as a finished process which is to be preserved. This is a more conservative and complacent deployment of similar ideas.

In either version, complacent or activist, there is a real de-historicisation. An original history (always debatable of course) is frozen as the historic, as heritage, as tradition. Such essences can be mislaid or lost but will surely be restored, fundamentally unchanged. Perhaps the most productive reading of these forms is in terms of the politics of identity. From this point of view, Whig history, discourses of heritage and stories of essences lost and found are about sustaining identities under severe pressures. We can see this, in the case of heritage for instance, if we refuse to focus on the pleasure we may get from 'the past' and consider instead how stories of heritage position us in the present. To be the subjects of heritage, in order to inherit, we must occupy a fixed position. An inheritor with an uncertain identity is liable to dispossession.

I hope I have shown that if we focus exclusively on either moment, public or local, in the construction of national identity, *without some critical theoretical correction*, we are likely to miss the full complexity of the processes we wish to grasp. Often our disciplinary orientations or theoretical frameworks reinforce our positionings and point of view. If we focus on sedimented or 'traditional' associations we may underestimate the constructedness, and therefore the changeability of all versions of the nation

---

Eastern Europe especially) with boasts about British democracy.

[61]   Examples quoted in Roel Kuiper's essay above.

including the most naturalised forms. These too have a history - of the longer duration maybe.[62] If they are 'essences', a notion which historians must *always* approach sceptically, it is because they are *constructed* as such! The danger is that we see national features, and nationalism itself, as given and unaccountable - 'just a natural and necessary feeling of belonging' perhaps.

If, on the other hand, we conduct an analysis mainly in terms of the publicly canvassed versions and their relative fluidity, we may underestimate the material rootedness of national identities, hidden from this point of view, and their complex relations, part regulatory, part parasitic, with other social identities. Everyday practices are not intrinsically 'national' in their meanings. They can be made to mean in a host of different non-national ways. National associations have to be worked for, produced, in a dynamic process. It is only when the labour of cultural nationalisation has some success that *some* ways of living *become* 'the British way of life,' some everyday meanings and values *become* the national culture, and that (in the severest and most oppressive reduction of all) Identity as such *becomes* the Nation.

Nationalism and National Identity as a Process or Circuit

Studies of images of the nation must include both highly articulated and more implicit forms; more importantly they should be informed by this difference theoretically. This *combination* is the particular interest of Annemieke Galema's and Barbara Henkes' studies. Once this juxtaposition is achieved, however, further

---

[62] The notion of a 'long duration' history comes from Fernand Braudel, *The Mediterranean and the Mediterranean World in the Reign of Philip II* (2 Vols, London, 1975) and more generally from structuralist conceptions of historical time. Such distinctions in temporal modality offer further dimensions of the differences between the public and the local.

questions emerge. How are the levels or instances related? Is the (rather binary) distinction adequate, or not? Is the distinction itself an historical one, an historical abstraction? Is it superseded today? Theoretically, therefore, does the distinction set limits? What might be a better idea?

It might be better to think of cultural nationalisation as a circuit or sequence of 'moments', each of which involve particular transformations of common materials. When we read public texts or private sources we break into this circuit at different points, and with tools of our own.

It could be that as some postmodern theorists argue, the distinction between lived culture and media representations has already broken down. These distinctions are historical after all. I would be more convinced of this if postmodern theory was itself less resolutely constructivist.[63] We might insist, more carefully, that public and private moments are necessarily *linked* today, which is why the idea of a circuit is useful. Local and particular cultures appear twice in the circuit: as endpoints and as beginnings. From one point of view they are a *product* of a history of struggles over public culture; from another they are a kind of *base* for all the specialised, public forms. No public version (Huizinga's view of the Dutch as burgerlijk for instance; or Mrs Thatcher's advocacy of courtesy or entrepreneurship) will acquire ideological effectivity unless it resonates with common sense meanings. No ideological form can succeed in the public sphere unless individuals and group invest in it, translating it into their inner speech. On the other hand, the forms of imagination associated with modern publicity are so powerful that no local version can remain immune from them. It remains a cardinal error, however, to read off local versions from the most public images, as if all were part of one flat cultural

---

[63]   I am thinking particularly here of the work of Jean Baudrillard, especially *In The Shadow of the Silent Majorities... Or the End of the Social and Other Essays* (trans. Paul Foss, Paul Patton and John Johnston, New York, 1983).

surface.[64] From a position of power in the public sphere, if only as an analyst of it, much of the cultural world simply does not appear. Particular ways of life, specific identities, are formed away from the grand national themes but always in a negotiated relation to them. Secrecy, masquerade, or a certain enforced inner-ness are necessary strategies in struggles with surveillance and control. Local cultures are not so much 'authentic' therefore, as formed as defences and alternatives.

There are two particularly productive moments. The first is the production of versions of the nation by 'intellectuals' in Gramsci's expanded sense, that is cultural organisers. Politicians and political parties are significant because of their privileged relation to the nation-state form, but not all nation-production is narrowly 'political'. Equally important have been the growing apparatuses, of publicity and the modern media, 'national' and commercial. Like education systems and other cultural institutions, these may acquire some independence from governments, and are struggled over constantly. There are also rituals which, though certainly public and national, present themselves as 'non-political'. Examples in Britain are the Queen's Speech at Christmas or international football matches. Then there are hosts of more modest practices, dispersed through civil society, which articulate versions of the nation to particular publics. I have in mind the writing of books about national or regional cuisine, or guides to the beauties and curiosities of the English countryside. Beyond this, in everyday speech and practice all of us may act as 'national intellectuals', connecting national meanings to our lives and ascribing them to others. Accumulatively these different productions, each with their own intersecting circuits, are of immense weight. To succeed in articulating them, at the most public level, is a great prize.

The second active moment, however, is when these versions return transformed to the social individuals and local publics from

---

[64]   e.g. some accounts of the postmodern, repeating features of mass culture theory in the past.

whose cultural life they arose in the first place: when, as it were, the politicians face their publics in parliaments and streets and living rooms. Now their words are refused, reappropriated or further transformed according to the pragmatic run of life of citizens and the identitifications and investments they have already made. It is important not to see this 'reading' as a smooth or functional set of transactions; rather it is full of tensions.[65] Disjunctions between public campaigns and local identities are endemic, normal. There is a struggle to conform ways of living to some national project; but it is a struggle that is always contested and rarely fully successful.

In the rest of this essay I want to explore some of the transformations involved at these two key points of cultural nationalisation. I will use the studies in this volume as the main source of examples and insights.

Transformations in the Public Sphere: Selection

What part is played by specialised agencies in the production of cultural nationality? What work do they do on the basis of everyday beliefs and existing articulations?

Nation construction at this level involves, first, a process of selection. Selections must be made from the heterogeneous mass of beliefs, practices, fantasies. What counts as British, and may even come to exemplify the nation, is not the same as the sum of activities among the people. 'British food', for example, is different from what people in Britain actually eat: it is a more restricted category. Food in Britain today is extraordinarily multicultural.

---

[65]   Studies of the 'readership' or 'audience' of popular-cultural and media forms are one (restricted) way into this problem. See, for example, David Morley, *Family Television: Cultural Power and Domestic Leisure* (London, 1986); Janice Radway, *Reading the Romance* (Chapel Hill, 1984).

This culinary heteroglossia derives from pressures towards both standardisation and diversification. In such a situation the search for an authentically native cuisine is more than usually hopeless; though far from being abandoned. 'British food' is strenuously pursued through pre-industrial byways, 'farmhouse', 'village', or regional cookery, and consumed on special occasions like Christmas. In one considerable genre of food journalism such survivals and inventions are regularly celebrated, sometimes with decidedly racist overtones.[66]

Selection always involves de-selection. De-selection, however, is by no means the end of the story. To follow a well-worn argument in cultural theory, apparently unselected categories are never simply absent; they are 'structuring absences'. Their 'difference' defines those identities which are all too insistently present. Moreover, these marginalised categories may come to figure in elaborate symbolic transactions which, in one sense, re-centre them again. As Stallybrass and White argue in a fine exploration of the formation of bourgeois social identity in post-Renaissance Europe, there is no automatic correspondence between what is socially central and what is culturally significant. The 'most powerful symbolic repertoires' are often located 'at borders, margins and edges, rather than at the accepted centres of the social body'.[67] The formation of the middle classes had specifically psychic as well as social dimensions. In order to constitute itself as separate and superior, the bourgeoisie expelled from its own social practices those 'low' and 'dirty' elements which figured in the carnivals of popular culture. Psychically, then, respectability involved internalising denigrated features in the form of disgust. This also meant, however, that they remained available as objects of fascination and desire - as testified by their reappearance in

---

[66]   I am particularly grateful to Mariette Clare (of the CCCS Popular Memory Group) for discussions on food and nationalism.

[67]   Peter Stallybrass and Allon White, *The Politics and Poetics of Transgression*, (London 1986), esp. p. 20.

literary and other 'high' forms.[68] Such an analysis draws attention
to the figures which lurk on the margins of our sources and histories, to the internal 'others' of the different versions of Dutchness: the 'uncivilised' lower classes whom Robert Fruin explicitly
excluded from the nation; the 'scum', 'dregs' or lumpenproletarians
of the cities who frightened and fascinated respectables everywhere
in the late nineteenth century; the disorderly youth and the 'weak,
scholarly nervous little fellows' that upset military men across
Europe; and that catalogue of working-class roughness and transgression (including 'sensual dancing') against which official Dutch
socialist youth defined itself in the inter-war years. The whole
discursive regime of burgerlijkheid, in its liberal, conservative and
socialist versions, depended on the evocation of an unrespectable
or 'undomesticated' Other - bohemian, hedonistic, sexy, im-
moderate, uneducated, excessive, dissolute, insolent and out of
control.[69]

It is important to add that very large social categories may
be marginalised (and symbolically valorised) in this way, not
merely a Bohemian fringe or an underclass. Almost all the public
discourses of nationhood discussed in this volume address a primarily masculine citizenry and exclude the world of women.
Sometimes this is implicit as in the continual address to public
affairs; sometimes it is more explicit, as in soldierly preoccupations
with 'virility'. In either case women are subsumed into a nation
described in male-centred terms: through male-exclusive occu-
pations ('lawyer and poet, baron and labourer alike'), through the
use of the male form to designate a national ('Dutchmen'), or
through the male metaphors of 'Fatherland' and 'brother'. Unal-

---

[68]   In this tracing of migrations of carnivalesque forms Stallybrass
and White follow the argument in Mikhail Bakhtin, *Rabelais and His
World* (trans. Helene Iswolsky, Bloomington, 1984).
[69]   All examples quoted or cited in this paragraph are drawn from
essays in this volume and especially from Henk te Velde's and Wim
Klinkert's.

luring exceptions were the discourses of the German philanthropic societies and, later, of the German Nazi state which did recognise some women, but only through a very oppressive reduction - as mothers for the nation and the race.[70]

At the same time gendered identities are continuously evoked in the languages of nation builders. If we treat 'Dutchman', 'Englishman' or even (in this period) 'citizen' not as abstract but as truly gendered categories with their own private faces and subjectivities, the presence of masculinities in these texts is quite overwhelming. This reaches a peak in the late nineteenth century material when challenges to the hegemonic masculinities were accumulating. Feminism challenged the power of men by criticising the forms of masculine sexuality, especially the double standard, and demanding an end to male monopolies of the professions, higher education and political life.[71] The same period saw the distinct emergence into discourse of the troubling figure of the

---

[70]   See Barbara Henkes' essay above and also her 'Changing Images of German Maids during the inter-war period in the Netherlands' in Raphael Samuel and Paul Thompson ed., *The Myths We Live By* (London, 1990), pp. 225-38. For Nationalist Socialist policies towards women more generally see Claudia Koonz, *Mothers in the Fatherland: Women, the Family and Nazi Politics* (New York, 1987) and Tim Mason, 'Women in Nazi Germany', *History Workshop Journal*, Nos 1 (Spring 1976) and 2 (Autumn, 1976). Thanks to Barbara Henkes for the first of these references.

[71]   For accounts of the late nineteenth century crisis in Britain see Mary Langan and Bill Schwarz ed., *Crises in the British State 1880s-- 1930* (London, 1987). For relevant aspects of feminism in this period see Jill Liddington and Jill Norris, *One Hand Tied Behind Us* (London, 1978) and Judith Walkowitz, *Prostitution and Victorian Society* (Cambridge, 1980).

homosexual man.[72] At the same time the socialist and working
-class mobilisations of this period offered complex possibilities for
new alliances across class and gender allegiances.[73] Imperial
competition and overseas adventures offered scenes, fictive and
real, for bolstering old masculinities and class repertoires and
inventing new. A host of significant others were offered to European men of the ruling groups: other subordinated 'races' in the
'uncivilised' world and their also frequently racialised imperial
rivals in Europe.[74]

The most obviously 'masculine' responses occurred in discourses
on the nation as an army, a pervasive social metaphor in the
decades up to World War I. In both the Netherlands and Britain
the Boer War unleashed a flood of 'manliness'.[75] Here a male
exclusive institution was used as the very model of nationhood;
manliness was defined in terms of your preparedness to fight and
die for your nation. Even in the unmilitaristic Netherlands strenu-
ous efforts were made to move the military from the symbolic and
institutional margin to a more central position. The army was to be

---

[72]   Jeffrey Weeks, *Sex, Politics and Society: The Regulation of
Sexuality since 1800* (London, 1981), esp. Ch. 6, but see also the
historical and theoretical controversies about the historical formation of
homosexualities in Duberman, Vicinus and Chauncey ed., *Hidden from
History*.

[73]   See Liddington and Norris, *One Hand Tied Behind Us* and
Caroline Rowan, '"Mothers, Vote Labour!" The State, the Labour
Movement and Working-Class Mothers, 1900 -1918' in Rosalind Brunt
and Caroline Rowan ed., *Feminism, Culture and Politics* (London,
1982), pp. 59-84.

[74]   For Britain see Dawson, 'Soldier Heroes', cited above note 10.

[75]   Also an intensification of preoccupations around 'motherhood'.
For Britain see the debates around the 'physical efficiency' of recruits to
the Boer War armies discussed in G. R. Searle, *The Quest for National
Efficiency* (London, 1971) and for further gendered ramifications see
Anna Davin, 'Imperialism and Motherhood', *History Workshop Journal*,
No. 5 (Spring 1978): 9-66 and the sources cited above, notes 10 and 74.

'the big national school, where order and duty are practised and transferred to civilian life'.[76] The tactical differences among military men which Wim Klinkert analyses are very interesting here: advocates of the cadre army sought to discipline the young male population by getting as many as possible into the barracks, where 'real soldiers' (real men?) were made. The advocates of conscription sought to diffuse military values through the society as a whole, colonising existing instititions like the family and the school, or inventing new ones like paramilitary youth movements. Common to both schools was a model of social relations and of masculine virtue that privileged hierarchy, obedience and physical strength, as defined against both unruly youth and more clerkly or 'mental' masculinities. All this amounted to a particularly complex structure of recognitions and exclusions in which 'the body of the nation' was always a cross-class, cross-generational and 'manly' alliance or 'fraternisation' of some kind.

Warfare is the apotheosis of public man, the ultimate test and adventure. It is also important to read the public texts of the nation for the private masculinities which they (and I am afraid their male historians) so often tuck away. What are we to make of the private sense of self of a man who scripts himself as the leader of the nation as Abraham Kuyper did? Or of the anxieties and pleasures which are (barely) contained in all that emphasis on virility and manliness? And how was failures of such overblown and 'epic' masculinities to be handled, personally, on a battlefield, under the arc-lights of some public performance or at home? And when heroes failed, who was to pick up the pieces?

Evaluation and Difference: Us and Others

The second crucial move is the attachment of value to all such selections. The nation is not only a cultural and imaginary con-

---

[76]   Quoted in Wim Klinkert's essay above.

struction; it is a highly normative or prescriptive one. When Abraham Kuyper or Mrs Thatcher described the nation they came up with a long list of *virtues*: for Kuyper the Dutch nation constituted itself around the key virtues of religiosity, historical sense, a thriving 'family life', self-government and freedom of conscience; Mrs Thatcher's Britons were 'naturally' enterprising (good neo-liberals), responsible and courteous.

Lists like this are always shadowed, more or less explicitly, by equally long lists of evils. These may be personified by internal or external others, sometimes by whole nations. In nineteenth-century Netherlands, 'Prussia' seems to have had this function. Fear was understandably strong at moments of military danger as in 1870, but Prussia, presented as autocratic and militaristic, was important as a point of reference in identity work too. As Tellegen put it in 1870 - 'no authority but selfgovernment, not German but Dutch.'[77] Through this comparison, Dutch intellectuals and politicians could hold up a self-image to their people as freedom- and peace-loving, as voters, arguers and negotiators rather than fighters.

'External' othering can be many-sided. It is fascinating, for example, to find middle-class intellectuals in France, Holland and Germany in the years during and after World War I constructing their respective bourgeois classes in relation to those of other nations.[78] Overarching this imaging of inter-European differences were global comparisons with America and the Soviet Union: Huizinga, Mann and Johannet (and, we might add, Stanley Baldwin)[79] defined their respective countries' identities in terms of the opposition to both Bolshevism and vulgar American capital-

---

[77]   Quoted in Rico op den Camp's essay above.

[78]   As discussed by Henk te Velde above.

[79]   For an acute discussion of the politics of Stanley Baldwin, the inter-war British Conservative Party leader, see Bill Schwarz, 'The Language of Constitutionalism: Baldwinite Conservatism' in *Formations of Nation and People* (London, 1984) pp. 1-18.

ism. Equally complex is the simultaneous construction of one national identity through many international others. The English, for example, developed a many-sided and often denigratory repertoire for Europeans, Americans, Africans and Indians, 'beginning' with the Irish 'at home'.[80] The wealth of material and cultural connections, the composite nature of nationality at home, and the rise and fall in super-power status made for a bellicose policing of identity boundaries too.

Identity construction was complex in Limburg, because internal differences of language and religion interacted with external relations. The province's political history and cultural heterogeneity offered a three or four way choice. Was Limburg to be Dutch or Belgian, French or German, or perhaps an independent state? Rico op den Camp argues convincingly that the Limburg elites, themselves culturally divided, opted to be another Dutch province as the best chance for their heterogeneity to be tolerated. They too made this choice through an over-arching Us/Other construction (the Netherlands versus 'Prussia'); but at the same time reproduced themselves and their people as members of a 'hybrid' province. Thus Limburg, like the Netherlands itself, is an interesting example of a way of handling diversities rather different from that of post-imperial Britain or racist Europe or indeed, contemporary Yugoslavia. Here differences were negotiated rather than extruded, albeit within the context of larger threats.

Constructions of Us and Others always have some material basis in historically produced differences within and between national formations. The more bizarre and imaginary representations may be aided by massive cultural difference and distance as

---

[80]   I am grateful to Chris Glen (of the CCCS Popular Memory Group) for first drawing my attention to the importance of cultural international relations of this kind in the production of national identities.

in the various phases of colonialisation.[81] But as Edward Said and others have argued, the grosser denigrations of Others must be seen against the ideological imperatives of imperial conquest, or inter-imperial rivalry, and, in recent times, the informal control of valuable resources like oil.[82] Othering is certainly explicable as a function of 'interest' in part, typically as a justification for rule and for the refusal of self-determination. It is no surprise that its workings are often detected across major discrepancies of power.

The most interesting accounts suggest that neither social distance nor ideology are sufficient explanations. To construe Us/Other relations as simple oppositions may even reproduce conservative theories of identity. Difference in a simple binary sense - opposed interests, strong boundaries, categorical separations - is thereby preserved. It is hard, within this framework, to comprehend the common elements between national formations, and all the boundary crossing especially characteristic of today's world: globalisation in economic life, culture and mass communications, physical migration and settlement, cultural borrowing or translation, and psychic introjections of and projections onto national or 'racial' Others.

A better starting-point is to see that we always have need of others, individually or collectively, imaginatively and materially, to constitute ourselves. Thus Edward Said also argues that the construction of the image of the Oriental by scholars in the West had

---

[81]   See, for an early example, Peter Mason, 'Portrayal and Betrayal: The Colonial Gaze in Seventeenth Century Brazil', *Culture and History*, No. 6, (1989): 37-62 and for later Sander L. Gilman, 'Black Bodies, White Bodies: Toward an Iconography of Female Sexuality in Late Nineteenth Century Art, Medecine, and Literature' in Henry Louis Gates ed., *'Race', Writing and Difference*, pp. 223-61. Thanks to Barbara Henkes for the first reference.

[82]   Said, *Orientalism*; see also the similar emphasis in Abdul R. JanMohammed, 'The Economy of Manichean Allegory: The Function of Racial Difference in Colonialist Literature' in Gates, *'Race', Writing and Difference*, pp. 78-106.

more to do with Western identity and preoccupations than with any of the peoples beyond the Mediterranean Sea. Orientalism involved an 'imaginative' and 'arbitrary' geography, important for anchoring Westernness in a negation of the East.[83] In the same way Britain's Others have been internal to the identity British, even when they have lived outside the British Isles. Later versions of this argument have drawn explicitly on psychoanalytic categories (like splitting and projection) to account for the imaginary or internal nature of the Other, especially in forms like colonial literatures. They have stressed the emotional ambivalences of Us/Other relationships, which involve fantasies of fascination and desire as well as fear and loathing.[84] This suggests that to stress the drawing of boundaries (identities as 'whole ways of life' for instance) is to grasp only one side of the process. The struggle for boundaries is itself conducted through personal, imaginary, cultural and material *relationships*. The hope of finally 'expelling' the Other is forlorn. This is one reason why contemporary theorists argue that identity is not only unstable and fragmentary, but is typically 'hybrid' too.[85] Indeed, identity is 'impossible' in the 'pure' forms in which it is so often sought.

The newer theories of identity construction, which focus on psychic process, may also explain why othering is so persistent a feature of self-production even where the 'we' involved does not wield major institutional powers. Experiences of migration are

---

[83]   Said, *Orientalism*, esp. pp. 54-55.

[84]   This difference (with Said) is clearly marked in Homi Bhabha's work where a shift is made from 'colonial discourse' to 'colonial fantasy'. See his 'The Other Question: The Stereotype in Colonial Discourse', *Screen*, Vol. 24, No. 6 (Nov.-Dec. 1983) and his post-structuralist re-reading of Frantz Fanon's *Black Skin, White Masks* (London, 1986), editor's foreword.

[85]   For the notion of hybridity as a general category and also in relation to Caribbean identities see Homi Bhabha, 'The Third Space' and Stuart Hall, 'Cultural Identity and Diaspora' both in Rutherford ed., *Identity, Comunity, Culture, Difference*, pp. 207-21 and 222-37.

particularly interesting here since they repeat, at an individual level, something of the dilemmas of the Limburgers - situations, in short, in which a 'choice' of nationality becomes possible. We will explore these dynamics further in the final sections of this essay which look at some of the consequences, in the private sphere, of nationalist constructions.

The Nation As a Structured Moral Community

Selection involves exclusion and inclusion, denigration and desire, but it may also operate through less binary distinctions. Generally, nationalist rhetoric puts all the citizens in their places in two particular ways. First, it places individuals and social groups in some evaluative grid, often by ranking the practices, sites or symbols with which they are particularly associated. Second and more dynamically it puts pressures on groups and individuals to behave in recognisable ways and even to change their identities.

Two moral maps of this kind are common in the (mainly nineteenth-century) materials discussed in this volume. The first evaluative scheme, which corresponds to essentialist conceptions of the nation, is a kind of moral map. Sometimes the geography is literal, as in the privileging of Holland in representations of the Netherlands and of the south and east in dominant versions of the British/English (the 'southern metaphor').[86] More generally, the nation is conceived as having an essential or ideal feature, and individuals, groups, institutions and practices are arranged in relation to it. Some are exemplary or quintessential. They are 'representatives of the true spirit of the nation'. They are practising Christians, quiet and virtuous citizens, hardy soldiers, frontiersmen, entrepeneurs, members of the Falklands 'task force'. Above all

---

[86]   For the 'Southern metaphor' see Martin J. Wiener, *English Culture and the Decline of the Industrial Spirit 1850-1980* (London, 1981).

perhaps, they are the statesmen and (rarely) stateswomen themselves. In societies with monarchical traditions, like the Netherlands and Britain, Queens or Kings may personify the nation, or its best attributes, or provide personalised materials for heart-searchings about national morality more generally.[87] In some versions, as in Abraham Kuyper's populism, it is the people, even the unenfranchised people, who represent the nation from 'outside the sultry atmosphere of a political lumber room'.[88] In other versions (times of moral danger indeed!) domestic exemplars are lacking and are sought elsewhere. The Boers seem to have functioned thus for some Dutch politicans at the turn of the century; the Falklands islanders (free of strikes and 'immigrants') were ideal or imaginary Britons for some Conservative newspapers in the 1980s.[89] Sometimes, as we have seen, such representatives have to be found in the past: 'Thank God we have a history to mirror ourselves' as *De Oranjevaan* put it in 1883.[90]

Of interest here, however, is less the familiar self-defining play around Others, and more the intermediate positionings, somewhere between core and margin. To focus only on centre and margin is to miss the presence of persuadable majorities, and fail to connect the texts with the political and rhetorical processes of which they are a part. Such constructions exert pressures, often towards assimilation. In the meantime intermediate categories may

---

[87]   On these aspects of monarchy in Britain today see Nairn, *The Enchanted Glass*; Ros Brunt, 'The Changing Face of Monarchy', *Marxism Today*, (July 1984); Rosalind Coward, 'The Royals' in *Female Desire* (London, 1984). For earlier periods see Dorothy Thompson, *Queen Victoria: Gender and Power* (London, 1990) and Henk te Velde, 'Het "roer van de staat" in "zwakke vrouwenhanden"': Emma en het imago van Oranje' in C. A. Tamse ed., *Koningin Emma: Opstellen over haar regentschap en voogdij* (Baarn, 1990).

[88]   Quoted in Roel Kuiper's essay above.

[89]   Notably for *The Sun*.

[90]   Quoted in Roel Kuiper's essay above.

be classed as 'erring', 'lost' or leaderless, victims of a loss of direction elsewhere.

Particular forms of narration are often associated with this core-periphery model, bodying out its moral character and point of view. Pervasive in texts discussed in this volume is what we may call the nationalist epic. Like all good adventure stories, this narrative centres on heroes and villains. Villains are powerful but fatally flawed assailants whom our heroes must defeat in battle. Heroes may be seen as the exemplary types who meet such challenges and develop their sterling characters in the process. But maybe the true heroes of this genre are the people-nations who have lost their identities but must recover them before the story ends. The military men's version of the Dutch as a people corrupted by prosperity, peace, poor leadership, anti-nationalism and book-learning, but winnable to martial virtue and a less 'wilting' form of masculinity is a particularly desperate example of this story-line. It is interesting to note that they saw the country's unwilling elites as also in need of reform.[91] Mrs Thatcher's deployment of a similar narrative in the aftermath of the Falkland/Malvinas war shows how persistently connected with nationalism this form of story-telling has been.[92]

Another way of understanding these less binary formations is in terms of Gramsci's account of hegemony as a form of rule.[93] In articulating versions of the nation, cultural organisers excercise power by constructing alliances of different kinds. Such alliances may involve exclusions and coercion, but are centrally built around forms of consent or ethico-political leadership. Alliances involve

---

[91]   See Wim Klinkert's essay above.

[92]   Margaret Thatcher, Speech to Conserative Party Rally, Cheltenham Race Course, 3 July 1982 in Margaret Thatcher, *The Revival of Britain*, pp. 160-78.

[93]   This account is based on my reading of *The Prison Notebooks*; for the notion of 'national popular' in Gramsci see esp. David Forgacs, 'National-Popular: Genealogy of a Concept' in *Formations of Nation and People*, pp. 83-121.

'leading' or 'directing' groups, subaltern groupings (which may perform subsiduary but indispensable functions) and subordinated groups. Those who are subordinated are not necessarily excluded from the dominant alliance. In more stable hegemonic moments their consent may be won by concessions from the directing groups. Subordination becomes problematic if subordinated groups develop a counter-hegemony which threatens the terms of consent and rejiggs alliances. From this point of view we can read nationalist articulations (the various versions of 'burgerlijk' for example) as strategies for building alliances, not only by exclusions and inclusions, but by subtle patterns of incitement, reward and punishment. Since nations are heterogeneous formations, unstably bounded, embodying profound antagonisms, and structured in dominance, it is very hard to find versions which do not discriminate on these lines.

The Nation as Social Recognition

I have stressed throughout this essay that to construct the nation is to work on other social identities, through a process of articulation for example. Articulation, however, is a rather formal category - it focuses on the connecting up of elements, not on qualitiative transformations. It is ill-adapted to account for changes in subjective investment for instance. This is why I prefer to use categories with a more psychological connotation, especially the language of recognition, familiar from both psychoanalytic and dialectical or dialogical discourse.[94] Social recognition is a ubiquitous social

---

[94]   Dialectical versions are often traced to Hegel's discussion of the master-slave relationship in *The Phenomenology of the Spirit*. A more specifically linguistic/literary version is to be found in the 'dialogism' of the Leningrad Circle of the 1920s, a grouping that included V. N. Volosinov and Mikhail Bakhtin. See especially M. M. Bakhtin, *The Dialogic Imagination* (ed. Michael Holquist, Austin, 1991) and Volosinov, *Marxism and the Philosophy of Language* (cited above note 26.) For

phenomenon, with strongly institutionalised forms. It is a fundamental condition of human communication and subjectivity. From this perspective, we may say that discourses of the nation act on other identifications by sorting through them in different ways, recognising some, refusing recognition to others. Recognition or non-recognition are not the only possibilities however: national discourses may systematically *misrecognise* previously formed identities. Indeed misrecognition seems a built-in probability of recognition processes since they are never simply communicative but are always crossed with power and desire. Misrecognised categories are neither approved nor excluded: they are offered alternatives under duress. They can strive to maintain their own subjective fictions in the face of neglect or retribution; or they can endeavour violently to conform to the recognitions that are on offer.[95]

'Recognition' has implications for understanding cultural nationality as a whole. National identity is not necessarily a direct form of loyalty to the nation or to national institutions or symbols. It may also attach itself to other identifications which are then nationalised in different ways. National identity is a meta-discourse or grand narrative that regulates or polices other identifications.

---

an account of the circle and their entangled authorships see Katerina Clark and Michael Holquist, *Mikhail Bakhtin* (Cambridge Mass., 1984), pp. 95-118. Though notions of recognition /misrecognition have been central in the contemporary revival of psychoanaysis across different currents, the Object Relations school has made the fullest use of this idea. For an interesting summary and critique, in relation to gender and power especially, see Jessica Benjamin, *The Bonds of Love: Psychoanalysis, Feminism and the Problem of Domination* (New York, 1988). The CCCS Popular Memory Group developed its own version of this theory.

[95]　In the Popular Memory Group we owed these insights to Pat McLernon particularly. From the group's own perspective there is too little stress on misrecognitions in the Object Relations versions, while Lacanians tend to ascribe misrecognition to psychic and linguistic relations in general rather than to particular power relations.

This applies both to 'nationalist' forms, where the nation is strongly preferred, and to a more modest 'patriotism' that leaves more space for other identities.[96] Discourses of the nation are only one source of recognition, but they have a particular power because often associated with citizenship, law and legitimised violence.[97] The power of national agencies to recognise citizen is one side of the condensation of powers which is the nation-state. These powers include the right to speak 'universally' for all within a national territory. This cultural role is backed by coercive powers: the criminal law and other disqualifications like the regulation of residence, citizenship or nationality. Of course, this articulation of other identities to nations through recognition processes has implications for ruling groups as well. If cultural organisers fail to colonise the everyday identities of the people, the forms of rule are weakened.

The essays in this volume offer many examples of recognition processes. By this stage in the argument we can restate familiar instances in a new language. The various deployments of burgerlijkheid can be understood as a form of differential recognition, in which unambiguously burgerlijk groups (according to any one version) are privileged, while other groups must prove their value in these terms. Such political interventions are only likely to have success, however, if social groups have already bought into the moral identifications involved. Similarly, we have seen how military signifiers were a means of making interventions into the field of meanings around gender, generation and class in the years before World War I. In the Netherlands this was clearly an attempt to install, from a relatively outsider position, new sources of public

---

[96] The whole distinction between nationalism and patriotism (in which the latter is morally preferable) seems shaky. Are nationalism/patriotism just the public/private faces of the same articulation?

[97] 'Usually' - because there are many instances in which nation and state do not coincide.

recognition. It seems that this form of 'military imaginary' did not acquire the centrality that the Christian soldier hero acquired in Britain over a longer period.[98] In Britain such versions were also strongly articulated to Empire and 'the race', an example of the larger presence of racism in European national traditions. From the point of view adopted in this essay racism is a form of non-recognition that makes thinkable the expulsion or obliteration of the other, from assimilation or repatriation to genocide.

There is a danger of restricting arguments about identity to a list of major social differences like class, gender, race and age/generation in a kind of 'new reformed' (but still conventional) Leftism. Such lists may themselves become prescriptive, with misrecognitions of their own. It is clear from our studies, for example, that regional identities are crucial in national articulations. Regionality and nationality are categories with many of the same features, but they may be more or less closely aligned. The story of Limburg in the later nineteenth century prompts us to think about the circumstances in which regional identities may be integrated with nationality (and so strengthen it as a focus of identifications) or to ask why, as in separatist movements all over the modern world, 'region' is an *alternative* to nationality, even a locus of lost or emergent nationhood? Again, recognition processes are a useful concept here: did Limburg become Dutch because its peculiarities were recognised? Are separatisms (of many different kinds) necessary resistances to mis- or non-recognitions?

In Roel Kuiper's study, religious identities occupy a similarly central place. The political history of Orthodox Protestantism turned on how far the national structures would privilege this form of Christian practice and belief. Its strategies were attempts to install 'Calvinism' (in its more or less secularised meanings) as the key point of national recognition and identification. Of course, as the concrete instance shows, the subjective implications of religious

---

[98]   For the notion of 'military imaginary' and the Christian soldier hero see Dawson, 'Soldier Heroes'.

doctrine and belief are themselves complex or composite. This is because religious forms have been another grand organising narrative of subjectivities, providing a main means of individual self-production. As Michel Foucault argued, Christianity provided ¸technologies for the self', like the confessional, which came to characterise ethical regimes in the West more generally.[99] Even in the twentieth century these have not been displaced by scientific discourses of the subject. Some historical settlement between the Churches and the Nations was a necessary moment, therefore, not just in a balance of institutional power but in the history of structures of subjectivity and social recognition. It is not surprising that God and the Nation are so often found as a double act or as rivals in the meta-discourses of identity, as in 'God, the Netherlands and Orange!' and 'God, for Harry, England and St George!'[100]

Nationalism and Everyday Identities.

Both of the studies in this volume which focus on the private sphere happen also to be about migration. We have to make two shifts of perspective instantaneously, with consequences which are hard to untangle. Migrants have made a break with their original home; they have chosen to adopt another country, if only as a place of residence and work. Of course the circumstances and subjective significance of migration may differ greatly, from forcible expulsion to movements of aspiration. The change of location in itself, however, involves a necessary double-take on questions of national identity - a more than usual ambivalence, 'hybridity' or 'translation'. It must certainly put the 'old Country' in a new light. It may make the migrant unusually self-reflexive

---

[99]   Michel Foucault, *The History of Sexuality*, Vol. I (Harmondsworth, 1981) pp. 58-70.
[100]   I am grateful to Henk te Velde for suggesting the Dutch version; the English battle-cry is from Shakespeare's *Henry V.*

about national and other cultural differences more generally. As Stuart Hall has argued, it has also become a more and more common experience, paradigmatic, perhaps, for identity in a postmodern world.[101]

Nonetheless many of the processes we have analysed in the public forms in one country can be discerned in the everyday stories of migrants. Economic calculation does not suddenly assert itself as a master motivation, with other subjective conditions revoked. As Annemieke Galema, quoting John Bodnar, argues, it is 'the realm of cultural construction' that has been most neglected in migration studies.[102] It is true that the signifiers of 'bacon-letters' are mundane and material; but, as we argued earlier, representations of everyday events and objects are used to solidify choices and preferences and to express hopes and aspirations.

The letters can certainly be analysed with terms drawn from our discussion of public forms: selection, evaluation, us/other opposition, forms of self-narration. The sharpest of distinctions are drawn between the promises and hopes of the new land ('abundance of work and food so cheap') and the distancing memories of the old country ('pitiful, poverty-striken and sorrowful existence'). In their cross-national positionings, indeed, migrants' letters resemble the negotiations of the Limburger press, though their internal dialogues are lit more by the glow of the chosen country (and the necessity of putting it in a good light) than by resistance to the homeland or hatred of an enemy. Here on the private side of public engagements it is the personal success story rather than the national epic which predominates, both how ever forms of adventure narrative, often linked to masculinity.[103] Similarly, Anna Haye's

---

[101]   Stuart Hall, 'Minimal Selves', *Institute of Contemporary Arts: Identity Documents*, No. 6, pp.15-17; for the metaphor of 'translation' see Brennan, *Rushdie*, esp. pp. 59-70.

[102]   Quoted in Annemieke Galema's essay above.

[103]   For an interesting discussion of adventure forms in autobiographical accounts of the masculine career see David Jackson, *Unmasking Masculinity: A Critical Autobiography* (London, 1990) pp. 18-22.

accounts use some classical forms of splitting in which 'good objects' are radically distinguished from 'bad objects' as she tries to position herself unambiguously in memories of 'moral danger': on one side there were good, proper, German girls from the country (including herself); on the Other there were bad, working-class, German girls from the big city , 'who had quite something behind them'.[104]

These studies do show very clearly that everyday identities do not have to be articulated through national categories - though these may be present in their negation. The use of regional rather than national referents by migrants is one instance of this. In looking back to the old country, migrants may orientate themselves to Yorkshire or to Friesland more than England or the Netherlands. But in the new country too they may continue to position themselves through a regional identity as did Frieslanders in the United States.[105] The most detailed account of such a disarticulation of national from other identities is Barbara Henkes' analysis of Anna Haye's stories.

Anna's story, as she tells it, in autobiographies and to her researcher, revolves around a set of personal identifications in which class and gender themes are uppermost. As Barbara Henkes puts it, '"Respectable"' is the denominator Anna Haye wished to be judged by'.[106] From a better-off working-class background, Anna seeks respectability, but respectability as a young woman of course, perhaps even, her interviewer suggests, a kind of lady-like gentility. Her assignment to training in a farmer's household cuts across her aspirations, or perhaps helps to form them by contrast and opposition. As Anna tells the story later, in an avalanche of

---

[104]   See Barbara Henkes essay above; for a classic discussion of splitting as a psychic defence see Juliet Mitchell ed., *The Selected Melanie Klein* (London, 1986) esp. pp.180-86; for an interesting application to ethnographic materials see Wendy Hollway, *Subjectivity and Method in Psychology*, pp. 70-80.

[105]   See Annemieke Galema's essay above.

[106]   See Barbara Henkes' essay above.

epithets and instances, she was struggling with a three-fold contradiction. Firstly, the work was below her in class terms: it contra-
dicted her fantasy of gentility. 'Toiling on the land', 'perspiring
horribly', 'awful lot of dust and you got horribly dirty', 'ruining
my finger nails', 'having my hair all knots and tangles' 'a farmer's
colour' - all these are signifiers of the disgust with which she puts
a possible, horrible self behind her. Secondly, and just as bad, farm
work transgresses her sense of propriety in gender terms: 'because
there were no men left' ... 'wearing boots' ... all of the men's
work' ... 'fill up shortage of male work force' ... 'we weren't men
were we?' Thirdly, this drudgery consigned her to the prospect of
work and marriage on the land, when many of her dreams, framed
against her mother's rural defeats, were associated with the town.
The tension between aspiration and actuality is caught through a
narrative in which best clothes are a metaphor for true identity: 'In
the evening, before dinner, I rushed up the stairs to put on a good
dress hastily'.

The particular twist in Anna's story is that she associated
these painful contradictions with Germany as a place and with the
policies of the wartime state. In interviews she quotes and parodies
official-sounding pronouncements with energy: 'had to drudge for
the fatherland' ... 'I heard that many a time'. Her refusal and its
attendent fears are recapitulated later in the story when the same
disavowed fatherland arrived on her Amsterdam doorstep in 1940 -
'so they have come after me after all'. Far from meaning Heimat,
or dutiful daughters and mothers of the nation, Germany stood for
'toiling on the land for the rest of her life'.

As Barbara Henkes puts it, in the language of articulation,
Anna Haye 'disconnected the notion of respectability from the
notion of patriotism.' This disarticulation might be understood,
dynamically, in terms of personal strategies in the face of misrecognition. Anna felt herself grotesquely misrecognised in the
official discourses of German society and in the place allotted to
her there. Her aspirations are formed in opposition to such a
destiny. She resists by working up conventional social codes of

gender and class differences in the form of individual aspiration. We could say she resists nationalist articulations by buying into respectable femininity. As is so often the case, her search for autonomy on one (national) side led her to more conforming choices on another (gendered) front.

Barbara Henkes also notes limits in Anna's adoption of the Netherlands. She refused to distinguish morally between the behaviour of people in Germany or Holland during the war. Nationality, it seems, was an unimportant signifier of identity for her. We are left, however, with questions about Anna's orientation to her country of adoption: what was her relation to the available images of Dutchness, other than those concerning war and collaboration? Did not the Netherlands, the land of quiet bourgeois virtues, figure in her life as 'respectability' writ large? Beyond this, lie more general and very complex questions about women's different relationships to nationalism, much discussed by feminists in different historical periods.

The America-Friesland letters suggest that resistance to national articulations may be quite a common component in migration, viewed as a cultural process. Annemieke Galema argues that the commonest comparison between the Old and New Countries, economic benefits apart, was in terms of the articulation of nation to class. America, it seemed, was a land without classes. Class relations and inequalities in Friesland were clearly a source of deep feelings of personal devaluation among migrants and some of their relatives at home: the Old World was associated with drudgery, deference and inequalities of opportunity. Migration was a way of escaping from the binding up of class and nation characteristic of European formations. Were the class structures of the new society also less visible to migrants, used to their own cultural map?

It is clear that migration profoundly modifies the terms of national identity both as an aspect of individual subjectivity and as a form of collectivity. If this was the case for European migrants in the nineteenth century, it is still more true for migration to Western Europe in the postcolonial age. Theorists of 'hybridity', like Stuart

Hall and Homi Bhabha, are undoubtedly correct that migration and settlement and the whole post-colonial scene profoundly complicate the 'simpler' models of nationality of the kind mainly analysed in these pages. Together with the other forms of fragmentation identified in theories of postmodernity, it may also modify the politics of identity more generally. Modern migrations, and especially the anti-racist and anti-assimilationist struggles which have followed them, have thrown into crisis European national formations of an absolutist kind. All over the world, and in Europe especially, we can expect a heightened struggle over these issues in the coming years.

From the point of view adopted in this essay, however, migration is only one of those everyday happenings from which national identities are made and unmade. It is also only one of the forms of resistance, one of the ways in which other identities may be disentangled from the web of national interpellations and given an independent force, even as a social alternative. There are many different degrees and forms of such resistance which are not discussed in the essays in this volume. I am thinking of the sustaining of an identity in the face of 'national' misrecognitions, with the daring inversions of dominant evaluations which this often involves: the idea of a 'black nation' or more recently a 'queer nation' in the United States for instance.[107] From a base in alternative or oppositional collectivities, it may also be possible to bid to define the nation in different more inclusive ways, or to construct a potentially hegemonic alliance on different terms as in nationalisms of the left. Alternatively movements and individuals may choose to de-emphasise the nation as a forum of politics and recognition; and to orientate towards international organisations and cross-national loyalties instead.

---

[107]   With more recent affirmations in mind, it is easy to forget that socialism began with a similar affirmation: of the working class who really produce the wealth.

Such resistances act back on the strategies of leading groups and institutions, shaping overall formations. Given our tendency to simplify, polarise and project around the image of the Other, national peculiarities, even if rooted in critical theory and history, must be advanced with some caution and irony. It may be, however, that rather than identifying single features of national difference, we should focus on the different ways in which key relationships are handled. Of most concern here, as throughout this volume, are relationships between the differences and contradictions of everyday life and the regulative work of publicity and state power. It may be that this dialectic not only moves a whole formation, but also creates its main distinguishing features.

British (especially English) institutions have, over a very long period, been based in cultural and social exclusions.[108] The dominant versions of Britishness have also been persistently monocultural. This mode of handling cultural relations has helped to create, paradoxically, a rich configuration of oppositional forms, in which social antagonisms of all kinds, not only those of 'race', are strongly marked culturally. In the Netherlands, it seems that differences of politics, belief, and 'community' have been handled more negotiatively, with some differences institutionalised. This may mean that the road to a genuinely open national culture or to something still more inclusive may be easier in the Netherlands than in Britain; but easier too may be the temptation to believe that antagonisms have been successfully resolved, sometimes without good reason.

---

[108]   For one discussion of this pattern, in English education, see Richard Johnson, 'Thatcherism and English Education: breaking the mould, or confirming the pattern?', *History of Education*, Vol. 18, No. 2, (1989): 91-121.

Notes on the contributors

NIEK VAN SAS (1950) is a senior lecturer in the department of history, University of Amsterdam. His special interests include the history of international relations (particularly 19th and 20th centuries), and the political culture of the Netherlands during the "long 19th century" in a comparative perspective.

WIM KLINKERT (1960) studied history at the State University Leiden from 1979 to 1985. He teaches history at the Royal Military Academy in Breda and is doing research as a member of the Military History Section of the Royal Netherlands Army. In 1992 he completed his thesis at the University of Leiden on Dutch defence policy 1874-1914: *Het vaderland verdedigd. Plannen en opvattingen over de verdediging van Nederland 1874-1914.*

ROEL KUIPER (1962) studied history and philosophy at the Free University in Amsterdam. In 1992 his thesis on Dutch orthodox protestants and their views on Dutch foreign policy was published: *Zelfbeeld en wereldbeeld. Antirevolutionairen en het buitenland, 1848-1905.* He is director of the Center for Reformational Philosophy in Utrecht.

HENK TE VELDE (1959) studied history at the University of Groningen, where he teaches in the Department of History. He wrote several articles on Dutch intellectual history and political culture. In 1992 his thesis on nationalism of Dutch liberals 1870-1918, was published: *Gemeenschapszin en plichtsbesef. Liberalisme en Nationalisme in Nederland, 1870-1918.*

RICO OP DEN CAMP (1960), studied history at the University of Utrecht, and is preparing a thesis about Social Liberalism and The Labour Movement in the Netherlands at the end of the nineteenth century. He published, among others, on the question of the definition of nationalism.

ANNEMIEKE GALEMA (1956) studied history at the University of Groningen. She got a N.W.O-Fellowship to make researches into Dutch migration to the United States at Kent State University (Ohio). She published several articles on this subject and wrote a book on the history of the schools of chemistry. For her doctorate she investigates Frisian migration to the United States (1880-1914) at the University of Groningen.

BARBARA HENKES (1955) studied history at the University of Groningen. She is working at the Centre for Contemporary History of the University of Amsterdam. She wrote several articles on women's history and oral history and is co-author of a book on Dutch domestic servants: *Kaatje ben je boven? Leven en werken van Nederlandse dienstbodes 1900-1940.* She is writing her thesis on German maids in the Netherlands, 1920-1950.

RICHARD JOHNSON (1939) was director of the Centre for Contemporary Cultural Studies, now the Department of Cultural Studies at the University of Birmingham. At present he teaches part-time at this Department. He has taken early retirement in order to write and research in the field of historiography and popular memory, cultural theory and theories of identity.